ASSEMBLING
MORAL MOBILITIES

Cycling, Cities, and the Common Good

NICHOLAS A. SCOTT

University of Nebraska Press | Lincoln

Library of Congress Cataloging-in-Publication Data
Names: Scott, Nicholas A., author.
Title: Assembling moral mobilities: cycling, cities, and the
common good / Nicholas A. Scott.
Description: Lincoln: University of Nebraska Press, [2020] |
Includes bibliographical references and index.
Identifiers: LCCN 2019015600
ISBN 9781496217127 (cloth: alk. paper)
ISBN 9781496219398 (epub)
ISBN 9781496219404 (mobi)
ISBN 9781496219411 (pdf)
Subjects: LCSH: Bicycles. |
Urban transportation—
Planning. | City planning.
Classification: LCC HE5736 .S296 2020 | DDC 388.3/472—dc23
LC record available at https://lccn.loc.gov/2019015600

Set in Minion Pro by Mikala R. Kolander.

To an urban planet without
roadkill, quietly revolving, rife
with more-than-human life.
To one less car. To one more bike.

Contents

Photographs

Acknowledgments

This book was written with the support of a heterogeneous actor-network, including scholars, cities, comrades, and their bicycles. I'm a slow typist, and the manuscript is already four days late, so I'll be brief. It couldn't have happened without financial support from Canada's Social Sciences and Humanities Research Council, and therefore the intrepid Natasha Wiebe at the University of Windsor, who helped me secure this funding, for which I am grateful. It also couldn't have happened without all the kind folks who invited me into their busy mobile lives to witness their work and intimate experiences with city cycling. I especially thank Ange, Matt, Colm, Meghan, Eric, Laena, Julia, Marja, Lisa, and Megan, whose stories and experiences somehow left me more inspired by cycling than I was when I began this book.

The book had a rocky start, to say the least. A stolen laptop in Montréal and no backup left its first incarnation, a proposal with two chapters evaporated into thin air, before a move and radical change of context a year later from Motor City to Vancouver shook its foundations again. But I couldn't shake the idea, originally inspired by Jim Conley, to develop connections between pragmatic sociology and urban mobilities (thanks, Jim). Working in reverse chronological order back to those humble beginnings: for her unwavering support, I extend my warmest thanks to my editor, Bridget Barry (who remains remarkably calm about my manuscript's slow arrival). It is with utmost gratitude that I also thank the anonymous reviewers who read the manuscript with persnickety care, and whose immensely thoughtful and constructive feedback helped me whittle my arguments into their final shape.

The project could not have happened without the conversations I had with my colleagues at Simon Fraser University, including Michael Hathaway and Kathleen Millar, who provided vital feedback on my proposal, as well as Ann Travers, Lindsey Freeman, and others (I'm blessed with amazing colleagues). I also thank my students at SFU who picked up pieces in the book in creative ways to help me sharpen it, including Dan Prisk and Morgaine Lee. I am especially thankful to Zoë Sanderson and Sharlie Clelland-Eicker, students who became research assistants and mobile ethnographers and who collected some of the data underpinning chapter 2.

While writing the book in Vancouver I drew indispensable support and encouragement from a global network of scholars specializing in mobilities. I thank Justin Spinney for a critical discussion about methodology at an AAG meeting in Chicago. I am sincerely grateful for long walks and meandering conversations about movement in London and Santiago (and bike rides in Vancouver) with Soledad Martinez Rodriguez. I am indebted to Stephanie Sodero for far-flung collaborations that advanced my thinking while lifting my spirits. The same goes for Phillip Vannini, another collaborator who never ceased to be a source of inspiration. Malene Freudendal-Pedersen gifted an early insight (not long after Jim's) at a conference in Caligari by connecting cycling to the common good. A recent talk by Mimi Sheller in Vancouver on mobility justice helped me close the book. Many, many other mobility folks, from Cycling and Society Symposium scholars to the Nordic Geographers, offered intellectual help along the way. An earlier version of some of the Ottawa material in the book was published in a 2016 article in the *Canadian Journal of Urban Research*, and I thank the anonymous reviewers for their insightful suggestions that helped move along my analysis.

"Back east," before I moved to Vancouver, colleagues in the University of Windsor's Sociology, Anthropology and Criminology Department generously offered comments, too, with which I refined early versions of the project; I especially thank Paul Datta. I am also grateful to Cristina Benneian, who helped open my eyes to the beauty of cycling in

Motor City at a critical juncture in my life. I am profoundly grateful to Christian Pasiak and Michael Christensen in Ottawa, both of whom offered critical sounding boards as I fashioned the book's underlying philosophical framework. And this project simply could not have happened without the longtime mentorship of Janet Siltanen, Fran Klodawsky, and Jacqueline Kennelly, whose formative guidance permeates the nature of this book.

Most of all, I am grateful for my family, for all their love and support, for teaching me how to bike and riding with me in the first place, and for listening to my never-ending stories about making this book.

ASSEMBLING MORAL MOBILITIES

1. Ruth gestures at an SUV on Laurier Avenue in Ottawa. Photo by author.

Introduction

In Search of the Good Bike Lane

"Moooove bitch. Get out da way! Get out da way!" thunders a voice out the windows of a black Chevrolet Suburban rolling into the intersection where Ruth is waiting to turn left. Traffic opens up for the Suburban to turn, but the enormous sport utility vehicle does not bite. Feeling a little annoyed toward the end of a frenetic ride home from work, Ruth gestures at the suv (see photo 1). She talks to it about the traffic lights, as if the suv might listen to her over the aggressive Ludacris lyrics.

"It's green."

Obnoxious suvs are not the most irritating thing on Ruth's commute this spring afternoon in Ottawa. She acknowledges that Canada's capital has done more than many other cities to promote cycling for everyday travel, taking impressive strides over the last ten years to build good bike lanes, including a new generation of dedicated cycle tracks that make cycling safer and more efficient for everyone. These cycle tracks promise Ruth a refuge, if not from the noise and pollution of motor vehicles then at least from their right hooks, door prizes, trampling wheels, and devastating strikes from behind. This is good news for Ruth. Like many ordinary cyclists in Canada, she has a nose for good infrastructure, and like many women (Aldred et al. 2017), she prefers the safety of dedicated lanes and pathways that physically remove and protect her from car traffic. Still, Ottawa's new cycle tracks, alluring as they are (and to be fair, they are very much a work in progress), are often themselves what frustrate Ruth most on her commute, and not simply because of their tendency to disappear when she needs them most.

1

On the way home Ruth confronts a patchwork of cycling infrastructures seeking by varying degrees to correct the inequality of space between driving and cycling. One new bike lane in particular, a cycle track, piques her sense of injustice: Mackenzie Avenue. Just mentioning the Mackenzie track makes her blood boil. The Mackenzie track opened on May 19, 2017, to much fanfare as a $4 million, 0.4-kilometer (0.2-mile) lane coproduced by the City of Ottawa, the National Capital Commission (NCC), the Province of Ontario, and the U.S. Embassy.[1] On the Mackenzie track, flanked by the U.S. Embassy's new security bollards, Ruth appreciates her physical separation from car traffic—she has not forgotten the ghost bike sitting in front of her last workplace, dedicated to a young woman killed after riding off a path into a river of cars—but the track is slow and complicated to access and too short—and then dumps her into just such a river. Averse to inefficiency and danger, she balances the two, and Mackenzie barely passes muster. Not helping are people who have yet to acknowledge its existence, a challenge (temporary, she hopes) for much of Ottawa's new cycling infrastructure. Nearing the end of Mackenzie, despite striking her bell, she almost hits a pedestrian lingering on the track for a selfie.

On cutting-edge cycle tracks, designed in Copenhagen and plunked down in Canada, Ruth feels like she is part of an engineering experiment trying to determine the future of her city. Later, after the Chevy Suburban finally roared away, she turns onto another new cycle track, the O'Connor Street Bikeway, for which she has even more ire. The O'Connor track runs beside a one-way, three-lane arterial road that was engineered in the last century to funnel cars from the business district and Parliament to a superhighway and the suburbs. After riding a few blocks, a cyclist in front of Ruth nearly gets struck by a car impatiently crossing the bike tracks into the powerful artery, an occurrence so common, given the number of access points, that solar-powered electronic billboards remind drivers to be aware of cyclists during traffic safety campaigns. The O'Connor cycle track, like the Mackenzie track, activates Ruth's sense of unjust engineering. Squeezing cyclists riding in opposite directions into close quarters while giving motorists ample access to cross the tracks into an artery off a superhighway, O'Connor's track guarantees cyclists neither safety nor efficiency.

Farther along the O'Connor cycle track, Ruth's gender equity alarm goes off. While approaching an intersection, a car suddenly drives into the track, stopping at the red light but blocking her path. Ruth, having the right-of-way, assumed the driver would have stopped before the track, and so "doing one of those wobbles," as she later describes, she barely catches herself to avoid a fall. The driver, "a muscly, tattooed man probably in his thirties," stares out his window. Ruth looks at him with a clear look of annoyance on her face. Over intense music on his stereo, he says, dripping with condescension, "Ohhhh. Sorry dear."

"Fine," she replies, coldly.

Ignoring the fact that he had interrupted Ruth's commute, her momentum, and her day, he continues to look at her, blocking her path. With a smirk he remarks, "You're kind of cute though."

The brief interaction leaves Ruth deeply frustrated. It means that cycle tracks, while safer and socially more inclusive than painted lines and sharrows, cannot be good bike lanes by virtue of their physical design alone. In some situations O'Connor is a bad place to cycle for Ruth, not because of its technical shortcomings but because of gender-based micro-aggressions that help reinforce cycling at large in Canada as male-dominated transport (Pucher et al. 2011). Unjust engineering merely compounds social inequity.

Between Mackenzie and O'Connor, outside the protected space of Ottawa's new cycle tracks, Ruth's commute changes dramatically. She had been riding home from work on lanes and paths separated from cars before reaching the end of Mackenzie, where the track suddenly dumps her during rush hour into seven lanes of motor vehicle traffic and powerful currents of pedestrians and other cyclists at peak flow. She pauses and starts making creative maneuvers for a better position to cross the river of cars. Circumventing a line of cyclists headed left, she weaves right, rolling slowly through a busy crosswalk like a pedestrian and raising a few eyebrows. With one foot on the opposite curb, she waits to ply the great river via a traffic island and multiple crosswalks.

A man walking home from work stops and unhelpfully explains to her why she should instead cycle the other way and turn left within traffic, classic "mansplaining," for which Ruth has little time. The light changes, and she enters what seems like a trial of democracy itself, meant to test the limits of human civility. Ruth confidently negotiates the busy public space without incident. As a careful cycling citizen, she defers to the slower speeds and trajectories of people walking in their own rights-of-way, always searching for eye contact. Her ability to accommodate and empathize with different road users allows her to hold on to her own flow. She makes excellent time, gliding through the river of cars and its tributaries on the crosscurrents of pedestrians.

In this slow, technically illegal shortcut on Ruth's ride home, she skirts Canada's memorial for its war dead and catches a glimpse of one of those beautiful urban vistas that help define a place, one that runs all the way to her apartment. While wheeling through this space of collective memory, she sees how her particular household connects to the wider city and its history, and her cycling momentarily transcends trials of democracy and engineering experiments as an extension of her home. In a testament to the way cycling has already redefined the place of her home within the city, at the end of her shortcut Ruth lands on Ottawa's first cycle track, the Laurier Avenue Segregated Bike Lane. In 2011 the birth of this segregated bike lane shook the foundations of Canadian urban mobility. On Laurier Ruth first tasted Northern European–style cycling infrastructure.

The good bike lane for Ruth, besides providing meaningful protection from inefficiency and danger, requires some kind of connection with nature, which she thinks does not oppose the city but rather helps animate it. Early on during her ride home, Ruth finds an ecological passageway on an interprovincial bridge over the Ottawa River along a narrow but separated pathway for cycling. Something about the river water—its spontaneous movement, its wildlife, its shadows and smells— connects her more closely with the more-than-human environment. She seeks out this closeness more directly on weekends by cycling along the river shorelines on Ottawa's multiuse pathway network. Still, the brief encounter with the river on her weekday commute helps bring nature into her daily life.

Ruth is aware of the privilege of being able to access protected cycling lanes and nature pathways in Ottawa. She expresses concern that less-affluent people in other, more gentrified cities like Toronto and Vancouver are being excluded from this beneficial type of cycling infrastructure, and holds on to a noble notion of cycling as the transport equivalent of soccer in global sports: cheap, accessible, and easy to pick up. At the same time, Ruth participates in the very sorts of stylish consumption that help drive high-end urban development in the first place, right down to her cool Brooklyn-designed bicycle. The same exposure and vulnerability to her surroundings, and ability to stop and engage the world, which brings Ruth closer to other citizens and nature, renders her consumption in the local marketplace more prolific than that of motorists.

At the end of her commute, Ruth turns onto her street, neatly hops the curb, and approaches the door of her apartment building while dismounting. In a strange blend of contrast and similarity to the Chevy Suburban blasting, *"Moooove bitch. Get out da way!"* a pedestrian passerby trying to be nice runs over and holds her door open. He does not realize that his behavior has made life physically and socially more difficult for Ruth, who can swing open that door by herself like a well-oiled machine. As she awkwardly shimmies with her bicycle by the oblivious, smiling man, Ruth cannot escape the feeling that though efforts have been made to empathize with people like her and build a better city for cycling, there is a long way to go.

Cycling, Driving, and the Mobilities Paradigm

What does a good city look like for cycling? What must change to move urban society from driving to cycling as a form of everyday travel? These questions bedevil city leaders and urban denizens around the world seeking more sustainable ways to live together. They are especially vexing for nations dominated by driving, such as Canada, one of the most highly urbanized countries in the world yet also one of the most car dependent, with 86 percent of Canadian workers using a car for their daily commute (Statistics Canada 2017a). Only a small minority of workers cycle in Canada, from a low of 0.2 percent in St. John's in Newfoundland to a national high of 6.6 percent in Victoria, British Columbia (Statistics Canada 2017b). Making cycling even more exclusive, within this small minority many more middle-aged people cycle than younger and older Canadians, as do many more men than women (Ledsham et al. 2012; Pucher et al. 2011; Winters et al. 2007). For example, in Ottawa, which offers many efficient, less stressful multiuse pathways outside car traffic, men outnumber women cycling by more than two-to-one (City of Ottawa 2013). Nevertheless, some hopeful signs of change lie just below the surface of this overall picture of car dependence.

National and city statistics overlook large variations in cycling within cities, where the rubber really hits the road. In certain parts of some cities, cycling is beginning to thrive, a trend expected to continue and broaden the socio-demographics of cycling through targeted investments in dedicated tracks and bikeways that appeal to women, immigrants, older folks, and children (Winters and Zanotto 2017; City of Ottawa 2013; Toronto Public Health 2012). The parts of the city in which cycling excursions by all people tend to concentrate are the sort of dense, mixed-use terrains that Jane Jacobs (1961) famously championed as vital for urban life, such as Vancouver's East End, Toronto's Queen Street West, Montréal's Plateau, and the complex urban fabric inside Ottawa's greenbelt, where Ruth rides for work and play. This large cluster of neighborhoods "located within a reasonable cycling distance from downtown," for example, had a cycling mode share (percentage of travelers who use a bicycle) that already rivaled that of any American city by 2011, at 8 percent, with plans in place to reach 12 percent by 2031 (City of Ottawa 2013, 26). In the same year, cycle mode share in particular neighborhoods in Montréal and Vancouver reached as high as 20.4 percent (Teschke et al. 2017). Taking account of these intra-city findings, Canada provides a strong case study of a cycling-developing nation.

Despite piecemeal signs of urban growth, cycling faces tremendous social and physical challenges in car-dominant contexts. As Ruth's ride home from work suggests, cities are struggling to find the right mix of cycling infrastructures and impose it on a preexisting twentieth-century city designed for driving, all while striving to update the habits and manners of the cycling and non-cycling masses. Making matters more challenging, even as many cities in Canada move toward fostering compact, transit-oriented development, expanding the kind of dense urban spaces that underpin cycling, Canada's prolific urban fabric continues to rapidly unravel around the edges. According to 2016 census data, cities are still sprawling along highways, advancing the suburban fringe where the single detached dwelling, cul-de-sac, and car remain king (McIntosh 2017). Even in Ottawa, a beacon of cycling development in North America, it can be easier for governments and industry to expand a superhighway than to build a bike lane (Scott 2016). These interscalar challenges, coupled with the tendency of policymakers to rely on narrow technical solutions (Hommels 2008), highlight the need for social scientists to historicize and unpack the dynamic, interwoven complexities of society and technology facing the expansion of cycling in the city built for driving.

To date, cycling scholarship in Canada has emphasized behavioral change, public health, and quantitative approaches to cycling. Behavioral studies, drawing on psychology and marketing (Yang et al. 2010), segment populations in order to identify target groups for strategic interventions that strive to remove barriers to cycling. Interventions such as public pledges, branding, marketing campaigns, community-based promotions, monetary incentives, training rides, and workplace cycling ambassadors or "champions" (Savan et al. 2017) aim to secure and sustain personal commitments to cycling. Public health research, like behavioral studies, draws heavily on quantitative methods, with which it shows strong evidence for the health benefits of cycling (Teschke et al. 2012). Health research supports, on a broad scale, the finding that both current and potential cyclists, particularly women, prefer dedicated tracks (Winters and Teschke 2010) and that proximity to this kind of infrastructure correlates with higher cycling rates (Teschke et al. 2017). These lines of valuable research face important limitations. Behavioral interventions emphasize personal plan making and tend to "target individual decision making as the point of change" (Spotswood et al. 2015), reinforcing prevailing neoliberal representations of cycling as a product of individual effort and environmental responsibility (Aldred 2013; Cupples and Ridley 2008). Public health studies recognize that personal behaviors reflect the larger socio-spacial contexts of which they are constitutive (Winters et al. 2007) but rely heavily on a traditional, deterministic, and positivistic approach that views cycling through a monolithic lens as something that can be explained through one objective model of reality. Consequently, Canadian cycling scholarship continues to neglect the systemic societal changes necessary for cities to displace driving with cycling.

This book provides a fresh perspective of cycling, drawing on the "new mobilities paradigm" (Sheller and Urry 2006). The mobilities paradigm applies multiple methods to define a sociological view of movement and stillness, and their mutual transformation (Hannam et al. 2006). First articulated in an editorial article by Mimi Sheller and John Urry (2006), the mobilities paradigm confronts the individualizing and positivistic models that dominate Canadian cycling scholarship and transport studies in general (Freudendal-Pedersen 2009). Turning conventional transport science on its head, the science of mobilities places movement (including the choice and capacity to move or not) in social, historical, and technological contexts. In contrast to the utilitarian notion of transport as being simply about getting from point A to point B, the concept of mobilities refers to movement (of people, ideas, and things) made socially meaningful in the context of systematically unequal power relations (Cresswell 2006; 2010; Jensen 2009). Among different systems of mobilities, the hegemonic system of automobility stands out as a coercive, self-organizing ensemble of actors (Dennis and Urry 2009; Featherstone 2004). It consists of not only cars and people but also cul-de-sacs, traffic computers, superhighways, petroleum networks, aluminum, jurisprudence, licensing, public subsidies, ubiquitous advertising, road rage, medical liabilities, ecological externalities, urban fragmentation, and suburban sprawl, which globally work to induce and conform human and nonhuman movement through motor vehicles (Conley and McLaren 2009). Changing one element of this complex, socio-technical ensemble requires modifying any other on which it depends (Hommels 2008). It is no accident then, that the car, and its impact on cities and societies, preoccupied the founders of the mobilities paradigm and continues to command attention (Sheller and Urry 2000; Walks 2014). Automobility impinges heavily upon the growth of most other mobilities, especially cycling (Longhurst 2015).

Through a mobilities lens, cycling does not appear as the isolated product of a personal, healthful choice, but rather as a distinctive, self-propelled system of travel continually developing in concert with wider mobility norms, infrastructures, and policies (Walks 2014; Furness 2010; Mapes 2009). On the one hand, cycling unfolds within the constraints of automobility, whose reorganization of work, consumption, home, and leisure has systematically eroded the dense interlinkages in cities that make cycling (as well as walking and public transit) feasible and desirable in the first place (Conley and McLaren 2009; Parusel and McLaren 2010; Paterson 2007). Within the matrix of these constraints, cycling may appear, and feel, like a deviant activity (Jones 2005). On the other hand, cycling embodies its own social, technological, and emotional affordances. Part of the distinctiveness of cycling owes to its physically demanding coordination, "kinaesthetic performance," and "sensuous intensities" tied to bodily exertion and exposure to weather and traffic (Spinney 2006). More than the motorist inside his metal cocoon and sonic envelope, the cyclist feels her environment, which, in turn, over time attunes her "affective capacities" (Larsen 2014) and competencies (Aldred 2012) for cycling. The intensities, capacities, and competencies of cycling can differ markedly by cultural and infrastructural context (Horton et al. 2007), ranging from easy-breezy, upright cruising in Copenhagen on seamless cycling tracks to cliff-hanging, hair-raising rides in Toronto traffic across disconnected bike lanes painted irregularly on the street. Together these differences point to cycling's animation of urban social worlds beyond the car.

Alongside and related to a concern with social practice and lived experience, a mobilities approach highlights the politics of cycling and public conflicts surrounding its uneven expansion (Bonham 2011). Cycling advocates have long battled the vested interests, spatial monopolies, and cultural boosters of automobility (Longhurst 2015; Norton 2009; Furness 2010; Paterson 2007). However, the politics of cycling are evolving and increasingly intersect with the politics of social justice and racialized gentrification (Golub et al. 2016; Hoffman 2016), climate change and ecological degradation (Horton 2007), and emerging forms of place, identity, and citizenship (Freudendal-Pedersen 2015; Aldred 2010). The "politics of mobility" is a broad idea that relates shifting representations of mobilities, "as adventure, as tedium, as education, as freedom, as modern, as threatening" (Cresswell 2010, 19), with differential access to mobilities in practice. Current growth in cycling comes at a time of globally intensifying neoliberal urbanism, with transport discourses repositioning cyclists as conscientious, self-reliant citizens with responsibilities to protect the environment while optimizing their own health and efficiency (Green et al. 2012). Such discourses reflect and reinforce growing unevenness in mobilities in general, "wherein carbon-hungry kinetic elites resort to the private jet, the helicopter, the high-speed train, the yacht, the cocooned limousine, [and] the semi-militarized sport utility vehicle" (Sheller 2016, 22) to secure and "offshore" (Urry 2014) their own prolific mobility and resources at the expense of others. The politics of cycling unfolds uneasily against this backdrop. Like the practice of cycling, cycling politics cannot be separated from, nor reduced to, the neoliberal politics of fossil fuel–driven automobility.

While the mobilities lens offers a powerful tool for advancing cycling research in Canada and around the world, it contains its own critical blind spot. What mobilities research does well is bring into focus the embodied practice of cycling, with its links to wider political changes in cities, technology, and society that push back against the social injustice of neoliberal car capitalism. It helps make sense of Ruth's cycling, placing the multisensorial capacities, strategies, and frustrations that animate her ride home from work inside a culturally and historically situated "constellation" (Cresswell 2010) of spatial representations and practices that privilege automobility. However, what the mobilities paradigm has failed to do is investigate the multiplicity of ways in which mobilities in general, and cycling in particular, become good. It fails to account for Ruth's ordinary yet finely textured sense of justice and the bricolage of things that, for her, make a bike lane good. In other words, while mobilities science helps explain what must change to move society from driving to cycling, it falls short of illuminating what a morally good city for cycling looks like and how it builds on, and diverges from, that of driving. This book steps into this blind spot, using the knowledge of experts and everyday cyclists to explore how mobilities animate the good city as a moral construct in which people flourish together (Fainstein 2010; Amin 2006). Instead of one monolithic manifestation of the good cycling city, I follow the engineering experiments, trials of democracy, extensions of home, ecological engagements, and routes of consumption in Ruth's search for the good bike lane as lines of flight for a multiplicity of good cycling cities.

Assembling Moral Mobilities

The concept of morality troubles social-scientific understandings of mobilities. Sociologists and anthropologists, weary of outdated Durkheimian notions of moral values masquerading as objective social facts, remain deeply divided over whether to revive its analysis (Fassin 2008; Stoczkowski 2008; Zigon 2010). Widespread unease with morality may reflect the zeitgeist of the twenty-first century (Bauman 2003), with its ever-shifting social attachments and skepticism for universal notions of the good life, the good society, and, indeed, "the good city," which condenses these ideas within an urban context (Fainstein 2010; Amin 2006). Mobilities, moreover, and mass driving in particular, are partly responsible. Forces of individualization, such as long commutes inside single occupied vehicles to scattered suburbs, undermine traditional forms of community (Putnam 2000). Even emerging communities, including the cycling community, with their shared experiences, green image, and "resistance identity" (Castells 1997; Green et al. 2012), often fail to create a strong moral connection with the common good—even in places like Copenhagen, where 35 percent of people commute by bike and cyclists build "project identities" based on common praxis (Castells 1997; Freudendal-Pedersen 2015). Despite, and perhaps because of, lingering notions of morality as universal laws that transcend space and time, the role of morality and moral judgment in transforming contemporary, fragmented societies is overlooked and ill understood.

And yet multiple moral notions of the good play an increasingly salient role in urban socio-technical change (Blok and Meilvang 2015; Blok 2013; Holden 2017), particularly moralities of the *common* good. Unlike eugenics and other widely discredited moralities that reject the dignity of some humans, moral appeals to the common good identify higher principles that appeal to a common humanity and the mutual flourishing of all people (Kymlicka 2001; Taylor 2004). Theories of the common good thus reject extreme forms of "cycling fundamentalism" (Cupples and Ridley 2008) that would place the moral worth of people who cycle over that of people who drive. For example, to publicly justify building new dedicated cycle tracks, planners frequently appeal to the market as a common good, because even if cycle tracks remove car parking, in the end cyclists spend more money at local businesses than motorists, which ultimately strengthens the collective and benefits everyone—even motorists and businesses who lose their parking (Sztabinski 2009). Underlying such a market "moral worth" is a vision of a common humanity based on the unique ability of people to flourish through their economic activity and consumption.

City officials, of course, do not always appeal to market worth to justify or critique new dedicated tracks. Sometimes they appeal to another common good based on civic equality, rooted in a concept of common flourishing based on democratic citizenship and the rule of law, because dedicated tracks often increase access to cycling and cycling inclusion. Less often, officials appeal to an ecological common good, where cycle tracks advance environmental knowledge and protection. The growing salience of such conflicting moral appeals—on issues ranging from new road construction (Thévenot 2002) and urban development (Blok and Meilvang 2015; Holden and Scerri 2015) to the various uses of streets and sidewalks (Conley 2015)—shows a fundamental lack of consensus over what actually constitutes the common good. The presence of conflicting common goods in contemporary liberal democracies injects uncertainty and anxiety into debates over new bike lanes and other urban controversies. However, the idea of a good city for cycling grows significantly stronger, I contend, through an intrinsically plural and sociological understanding of morality, judgment, and the common good. To show how, this book places cycling and the mobilities paradigm in conversation with the "pragmatic sociology" crafted initially by Luc Boltanski and Laurent Thévenot (2006[1991]).

Pragmatic sociology holds that people in practice develop a nuanced, everyday sense of (in)justice and become adept at moving between different moral situations to which incompatible notions of the common good apply. What makes such a sociological approach to morality so appealing is that it follows multiple moralities out of the minds and books of philosophers by recognizing how "laypeople" already exercise a surprisingly nuanced ability to cast moral judgment, albeit an imperfect one that requires gaining the capacity to naturally grasp different moral situations through repeated practice in everyday life. For example,

> an excited consumer who has just bought his first car exults in the plentitude of the market world; that same feeling will come back the next time he hears about a sale, a promotional event, or huge discounts in a department store. In short, this person will acquire the ability to involve himself in situations based on a market principle of justification by going to an automobile showroom or a supermarket, not by going to a library to read Adam Smith. (Boltanski and Thévenot 2006[1991], 148)

Which moral worths become relevant depends on the nature of the situation—acceptable practices for the automobile showroom do not necessarily apply to a public park or legislative assembly. In one moment a cyclist plays the good consumer, in the next the good citizen, in the next the good commuter, in the next the good mother, and so on. Not all situations invite moral judgment (and not all moral judgments, of course, appeal to our better, common humanities). That so many of them, upon observation, do, suggests that morality itself forms a far more dynamic and open-ended site of world-making than is often assumed.

Informed as much by sociological observation as political philosophy, this morality, as I explore it through mobilities, no doubt challenges its conventional meanings. Contesting, in particular, religious and universalizing views of morality as one objective truth or mode of behavior, an irreducibly plural, situationally dependent, and, indeed, mobile approach to morality notably "abandons any strong, Durkheimian emphasis on a homogeneous, shared commonality in society," as Paul Blokker (2011, 253) puts it, in favor of "a rather profound indetermination of social life." Moral mobilities come out of a long line of liberal and democratic philosophical thought on the nature of the common good (Kymlicka 2001; Taylor 2004). I build on this thought by pulling incompatible lines of it together through a close examination of how different common goods are assembled through the daily practice and politics of mobility. This plural idea of morality overlaps with, and extends, the idea of justice—where "justice itself is a mobile assemblage of contingent subjects, enacted contexts, and fleeting moments of practice and political engagement" (Sheller 2018, 20). While justice and morality share the same unmistakable quality of an open-ended, mobile "becoming" of practice and politics, what is *just* and what is *good* nevertheless embark on diverging avenues of analysis. Whereas mobility justice, in Sheller's (2018) capacious rendering, encompasses the distributive, deliberative, procedural, restorative, and epistemic networks related to (in)equity in a postcolonial context of reconciliation and geo-ecology, moral mobilities wonders how widely shared imaginaries of the good life (including social justice) come about in the first place, and why some imaginaries expand and become more dominant than others.

Moral plurality means the moral nature of any situation is inherently contested, the endemic uncertainty of which necessitates a reliance on qualified objects. During formal public situations in which competing judgments are "put to the test," people mobilize nonhuman "mediators" (Latour 2007), material equipment, and complex infrastructures (Harvey and Knox 2015), which reciprocally transform people. Each common good provides a distinctive moral language with which actors actively qualify and judge persons but also things associated with a particular good. Learning to act naturally and involve oneself in multiple moral situations invites people into wider "common worlds" populated by different moral beings, in which people gradually learn "which beings matter" (Boltanski and Thévenot 2006[1991], 147). Just like social practices, objects that belong in one world do not fit easily into another. For instance, planners seeking to judge the market value of a cycle track follow shopping spaces, commodities, and dollars, and for judging civic worth look instead to laws, street signs, and the bollards, flower planters, and curbs that protect people cycling from people driving. By leaning either on dollars or bollards, actors in public conflicts over new bike lanes not only qualify objects; they "attempt to verify the solidity of bonds that confer value (grandeur) on particular social and material arrangements" (Blok and Meilvang 2015, 22). In this way a plurality of abstract common goods becomes "morally equipped" (Thévenot 2002). Nonhuman actors help physically furnish competing common worlds wherein "infrastructuring" unfolds as an active, contested, and everyday process (Star 1999; Guy and Shove 2000; Sheller 2016).

From a moral mobilities perspective, cycling will not easily substitute for driving in the sprawling urban habitats of North America (Furness 2010; Sheller and Urry 2000). As the dominant culture and infrastructuring of terrestrial mobility, the car holds a major moral advantage in defining "what constitutes the good life, [and] what is necessary for an appropriate citizenship of mobility" (Sheller and Urry 2000, 739). Where cycling and driving are talked about together, sensational media and politicians quickly pit cyclists against motorists in a zero sum "street fight" (Sadik-Khan and Solomonow 2016) for scarce road supply. To open up the moral analysis of mobilities, and cycling in particular, scholars should resist the default "balkanisation of transport history into modal specialisms," as if driving and cycling only compete with one another as separate "modalities" (Pirie 2016, 3). In fact cycling and driving interconnect, enable as well as hinder one another, and the diverse practices that grew up around the car offer clues for expanding cycling. Rather than competing modes or binary mobility systems, I propose ontologically distinguishing mobilities by moralities, wherein competing modes of transport can become good in the same way. To advance a morally nuanced notion of mobilities with new tools for a mobilities–pragmatic sociology framework, I introduce the concepts of "moral assemblage" and "moral friction."

Moral assemblages entail durable configurations of public judgments, social practices, and qualified infrastructures that advance particular moral worths.[2] The power of these parts—judgments, practices, and infrastructures—is not equatable to their functions in any one "whole" assemblage (indeed, they may play parts in other assemblages). However, these parts "are deeply shaped by their finite properties and their infinite relations within the whole" (Vannini and Vannini 2016, 194). For example, a single bike lane can take on market, civic, ecological, and other roles, depending on the situation, as can a single bicycle. The point is, the roles that these roads and vehicles play in separate moral assemblages profoundly shape their impact through associations with morally equivalent beings. The concept of moral assemblages builds on Boltanski and Thévenot's (2006[1991]) notion of "common worlds" by showing how moral assembling leads to more variation *within* each world of worth than is commonly assumed, particularly as dramatic relations *between* worlds unfold. Anders Blok (2013), for instance, has explored significant ontological variation in the world of ecology as ecology negotiates complex political alliances and tensions with market, civic, and other moral worths. Thinking through moral assemblages, I explore whether similar moral multiplicity characterizes every world of worth, rendering moral worth in general more open-ended and politically less coherent than is often understood. To this end I focus on high-stakes political judgments, or formal "confrontations" with reality (Blokker 2011) in which moral worth is attributed to, or extracted from, particular projects, people, and material arrangements (e.g., major policy and planning decisions). But I also trace informal banal cases of moral judgment, such as the rich (dis)approbation that occurs in everyday traffic, as they, too, interconnect with the qualification of mobility infrastructures and practices.

Adding to their multiplicity and political complexity, moral mobilities clash and compete with one another for finite moral territory. As some moral assemblages grow, others wither. I introduce the additional concept of "moral friction" to account for this territorial conflict between, but also within, moral assemblages. In some cases when differently worthy objects and people come into contact, their friction leads to outright conflict and formal public judgments wherein the moral worth of a given situation may be either unclear (market or civic?) and question which beings matter (dollars or bollards?), or the situation is crystal clear and controversy swirls instead around living up to its worth (is a cycle track sufficiently democratic?). In other cases moral friction holds differently worthy beings together in tension without sparking much public controversy, affording a measure of stability. For example, some good cycle tracks connect people to local businesses, upholding a delicate balance between market and civic infrastructure. The different scales of moral friction, global and local, remain interconnected. Like a stream overtaken by a flooding river, larger territorial dynamics can swallow up and sweep away local actors. For example, in Canada, if a city elects a car- and suburb-oriented, right-leaning government, plans for new bike lanes, and even existing cycle tracks, can suddenly face the chopping block (CBC News 2011). Ultimately moral friction elaborates how moral assemblages, across multiple scales, can both reinforce one another and break each other apart.

In what follows I introduce five moral assemblages of mobility based on five canonical understandings of the common good (Boltanski and Thévenot 2006[1991]; Latour 1998): industrial, market, domestic, civic, and ecological mobilities. These five moral assemblages of mobility compose a plurality of good cities for cycling and driving, and they generate significant moral friction. Rather than situate each moral assemblage as its own unique, open-ended world—something each subsequent chapter will do—I introduce the five assemblages within the particular contexts of driving and cycling in which they are later explored, taking inspiration from early twentieth-century fine art, early twenty-first-century advertising, and a brief vignette of a man getting ready to cycle in downtown Toronto. After plotting these points of entry for this book, and tracing the book's metanarrative about territorial conflict between moral assemblages of mobility, I then offer a less conventional retelling of this metanarrative in the form of a fable in which I personify the five moral worths underlying each assemblage as nonhuman animals.

Driving for Capitalism

What is driving worth to society? A compelling place to contemplate this question is Rivera Court, inside the Detroit Institute of Arts (see photo 2). Across the walls of the Court span Diego Rivera's *Detroit Industry Murals*, a series of frescoes he painted between 1932 and 1933. The frescoes depict brawny factory workers alongside gigantic spindles heaving and punching holes into v8 engine blocks on Ford's revolutionary comprehensive assembly lines. The frescoes also show scientists harnessing mass-production techniques to manufacture poisonous gas bombs and life-saving medical vaccines. Personally, I like to stand near the middle of Rivera Court. From the middle, if you swivel your head north and south you suddenly find yourself ensconced in a vast industrial-manufacturing complex. Human bodies and machines and car parts, all working in disturbingly close rhythm, recede like a perfectly timed procession up toward blast furnaces, foundries, and finished molds gliding on a distant conveyer belt. *Detroit Industry* punctuates the terrible, lifesaving, and altogether awesome power of modern factories, science, and commerce. Rivera used the murals during the Great Depression to announce the arrival of a new kind of civilization, one that transitioned from a religious and animistic higher calling for supernatural authority to one obsessed with techno-scientific production, mass consumption, and future progress.[3]

2. *Detroit Industry Murals.* Photo by author.

The limits of *Detroit Industry's* vision of civilization become clear when you step outside Rivera Court, descend the stairs in front of the Detroit Institute of Arts, and walk down Woodward Avenue (see photo 3). The 2008 financial crash shattered North America's "Big Three" automakers: General Motors (GM), Ford, and Chrysler. GM, Chrysler, and Detroit itself eventually filed for bankruptcy. But Detroit and its auto-industrial complex were crumbling long before America's sub-prime mortgage crisis suddenly hobbled the economy in 2008. Detroit's population shrank from its peak in the mid-twentieth century of almost two million people to about 700,000 today. An unmistakable absence hovers over Woodward Avenue. Woodward's excessive six lanes beckon to a bygone era—as does, more optimistically, its new five-kilometer (three-mile) streetcar line that opened in 2017. In the midst of unprece-dented urban depopulation Detroit made history in 2013 as the largest U.S. metropolis ever to file for bankruptcy. City-owned masterpieces in the Detroit Institute of Arts nearly became collateral damage. For-

3. Woodward Avenue, Detroit, 2015. Photo by author.

tunately a U.S. judge fought off their liquidation in the eleventh hour, arguing that "to sell the DIA art would be to forfeit Detroit's future" (Rosenbaum 2014).

Detroit shines a sobering light on the capitalist value that has come to dominate North American approaches to urban mobility and the good life. Along with Windsor, whose casino-dominated skyline you can see across the river in Canada from inside GM's Renaissance Centre, Detroit hitched its economic future to automobility. Like nowhere else Motor City endures the car's "creative destruction" (Schumpeter 2008[1942]), revealing capitalism's deeply conflicted approach to reassembling the good city.

Capitalism, on one hand, thrives on industrial worth. The common good of industry, for example, according to philosopher Henri de Saint-Simon in 1817, lies in long-term scientific planning of work and production to increase efficiency and productivity. Worthy, industrious people "work to discover and coordinate the general facts apt to serve as a basis for all combinations of agriculture, trade and manufacturing" (Saint-Simon, in Boltanski and Thévenot 2006[1991]). If industry built the car into the "quintessential manufactured object" of the twentieth century and refashioned the car-city into a "machinic complex," industrialized automobility also animates a dominant culture with "potent literary and artistic images and symbols," not to mention ubiquitous advertising (Sheller and Urry 2000, 739; Conley 2009). For example, Clint Eastwood preaches industrial moral worth to the masses through advertising in a TV commercial for Chrysler during halftime of the 2012 Super Bowl (an American football game watched by 111 million people) when he intones in his gravelly *sotto voce,*

> It's half-time in *America*, too. People are out of work and they are hurting. And they're all wondering what they can do to make a comeback. And we're all scared, because this isn't a game. The people of Detroit know a little something about this. They almost lost everything. But we all pulled together, now Motor City is fighting again. I've seen a lot of tough eras, a lot of downturns in my life. And, times when we didn't understand each other . . . we've lost our heart. When the fog of division, discord, and blame made it hard to see what lies ahead. But after those trials, we all rallied around what was right, and acted as one. Because that's what we do. We find a way through tough times, and if we can't find a way, then we'll make one. All that matters now is what's ahead. How do we come from behind? How do we come together? And, how do we win? Detroit's showing us it can be done. . . . This country can't be knocked out with one punch. We get right back up again and when we do the world is going to hear the roar of our engines. Yeah, it's half-time America. And, our second half is about to begin. (Chrysler 2012, my italics)

Eastwood delivers Chrysler's halftime pep talk with images of people driving and making cars with blast furnaces, manufacturing tools, and modern factories. Eastwood maps the personal pain of Detroit's industrial recovery onto the wider good in plain, cheap bromides: lose heart; pull together; overcome division; act as one; focus on the future; and roar of engines. At halftime there's still time left to turn it around.

Capitalism, on the other hand, thrives on market worth, which creates moral friction and alliances with industrial worth. Unlike industry's long-term horizons, good markets depend on competitive enterprise and short-term exchanges, selling and buying. The common good of the market, for Adam Smith in 1759 (2011), lay in free competition driven by deep desires in all people for inalienable ownership over rare goods. As Boltanski and Thévenot (2006[1991], 196) elaborate, "worthy objects are *salable* goods that have a *strong position* in the market. Worthy persons are rich, *millionaires*, and they *live the high life*." To see this distinction play out in the language of mass production, consider the pricey televised sermon delivered by General Motors when North America's Big Three automakers were up against financial ruin:

> Let's be completely honest. No company wants to go through this. But we're not witnessing the end of the American car. We're witnessing the *rebirth* of the American car. General Motors needs to start over in order to get stronger. . . . Reinvention is the only way to fix this, and fix it we will. So here is what the new GM will be: fewer, stronger, brands; fewer, stronger, models; greater efficiencies, better fuel economy, and new technologies; leaner, greener, faster, smarter. This is not about going out of business; it's about getting down to business. Because the only chapter we're focused on, is chapter one. (General Motors 2009, my italics)

It is no longer halftime in America. GM as we knew it is over and going back to the beginning. This television ad led a campaign called "GM Reinvention" that argued the automaker, after its insolvency and significant government bailouts, was reborn as a profitable concern. GM's projected sense of wholesale reinvention reflects the political urgency of its insolvency. It also encapsulates how markets focus on the present to accelerate new sales, even if this means uprooting Motor City's carmaking capacity and moving it to Mexico (Keenan 2015). Detroit shows how capitalist mobilities, torn between market and industrial worths, are capable of building entire cities and burning them down.

If industrial capitalism constitutes the dominant moral formation of twentieth-century automobility, neoliberal capitalism (Harvey 2005) threatens to reinvent the weal, as it were, yet again. By the 1970s, when Western welfare states were weakening and Earth Day signaled the arrival of a new form of ecological politics, the role of government started shifting toward facilitating the growth of business and privileging market solutions for complex social problems. Privatizing state assets, deregulating industry, marketizing infrastructure, and globalizing competition for scarce capital came to characterize the political ideology of neoliberal capitalism (Peck 2010; 2011; Walks 2009; Hackworth 2007), whose sails were filled by rightward political winds in many wealthy nations over the last four decades. By slowly eclipsing other moral worths championed by the Canadian state (Brodie 2002), neoliberal capitalism threatens to enshrine the open market as the principal arbiter of the common good. This isolated form of market worth differs from the markets of the mid-twentieth century that were tempered by Keynesian interventions and welfare state redistribution. Neoliberal market worth boils down the good city into short-term monetary exchanges that generate and justify extraordinary inequalities of income and capital in a globalized economy (Piketty 2014).

Freed from the fetters of public regulations and long-term planning horizons, neoliberal capitalism privileges a morally myopic practice. Good mobility in the world of neoliberal capitalism entails chasing market signals and elusive gains, for which individuals focus on coordinating themselves through intentional, enterprising actions and prudent choices. More important, by undermining moral difference, market moral hegemony may reduce the number of public judgments in which people think to appeal to the common good in the first place, any common good, including Adam Smith's competitive marketplace. Rising socioeconomic inequality, income polarization, and egregious levels of luxury are, for neoliberal market worth, publicly justifiable so long as wealthy people maintain market competition for all. But in reality "elite mobilities" (Birtchnell and Caletrio 2013) proliferate through exclusive spaces and networks wherein "organising elites in a global market society are largely responsible only to themselves and their like, [and are] no longer interested in societal projects" (Amin 2006, 1010). As a mere race between individual consumers and corporations to purchase and sell monistic worth, the common good grows emaciated. Undermining the plurality of morality, in short, augurs its political collapse.

Cycling for Home, Citizenship, and Nature

What is cycling worth to society? A compelling place to contemplate this question is Mike's apartment in Toronto's downtown eastside (see photo 4). In stark contrast to the robotic efficiency of a Ford assembly plant and the canned perfection of an automobile showroom, Mike's home bears no obvious signs as to why objects are where they are, when they arrived, or what they are for. Unlike the army of auto parts in Diego Rivera's *Detroit Industry Murals*, the cycling pieces in Mike's frugal apartment lack obvious functions and order, and it is not clear how they hold together. Cycling pieces mingle with sheet music, cacti, and crumply old receipts. Chainrings spin from the ceiling over a kitchen table teeming with (in)organic things. At first it seems like chaos. Upon closer inspection, Mike's apartment grows into a pattern of imaginative practice.

In Mike's living room and shared backyard, he takes apart and reassembles his bicycle with different tools and pieces according to the sort of voyage he imagines. He calibrates his cycling according to how many motorists he might encounter, on what sorts of infrastructure, and whether he expects to find water and trees. When Mike envisions commuting to work in car traffic, he includes gears to increase his speed and render his trips smooth, quick, and linear, and never forgets a helmet to protect himself against violent encounters with cars (especially after suffering a horrible door prize). Conversely, when Mike imagines a relaxed "Sunday ride" on dedicated pathways by the river away from fast-moving cars, he configures a fixed-gear bicycle or

4 & 5. Mike
reassembles his
bicycle at his
apartment in
Toronto. Photo
by author.

"fixie" (see photo 5). The reason Mike prefers a fixie for cycling with nature (even when this cycling takes him to work) is the extra "feel" it provides, or the sense of spatial intimacy that helps him become attuned to a wider surrounding habitat of humans and nonhumans. Mike's "cycling habitat," as it were, tends to grow as he pays it attention.

Mike's humble apartment in Toronto is morally intriguing. It hints at three moral worths outside of capitalism, the dominant moral formation of automobility. The first, domestic worth, emphasizes tradition, place, and home. Like industrial worth, domestic worth envisions an expansive view of time but toward the past. In an important sense the pieces of cycling around Mike's old apartment are not only signatures of his home but pieces of himself and local extensions of his biography. On a larger, collective scale, how and where things were done, by particular kin in unique places with specific objects, creates moral worth and a vocabulary for publicly judging change. Going against the flow of elders' mobility knowledge and conventions can prove difficult. After more than a century of driving, people view the car itself as an extension of family and home (Urry 2006). And yet Mike thinks the same of his cycling. The problem is, like Henry Ford's motorcar before it—when the car, too, was an upstart—Mike's cycling "ruffles feathers," especially when he feels entitled and rides through streets "like he owns the place," or is at least perceived that way by others. Strife, for domestic worth, entails "interrupting the chain of generations that unites and classifies beings according to tradition," such that "innovation becomes an intrinsic source of discord" (Boltanski and Thévenot 2006[1991], 94). Mike generates discord when motorists view his cycling as taking away road space that traditionally, if not by divine right, has belonged to them. At the same time, Mike is constantly tempted to become territorial himself in places outside his home where cycling is becoming conventionally prioritized.

The second moral worth outside capitalism glimpsed in Mike's apartment is civic worth. The care with which Mike calibrates and tailors his cycling to different urban environments while carrying on informal conversations outside with his neighbors, betrays an engagement

with his community and concern for civility and public space. Phil-
osophically speaking, moral authority for civic worth lies in a shared
sovereignty held above private interests. Rather than bloodlines or
company towns, the civic sovereign, as articulated by Rousseau in
The Social Contract, is "disembodied, . . . created by the convergence
of human wills" around "the general will" (Boltanski and Thévenot
2006[1991], 108). In practice, finding commonality demands community participation, the ongoing protection of public space and fighting
for distributive and procedural forms of "mobility justice" (Sheller
2017). For example, a great challenge for converging North America's
"general will" around cycling is the unequal concentration of cycling
and good bike lanes among well-off Caucasians, especially middle-
aged white men (Hoffman 2016; Pucher et al. 2011). Mobility justice
requires a complex intersectional lens, through which some aspects of
Mike's own identity align with privilege in a white settler society. Civic
worth expands where people stake out rights to the city and contest
sexist, racist, ageist, ableist, and otherwise exclusive infrastructure—
for example, restricted access highways—and use liberal democratic
procedures like laws and social movements to advance equality and
solidarity. Civic articulations of worth based on equity and democracy
arguably play an increasingly powerful role in challenging capitalistic
notions of the good city (Golub et al. 2016).

Finally, the third, and strangest, moral worth outside of capitalism, a
kind of black sheep that wanders away from the rest, is that of ecology.
Traces of it lie all around Mike's apartment in the houseplants, compost, and vegetable gardens outside that mingle with his cycling pieces.
It also lies in the calibration of his slower, more outwardly sensorial
cycling for encountering and paying attention to nonhuman beings
such as rivers, birds, and trees. Ecological moral worth acts unlike any
other. It tips over the table set by industrial and market worths by dis-
pensing with the hedonistic utilitarian value theoretically underlying
the economics of capitalism (Price 2004). As if this were not enough,
ecological worth burns down the entire house people built for all their
common goods. Civic, domestic, and industrial worths all generate

moral friction with hedonistic utilitarian value where it undermines equity, heritage, and long-term planning. Only ecology, however, rejects the basic idea behind them all: the existence of a higher moral principle of humanity based on "models of the shared competence required of persons in order for agreement to be possible" (Boltanski and Thévenot 2006[1991], 66). If shared competences lie at the core of a common humanity, what stops this commonality from spilling over into other species of life? If nonhuman great apes, microbiomes, and mycelia might also be competent "persons," ecology, in principle, might be as politically disruptive as neoliberal capitalism. Unlike markets and industry, however, ecology, rooted in complex associations across time and space scales that largely elude humans, lacks a clear strategy for becoming a politically formidable force.

Ecology could ape neoliberal capitalism. It could simply try to devour the other moral worths, drawing heavily on its absolutist faction of deep, dyed-in-the-wool ecologists who allow "little compromise with other human concerns" (Price 2004, 201). Taking over, however, would make "ecology responsible for all of politics and all of the economy on the basis that everything is interrelated" in "a single system of nature and society" (Latour 1998, 2). Without centuries of political philosophy or popular political parties to stand on, ecology could, alternatively, simply compromise with, and become a conventional part of, other moral worths (Lamont and Thévenot 2000; Blok 2013)—effectively conceding its own identity. For example, ecologists could monitor the health of watersheds and species the way factory workers do, extend rights to ever more species of life, and abandon ecology's formative political history of criticizing the market's environmentally devastating externalities in favor of an unprecedented "ecofiscal" marriage built on correcting market signals (Canada's Ecofiscal Commission 2014). None of these options are politically tenable for ecology. Humans lack both the super experts to manage a single nature-society system and the political will to face "one's electorate with a programme that envisages the possibility of making them disappear in favour of a 'congress for animals' who don't even vote or pay taxes!" (Latour 1998, 11). Reducing rivers, forests, animals, and other living beings into hedonistic utilitarian value, moreover, rubs ecology fundamentally the wrong way.

Ecology escapes this political cul-de-sac, I contend, by cultivating its own common good and moral assemblage that abandons outdated modernist notions of a common humanity (Latour 1998) in favor of new ways of coordinating human and nonhuman beings (Thévenot 2002; Blok 2013). To consolidate a stable moral force in the world, ecology cannot rigidly oppose human against nonhuman natures. Rather, ecological worth must openly question a common humanity by never treating nonhuman beings simply as means "but always also as ends" (Latour 1998, 15–17). Ecological worth, following Latour by extending Kant's basic "ends-in-themselves" moral principle to nonhumans, blows a fierce counterwind throughout this book against neoliberal capitalism, a force of moral opening up against a force of moral closure. Against the drumbeat of overreaching markets and urban financialization, ecology proclaims: not for sale! If this counterwind tips over a table (set by market-industrial capitalism) or burns down a house (built on a higher common humanity), it could spark a much larger fire that takes down a parched and cluttered landscape full of valuable structures. What might grow back after a forest fire of moral virtues? If the century of the car has closed and the century of cycling has just begun, what moral lessons can cycling learn from driving?

The following fable is a story that traces the book's metanarrative by personifying the moral worths underlying the assemblages of mobility as nonhuman animals. By metanarrative, I mean my interpretation of territorial conflict between five moral assemblages, one rooted in the experience of urban Canada and to a lesser degree the United States that will not necessarily generalize to other countries. You might come to a different interpretation based on my evidence—I am not offering mine as the only right way to parse the facts. But it flows directly from my analysis. Fables are not a conventional, social-scientific way of presenting an overarching thesis. But nor is political morality simply a matter of social science. As it happens, fables and the personification of moralities (e.g., Aesop's Fables in ancient Greece; medieval morality plays) have a long history of synthesizing complex moral dilemmas. It seems that capturing the complexity of multiple moralities in discrete characters helps provoke insightful thinking around their relations.

The Black Coyote

Cast (in order of appearance)

Crows . . . . Domestic
Foxes . . . . Market
Raccoons . . . . . . Industrial
Bees Civic
Beavers . . . . Industrial
Coyote . . . . Ecological

Crows on a wire whisper an old story to each other. It tells of a long-forgotten time before the City had yet caught on fire, a time that existed before the black coyote came and all the great neighborhoods in the City burned down.

Countless blue moons ago, the story goes, during an urban planning meeting about garbage collection, crows found themselves interrupted by a most unfamiliar sound. From their alleyway perch they could see the source of the queer sound: a fox, molesting a City compost bin, a bin to whose construction crows had devoted considerable energy and political capital (appealing to the industrial skills and better nature of raccoons). A raucous murder of crows suddenly turned into a devastating dive-bomb. Once dispatched, the fox fell from the crows' minds—until they spotted four fleeting foxes the following week, and fourscore more not long thereafter.

At first most did not know what to think of foxes. Crows with the longest memories fretted that foxes would undermine the City's Old Ways. Bees worried that foxes might undermine equality among the City's residents. Beavers were distressed that foxes could be wasteful with materials, but they also noted that foxes did not look that different from everyone else. Raccoons quickly defended foxes, having recently arrived to the City themselves. Only coyotes, watching in the background and listening to the winds change, sensed that something small was amiss. They creeped up on foxes moving cunningly within the forest and watched as they co-opted forgotten spaces between the City and the countryside. But nobody talked to coyotes.

More and more foxes came. They brought tasty food, strange machines, and protected property, increasing trade between the great neighborhoods while generating new work and wealth. Before long every part of the City began working with foxes. With fox financing, beavers bought better tools and began cutting down bigger trees to build larger lodges, dams, and highways. Bees allied with foxes in private-public partnerships for the City's pollination. Raccoons started producing their own dens before flipping them onto the market for a healthy return. Even the most miserly crows agreed that tourism dollars sustained local heritage sites. There were fights with foxes, who insisted everything was for sale. But before long foxes had built their own great neighborhood, and everyone agreed that foxes formed a valuable part of the City.

Flush with fox capital, the City rapidly grew upward and outward, spreading affluence while sparking conflicts between neighbors old and new. Amid skyrocketing property values many bees and crows could no longer afford to live and raise families downtown in the City's coolest high towers. Renovictions were rife. To the horror of crows, mom-and-pop shops and green grocers that had existed for many generations gave way to sleek new bicycle repair coffeehouses. Raccoons and beavers in the sprawling suburbs suffered long commutes during increasingly hot and dry weather, chafing under new toll roads that seemed to unfairly target them. The rain never really rolled over like it used to, all the way from the coast through the forest and up the mountains. At one point tensions flickering around foxes and fox-owned enterprises became so numerous that crows felt like they had no choice but to call an emergency session of the old City Council. To everyone's surprise, coyotes showed up.

"Foxes," slowly intoned old crows into creaky microphones at the Council, "have become too many. At first they brought opportunity and improved livelihoods. But now, unchecked, they threaten to usurp the values and traditions of our homeland. With shadowy money from the countryside, foxes are remaking a City we no longer recognize as our own." Lowering their voices, "Something must be done."

"Something in the ambit of City laws," bees concurred. "It is true, the growth of fox enterprises and its effect on our community should give the Council pause. Are foxes threatening to undermine the civil way of life on which our fair and equal City was built?"

"Now wait," protested beavers. "While we agree the City has changed dramatically under the influence of foxes, we believe this influence has generally been positive. Net profits and enjoyment from woodworks and waterworks have grown prodigiously since foxes arrived."

"And the price of pizza has fallen precipitously, which in turn lowers compost bin overheads and motivates workers," raccoons chimed in. "And don't the City's Old Ways include embracing change?"

"And we have more choice in materials for better houses, roads, and dams than ever before," continued beavers and raccoons in unison. "Not to mention the fact that foxes are financing much needed infra-structure for our City's future."

"A threat to our way of life!" crows and bees bellowed.

"A chance to upgrade our City!" beavers and raccoons shouted back.

"Friends," coyotes broke in, creating a moment of bewilderment, "singling out foxes is dangerous. And a red herring. You fail to notice the City unraveling while everyone defines, and is defined by—"

"Foxes," crows angrily interrupted, "are social aberrants and can-cerous to the City." Hastily tabling a bold motion, crows proclaimed, "All foxes who fail to plead allegiance to the City's Old Ways are to be deported, effective immediately, full stop." City Council voted on the motion:

Crows: *Yea!*
Beavers: *Nay!*
Raccoons: *Nay!*
Bees: *Yea!*
Coyotes: *Abstain.*

(As was the custom in the event of a tie at Council, the motion was rescinded and sent back to committee, where it later died a slow, painful death.)

With the support of innovative beavers, entrepreneurial raccoons, and a handful of well-endowed crows from the old Council, foxes transformed the entire City. Fox-run enterprises razed and revitalized slums for new convention centers, stadiums, and ports for containers and cruises. Billboards everywhere shouted, "City Economic Action Plan." Luxury lodges, high-end trees, and property value debates became the norm. A thriving underground economy emerged for industrial compost bins and luxury lodge rentals. Bees were suspicious: Where did foxes keep securing liquid capital? The City became a perpetual construction project fully leveraged on borrowed money from who knew where. (Coyotes had some good ideas about where but not enough ears in Council to hear them.)

One night, meeting in secret on top of the City Hall, a group of powerful bees and crows hatched a plan to forcibly deport foxes. Before dawn, knowing the old City better than anyone, crows and bees dispatched devastating dive-bombers and swarms of suicide stingers. In a desperate attempt to reassert control of a just Council and recover the Old Ways, they culled corrupt foxes and took over fox-owned properties. Innards spilled on both sides, before the plan backfired. The coup was lost in the suburban battlegrounds, where crows and bees were repelled by an Alliance of foxes, beavers, and raccoons surrounding the City. Then the Alliance, spying an irresistible opportunity, moved in and mounted City Hall. In a hostile takeover (that became an unexpectedly close call when coyotes arrived from nowhere and important foxes were assassinated), foxes acquired the great neighborhoods of crows and bees.

With crow judges and priests and pesky bee lawmakers out of view, foxes acted with neither restraint nor reserve. The Alliance outsourced the fire department, garbage collection, and other public services to private fox-controlled subsidiaries and shell companies under the banner of City austerity. Declaring a permanent state of emergency, fox leaders took possession over the great neighborhoods of beavers and raccoons, right after arresting and unceremoniously executing the crows and bees responsible for planning the coup. In the ever-hotter seasons that followed, the Alliance purged the City of any journalist, teacher, doctor, or lawyer suspected of anti-Alliance sentiments. With a Machiavellian touch, fox leaders flooded social media with stories that played hardworking beavers and taxpaying raccoons against entitled crows and elitist bees.

As the City paved over the countryside, the tranquil rain forest became a tinder-dry savanna. Rain came only infrequently and tried to drown the City when it did. Crows and bees would no longer nest or do business with beavers and raccoons—and vice versa. For a time, while in hiding, bees and crows ran a college radio station, trying to convince City dissidents that foxes were fascist vermin who would run the City bone-dry with their mendacity. Foxes, of course, found out about it. With a cunning they were known to possess during important situations, foxes lit small fires across the City while leaking stories about offshore accounts used by wealthy crows and bees on private island banks owned by foxes. Wealthy crows and bees were rounded up in their last high offices by those in whose eyes they finally saw themselves. A Pyrrhic pogrom ensued. Every day at dusk, coyotes and foxes in the distance cried horrible sounds over the whirs of hundred-year cicadas.

One day, during the driest dregs of summer, the entire savanna exploded into an inferno of its own weather and design, and the City burned to the ground. Noble persons and structures were incinerated. The City and all of its great neighborhoods were about to lay fallow for countless blue moons. Before the City fell asleep, an injured young crow woke up after the last fight, startled by a most unfamiliar sound. The ashes surrounding the crow suddenly shifted into a black coyote, who said flatly, "It's gone."

"Why," the crow groaned, "why is it gone?"

Covered in soot, the coyote stared at the dying crow with concern. After a long pause the coyote explained, "The City lived in all of its great neighborhoods. When the great neighborhoods had a lot but wanted more, everybody lost everything."

"But you, coyote, are not outside the City, are you?" gasped the quiet crow. "Can you not say if the City will ever return?"

"I do not know," the coyote pondered. "Slowly, perhaps. Like the rain forest."

Itinerary: Five Good Cities

This book argues that cycling can learn from driving in five salient ways. The expansion of twenty-first-century cycling can build on the domestic, industrial, market, civic, and ecological assembling of twentieth-century driving. Over and above these five moral assemblages, cycling can draw a deeper metalesson from driving: given the political diminution of moral plurality via industrial and then neoliberal capitalism, cycling ought to recalibrate the good city by emphasizing domestic, civic, and ecological worth. In this opening chapter I introduce industrial and market worth through driving, and domestic, civic, and ecological worth through cycling, not because driving fails to generate home, nature, or citizenship, or because capitalism will not be critical for the growth of cycling—quite the contrary. But for the sake of moral plurality and a multiplicity of good cycling cities, I am proposing the expansion of cycling, as a whole, ought to diverge from the dominant moral formation and trajectory of automobility.

The book follows two intertwining arcs. First it flows along a non-linear chronological arc, between two centuries. In each chapter I juxtapose a "critical planning moment of automobility" (Scott 2012) from the twentieth century (and one from the future), featuring leaps of infrastructure, politics, and practice, what I call "driving lessons," against the socio-technical and political rise of cycling in the twenty-first century. The second arc of the book follows moral friction between competing moral assemblages of mobility, and elucidates how cycling might learn from old crows whispering on a wire. To bring each moral assemblage of mobility to life I rely on a comparative mix of ethno-graphic ride-alongs, case studies of cities, case studies of infrastructure, and interviews with experts—the precise mix and weighting of which varies by chapter. Each chapter features three carefully selected cases (Flyvbjerg 2006) for empirical analysis whose contrasts illuminate the multiplicity inside each unique moral assemblage of cycling.

Chapter 1 traces how mobilities domesticate the city through cultural traditions, historic roads, and the socio-technical expansion of home. Domestic mobilities bring home, local political hierarchies, and an intergenerational sense of place into vehicles, landscapes, and urban policy. The driving lesson here is to construct "good roads" that animate home and local history without undermining selective traditions or existing attachments to urban places. To draw out this lesson for cycling, I follow the Canadian good roads movement in the 1920s as it reimagines home as happening between the city and the "unspoiled" colonial countryside via circuits of the motorcar tour, and I compare this movement with contemporary ways of animating home and local tradition through (and on) bikeways, or "good roads for cycling." I focus on Vancouver's bikeways and burgeoning cargo bike culture, using ethnographic data of parents cycling with their young children to school and work using different kinds of vehicles and roads. To further illustrate how domestic mobilities weave collective memory and home across generations into material cycling infrastructure, I shadow a woman riding the length of the Adanac-Union Bikeway, Vancouver's busiest bikeway that forms her "umbilical cycling route" between home and the city. Chapter 1 concludes by exploring possibilities for domestic cycling to enliven ecological ways of remembering the city and generate friction with industrial visions of generic infrastructural solutions that transcend locale.

Chapter 2 examines how mobilities industrialize time-space through road engineering, urban planning, and the infrastructuring of efficiency. Industrial mobilities turn the city into abstract space, a clean tabula rasa on which to write hierarchical, functionalist mobility systems that rationalize circulation. The driving lesson here is to avoid the hubris of high modernism and excesses of industrial capitalism while mobilizing the capacity of engineers and city planners to assemble good infrastructure.

Applying this lesson to cycling, I follow the engineering and planning of cycling in Motor City—both Windsor and Detroit—outlining the features of what I call "first-wave cycling planning" (2000–2010). In Motor City I also examine the figure of the cycling "engineer-bricoleur" (Harvey and Knox 2015). I then analyze Ottawa, tracing the repercussions of postwar planning for modern-day cycling through Jacques Gréber's 1950 Plan for National Capital and subsequent developments in population growth forecasting. I explore how Ottawa has learned from the mistakes of its first-wave cycling planning and is already taking the industrial production of cycling to the next level. Finally, to show what abstract industrial infrastructure feels like when you are riding on it and how the everyday experience of cycling becomes embroiled with industrial legacies of the car, I shadow a man who cycles to the "mall on the highway" in Dartmouth, Nova Scotia.

Chapter 3 analyzes how mobilities generate justice through social equality, democratic infrastructure, and solidarity. Civic mobilities transform roads into rights-of-way and road users into citizens of nations. The driving lesson here is to make mobility good by strengthening democratic forms of community without creating tyrannies of the majority or making permanent any social exclusion presupposed by citizenship. To trace this lesson out for cycling I follow the car taking hold of Canada's postwar civic identity through national infrastructure, especially the Trans-Canada Highway, and compare it to ongoing efforts to reinvent urban citizenship through cycling. I argue that, like driving, cycling constitutes a "civilizing process" (Elias 2000) that forges territorial equivalence and reassembles manners through socially exclusive practices and considerations of the self in relation to the cycling and driving communities (Aldred 2010). Specifically I follow the political and material construction of one of Canada's first dedicated bike lanes (Laurier Avenue in Ottawa), different cycling social movements as they wrestle with cycling inclusion in Motor City, and the rise of cycling gentrification as it threatens to limit prime cycling environments to those who can afford to live in the central city. Canadian cities are making cycling more inclusive by reducing cycling inequalities through what I call "second-wave cycling planning" (2011–20). Second-wave planning emphasizes dedicated cycling infrastructure that addresses some inequalities around age and gender, while exacerbating others through racialized cycling gentrification. This complexity of cycling inequality, I contend, shows the need for an intersectionality-based approach to cycling equity that explicitly problematizes cycling gentrification (Lubitow 2016) and design through a "third-wave cycling planning." Complex cycling inequalities also show the ongoing need for cycling social movements, like Slow Roll in Detroit, Tweed Ride in Windsor, and the Trans-Canada Trail, to further democratize cycling.

Chapter 4 examines how mobilities marketize urban society as a competition for inalienable ownership over rare things and elite experiences. Market mobilities convert streets, housing, and people into ventures, currencies, and consumers. The driving lesson here is to construct a competitive market that incentivizes innovation without triggering the political collapse of morality via hegemonic neoliberal capitalism. To elaborate this lesson I follow fiscal austerity in Motor City and the "attritional automobility" of billionaire Matty Maroun's expansion of the Ambassador Bridge by expropriating a Windsor neighborhood, and I compare the "authoritarian populism" (Walks 2015) of Rob Ford's regime in Toronto to what I call the "taxpayer tyranny" of Vancouver's failed 2015 referendum to finance non-car mobilities. I then use these "critical neoliberal moments of automobility" to contextualize efforts by Canadian cities, developers, and businesses to justify new cycling policies and infrastructure as a way to advance consumption and commercial profit. Juxtaposing Detroit's insolvency with that of the Bixi bike share brand, precipitated by investments in "new proprietary technology for international clients" (CBC News 2014), I examine how cyclists are positioned broadly by bicycle sharing systems, city planners, and urban developers as good consumers who advance wealth creation and luxury ways of living, drawing on Vancouver as a model of market cycling and cycling gentrification. Chapter 4 concludes by discussing how "elite secession" (Sheller 2016) by the kinetically privileged occurs not only through motorized vehicles but also through cycling.

Chapter 5 illuminates how mobilities ecologize the city by assembling cosmopolitan habitats through the enactment of nature and wilderness. Ecological mobilities turn people into human beings and mobilities into moments of encounter with nonhuman beings. The driving lesson here is to facilitate access to wild nature in the city through infrastructure without destroying habitat for nonhumans and ramping up anthropogenic climate change. To draw out this lesson for cycling, I compare parkways designed for driving nature in the early twentieth-century city to different pathways constructed since the 1970s in Ottawa and Toronto that afford "cycling nature." While environmental devastation is not motivating many people to cycle, people across Canada incorporate nature into their regular cycling. I seize on this insight to illuminate how cycling becomes ecologically worthy by enacting wild nature, not as something opposed to urban life, like previous forms of ecological automobility, but as something fundamentally imbued with the city, even its wastelands. In Ottawa and Toronto I show how cycling ecologizes the city by creating "cycling habitats" in which humans become familiar with, even concerned for, nonhuman beings in their vicinity. To accentuate urban possibilities for ecological mobilities, I then embark on a brief foray to Oulu in northern Finland, where infrastructure for cycling with nature reaches into the city's bones. The chapter concludes that ecological mobilities contest conventional notions of city and nature and strongly justify an expansion of cycling the urban wild at the expense of driving it.

The conclusion explores good mobility futures through moral vectors that cross multiple moral assemblages of cycling and proposes a progressive coalition for the moral assembly of cycling. Drawing on findings from each chapter, I conclude that impending pressure to gear cycling in Canada toward capitalistic expansion will be overwhelming under the gravity of market and industrial mobilities. However, I suggest—without discounting a role for cycling business and cycling techno-science—that what the car's experience really teaches humans about urban mobility expansion is to follow the political lead of ecology. A morally compelling path forward for cycling, I contend, depends on ecological mobilities leading the expansion of cycling along with civic and domestic mobilities so as to contest neoliberal capitalism. A postcapitalist détente must mitigate complex internal frictions, for example, where greater access to nature undermines it and ecological knowledge perpetuates colonial power. Its greater task, however, entails countering the external production of a hegemonic cycling space that not only erases distinctions between bodies, natures, and histories but also reduces cycling to a competitive vehicle for expanding individualistic consumption. Before fleshing out an aspirational and progressive politics of cycling based on implementing a national city cycling plan and a liberal democratic cycling education housed in public school, the book finishes off by retelling the fable of "The Black Coyote," this time from the perspective of its eponymous character.

6. Helena points to the Forks in Winnipeg, Manitoba. Photo by author.

1. Domestic Mobilities

Local Tradition, Urban Place, and Good Roads

What makes mobilities domestically good? What makes a bike lane good for creating "home"? What domestic lessons can cycling glean from driving? These questions lead to consideration of a time-honored moral assemblage of mobility, one rooted (and routed) in the generation of home, family, and the past. Domestic mobilities animate tradition and a sense of place. In popular judgments, however, they might come across as anti-innovation. For example, domestic worth informs not-in-my-backyard-style attacks on new development, like condos and cycle tracks, waged by local communities against top-down changes to their neighborhoods. However, not all domestic judgments entail knee-jerk reactions to change. As an expansive moral assemblage, domestic mobilities encompass long-standing relations among families, dwellings, roads, animals, plants, and affective atmospheres (Pink and Mackley 2016). The longer and deeper these relations are in time and place, the higher the domestic worth of mobilities. With a philosophical pedigree that predates liberal, modern social imaginaries (Taylor 2004), domestic worth links families and their infrastructures to great cosmic chains of beings that have come before. The car, itself a relatively new artifact in human history, mobilizes domestic judgment against cycling. For example, wealthy enclaves have been known to fight bike lane construction in the name of local tradition. At the same time, cars offer inspiration for cycling as an assemblage to keep people in touch with their roots.

Who taught you how to cycle—do you remember? For many people this question leads to a pivotal intergenerational moment of mobility that connects people's cycling to their elders, their families, and their homes. Most of my respondents say it was mainly their father who taught them how to ride, morphing a keen sense of vulnerability into something more like independence. I remember that my mother played a critical role for me. Deep in the Canadian suburbs of 1987, wearing knitted slippers and gigantic glasses as she stood in the driveway amid the dregs of winter (see photo 7), my mother helped launch my lifelong relationship with cycling. Two years ago I suddenly thought to inquire about that little bike in photo 7. It turned out that my parents, while purging the attic only a month earlier, had thrown it to the curb. To my surprise I was upset, as if it had been stolen. That memorable bike embodied a powerful affective bond between my parents, my siblings (some of whom also learned how to ride on it), my home, and me. In modern liberal societies parents often romanticize the moment when they let go of their children on two wheels for the first time as a pro-verbial cutting of the umbilical cord, the making of an individual self. Another way to look at it—one that resonates more strongly with the sense of loss I felt over that little red bike—is the reverse: the moment when home starts unfurling and flowing out of the driveway, down the street, and, by way of only the most familiar and well-worn routes, into the city itself.

The articulation of domestic mobilities, wherein home flows and circulates beyond particular hearths and dwellings, is executed by most Canadians via their cars—drives to churches, mosques, synagogues, and sundry other temples; drives to resolve domestic concerns and chores at the mall and community engagements; drives to be with old branches and new twigs on the family tree; drives to just spend time driving with family. However, as ever more people sync their roots with cycling routes and cycling routines, the urban nature of domestic mobilities is itself changing, offering new ways of translating home into wider, translocal places (Massey 1993) and multicentered worlds (Williams and Patten 2006). This ongoing domestic transformation begs the question: What kinds of intergenerational flows of home can cycling afford?

7. My mother teaches me to cycle in 1987. Photo by Stephen Scott.

Flowing Home

Domestic mobilities animate households, hearths, and homes, quilting the past and a sense of place into the present. In the classic understanding of domestic morality, "people's worth depends on their hierarchical position in a chain of personal dependencies" that leads all the way up to a godhead (Boltanski and Thévenot 2006[1991], 90). Each individual forms only a part of a vast corporate body, a body made up of many households with their own lineages and hierarchical bonds between human and nonhuman beings that, to an extent, resemble and generalize familial relations:

Each man is a father to his subordinates and a son to his superiors. But the familial analogy refers less to blood ties, here, than the fact of belonging to the same household, as a territory in which the relation of domestic dependence is inscribed. . . . His house is a second skin. . . . Beings are distributed according to the relation they maintain to a house (as evidenced by the distinction—a very pertinent one in [the domestic] polity—between domestic animals and wild animals) and, inside the household, according to the role they play in the reproduction of the family line. (Boltanski and Thévenot 2006[1991], 90)

Even in classic teleological conceptions of domestic worth, as exemplified by biblical texts and the institutions of monarchy, those on the lower rungs of the great chain of being—children, sinners, women, servants, slaves, the family dog and cat—are better off than they would have been without a household. However, this does not mean that people (or pets) in households enjoy individual rights or the freedom to choose and revise what kind of good life they wish to lead. Classic chains of this household dependence—versions of which still play out in small pockets of religious and ethnocultural fundamentalism across Western democracies—clash strongly with contemporary rights and freedoms in liberal societies such as Canada. Given the illiberal, blood-bound nature of classic households, to theorize domestic mobilities I draw on the related yet distinctive idea of home.

Mobilities become domestically good, I propose, by assembling home. Home offers an evocative way to associate mobilities with tradition, place, and familial ways of life without permanently locking the domestic worth of persons and places into these ways of life forever, as they are in the classic household. Home is revisable. Home forms but one transposable situation in which people judge and assemble the good life. People not only revise the particular homes for which they enact relations of care and belonging; home itself is contested by other ways of assembling worth. For example, traditional ways of making home through co-presence, especially among mothers and children, are challenged by women participating in the workforce at unprecedented levels. When governments in wealthy countries define "good mothering" as gaining paid employment or self-enterprise but do not publicly support working mothers by granting parental leave, child care, and flexible work hours, home life may suffer. Some experts worry that neoliberal pressures and the marketization of child care are turning home into "a site of financially recompensed interactions, rather than a locus in which all the social relations and interactions [are] assumed to be based on ties of love and affection and largely performed outside a cash nexus" (McDowell 2007, 132). This moral friction between domestic and market worths is only one way in which home is becoming distanciated and practiced at a distance through mobility. And yet home finds it difficult to embrace its place on the move.

Domestic mobilities are unique among moral assemblages and somewhat oxymoronic, causing intractable tension between moral worth and mobility itself. Home, and its companion ideas of place and dwelling, has long been viewed by social scientists as something that, by and large, stays put. By remaining rooted in one place, the thinking goes, home and neighborhoods thrive over time. According to the Chicago School of Urban Studies, too much mobility overwhelms and degenerates modern urban societies (Burgess 1925[1970]). Some level of free-flowing locomotion is important for a healthy city metabolism, "but ha[s] to be stabilized by association and anchored within place" (Sheller and Urry 2000, 741). Without roots people become rudderless, like the figurative hobo (Cresswell 2010). This narrative of the city as undermined by excessive mobility later resonates with theories of civil society in which places of dwelling supported by local associations that strengthen community keep people bonded and trustful of one another and prevent authentic places from becoming homogenized (Heidegger 2002[1954]; Putnam 2000; Relph 1976). The mobilities paradigm (Sheller and Urry 2006; 2000) articulates a strong counter perspective of movement that challenges such sedentary thinking wherein only rooted places of dwelling and associating are normal and healthy for urban people but not migrations, pilgrimages, wilderness holidays, or everyday journeys through the city. Still, while the mobilities paradigm has opened up new avenues for understanding place, community, and dwelling—as loci of exchange and translocal interaction rather than as bounded containers (Massey 1993)—home remains underexplored. Where home has been creatively investigated as a matter of mobilities, it is often equated with houses (Anderson et al. 2016; Pink and Mackley 2016) and, by extension, with cars (Wagner 2017; Ellingsen and Hidle 2013).

Home exceeds the house—and not only by car (Moore 2016). On one hand, the expansion of long-distance mobilities and virtual travel continues to disrupt the notion of home as a particular place. From domestic migrant labor (Cox 2006) and annual diasporic flows (Wagner 2017) to the rapid multiplication of private homes among the kinetic elite (Birtchnell and Caletrio 2013), mobilities are actively making new forms of home and dwellingness on the move. People not only dwell in a "multi-centred world" (Williams and Patten 2006); they find home *in* mobility. On the other hand, even homes that constitute particular houses in specific places transcend local space and present time. As Henri Lefebvre argues, the house has an "air of stability about it. One might almost see it as the epitome of immovability, with its concrete and its stark, cold and rigid outlines" (1991, 92–93). But this solidity quickly dissolves, when the house is "permeated from every direction by streams of energy which run in and out of it by every direction: water, gas, electricity, telephone lines, radio and television signals, and so on." Especially in the digital era, the house's "image of immobility" should be "replaced by an image of a complex of mobilities, a nexus of in and out conduits." It is worth noting that in this often-quoted passage, Lefebvre was describing home as a machine.

In a less-cited but domestically richer description inspired by Gaston Bachelard's (1994[1958]) ideas on the poetics of space, Lefebvre defines home as a richly temporal (and representational) space of memory:

> Consider the house, the dwelling. In the cities—and even more so in the "urban fabric" which proliferates around the cities precisely

because of their disintegration—the House has a merely historico-poetic reality rooted in folklore, or (to put the best face on it) in ethnology. This *memory*, however, has an obsessive quality: it persists in art, poetry, drama and philosophy. What is more, it runs through the terrible urban reality which the twentieth century has instituted, embellishing it with a nostalgic aura while also suffusing the work of its critics. . . . The dwelling passes everywhere for a special, still sacred, quasi-religious and in fact almost absolute space. . . . The contents of the House have an almost ontological dignity in Bachelard: drawers, chests and cabinets are not far removed from their natural analogues, perceived by the philosopher—poet, namely the basic figures of nest, corner, roundness, and so on. In the background, so to speak, stands Nature—maternal if not uterine. The House is as much cosmic as it is human. (Lefebvre 1991, 120–21)

The "House" flows and spills over the walls of dwellings into the streets while furnishing the city with ontological dignity and a cosmic connection. Lefebvre's rendering of home as memory shows that, in addition to moral friction with market worth, domestic mobilities share a strong temporal and process-related affinity with ecology, including a shared vision of place as an ever- and always-unfolding process formed through movement (Ingold 2008). If home exceeds the static house, as well as the sedentary conceptions of place and dwelling, where does home flow to? More important, how does it flow? How do mobility and home become together?

I imagine home as flowing through familial roots, familiar routes and the everyday routines by which roots are remade and remembered. Domestic assemblages of mobility take on more multiplicity than we often realize. Sometimes familial roots take on a physical co-presence, as when parents cycle with their children. At other times roots link generations but under conditions of absence, as when traveling on a familiar route brings about the reliving of an earlier familial voyage, like leaving the den, losing a parent, or an irreversible transatlantic emigration. At still other times roots entwine different communities and cultures, as when a confluence of rivers seasonally draws together a diverse city of people for thousands of years. Regardless of form, putting down one's roots constitutes a flowing, quite ordinary process reinforced by routine movement and well-worn pathways that map people onto place. The very act of longing for roots comprises an important affective piece of this process, where searching "for an authentic identity, a romantic dream of going back to roots, generates connections and links between the urban and the rural, the modern and the traditional, between 'routes and roots' " (Ellingsen and Hidle 2013, 255, citing Clifford 1997).

At first glance, traveling with children, riding and remembering familial routes, visiting traditional gathering places, and feeling nostalgic about home may all seem a bit thin as a domestic foundation for human flourishing. But consider the extensive synchronicity with which families enact domestic mobilities in the same seasons and rhythms between school and work, between weekends and holidays, between using shared equipment and infrastructure. Small-scale, local-level domestic routes and routines, when assembled together en masse, support a larger, common domestic good—one compatible with a liberal society. Inflating home and nostalgia into higher political registers, for example, by restoring a nativist fatherland with a manifest destiny, simply takes us back to where we started in the classic teleological household where domestic worth depends on being born into the right body bloodline. On the (trans)local scale, domestic mobilities instead assemble open-ended and ultimately fleeting associations. Nobody really knows where home will flow.

Driving Lessons

Imagine yourself in the summer of 1925, flowing with your family west across Canada on roads, paved and unpaved, swelling with American tourists, freight trucks, local migrants, and European immigrants. You find yourself easily and strangely at home in your five-passenger touring car, a McLaughlin Master Six. The Toronto newspaper ad that convinced you to own one shows a smartly dressed couple smiling inside a Master Six in front of Banff Springs Hotel with the snowcapped Rocky Mountains towering in the background. Something about that majestic old railway hotel combined with the creature comforts of your touring car (which has a roof on it and fits all your luggage), on top of the growing supply of good roads, pulls you into an adventurous family holiday.[1] Now you invent your own family routes across the countryside at twenty miles an hour. As the prairie roads rumble beneath your feet, you daydream of your family laughing at Indian Days in Banff, a multiday carnival for tourists showing Indians as they traditionally lived in the untamed wilderness. You cannot wait to see the looks on your kids' faces when they see their first moose.

The traffic congestion on the colonial highways states the obvious: the touring car has become more than just a "summer toy" ("*Automobiles More than Summer Toy*" 1920) or a "new sport of the rich" (CAA 2010). The Master Six is "Canada's Standard Car" said the ad, although very little seems standard about the horseless carriage. Its plainspoken manual says, "like any other fine piece of machinery, an automobile requires a certain amount of regular attention," and "in a short time a driver gets a 'feel' for his car" (McLaughlin Motor Car Co 1922, 11). But it took a long while for you to form the new habit of driving. Mistakes were made. "Never try to start an engine by pushing down on the starting crank as a back-fire is likely to result in a broken arm." Oops. "Never attempt to reverse the motion of the car before it has come to a complete stop. The car cannot move in two directions at the same time and the result is certain to be serious if this is attempted." Confirmed. "Form the habit of locking the ignition switch when leaving the car standing alone. Never leave the car with the engine running, as this is a useless waste of gasoline and there is always a chance that children or others may throw the transmission gears into mesh" (McLaughlin Motor Car Co. 1922, 12). "Others" included you, too, as it happened. But, eventually, driving your fine machinery became as familiar to your body's memory as climbing the stairs, turning off the light, and crawling into bed.

Thanks to the good roads movement there are more roads than ever before by which your family can escape your house in the city and drive to colonial countrysides, if not primeval wilderness. Grassroots movements for good roads, fueled by adventurous tourists like yourself, are in full throttle, galvanized by the high-profile race to be the first to drive across Canada and some local automobile clubs lobbying for better roads and fashioning them in their hometowns. When you reach Alberta's border your family encounters some activists who are so passionate about good roads that they are cruising the countryside nailing road signs onto posts and distributing homemade road maps. But it is not just good roads, wild nature, and sketchy maps that bring you west. It is also the gas stations, the full-service garages, the auto-camps with laundry, the mom-and-pop motels with showers, and the very idea of luxury in the wilderness at Banff Springs Hotel in Canada's first national park (founded in 1885). Touring an eclectic, idiosyncratic route to Banff in your Master Six feels like traveling around with the emotional atmosphere of home somehow kept intact. Your family embodies driving between the city and nature as an intimate flowing extension of itself, memories and images of which quickly punctuate your kids' lore.

At last you roll to the front of Banff's hotel. Dragging your luggage through the lobby, it vaguely dawns on you how lucky your family is. Your kids just asked you why Slavic enemies of Canada built the roads around Banff, and why a loudmouthed trophy hunter dressed like Theodore Roosevelt is running around the lobby decrying with horror the unethical way Indians ruthlessly hunt big game. Soon enough the whole family is fast asleep, lost in wild and unsettling dreams of Indian Days.

The birth of driving in North America, and its rapid extension via touring cars and good roads for families circulating between the city and wild nature, I suggest, offers two deep domestic lessons for twenty-first-century cycling. The first lesson is to put down roots and roads without severing and ripping up the existing routes and root structures of others like an invasive, banishing species. The illiberal state-sanctioned brutality with which Canada constructed its "home and native land," to quote the nation's anthem, was on full display in the First World War as thousands of Austro-Hungarian immigrants, deemed "enemy aliens," were banished by the federal government to internment camps—including the Ukrainians forced to build Banff's roads for motor tourists. Even more domestically destructive was the violent dispossession and assimilation of Indigenous peoples by European settlers, the intergenerational trauma that Canada has only just begun to address. Banff offers a salient Canadian case of "seeing like" a settler-colonial state (Scott 1998). In the United States romantic ideas of wilderness as pristine and untouched by humans helped justify the removal of Indigenous communities from what would become national parks. But in Banff, at this time, it was not unusual for people to make permanent homes in the park. It just depended on what sort of people. Despite their long history with the land, Indigenous peoples were evicted and simultaneously objectified by motorized visitors, not for wildlife and wilderness preservation but for game conservation, "sport hunting, tourism, and aboriginal civilization" (Binnema and Niemi 2006, 725).

This first domestic driving lesson for cycling is not simply to respect others' roots. It also entails remembering and honoring those whose roots were frayed and reweaving home through new roots and roads wherein various definitions of home can flow and thrive. Canada's wartime treatment of immigrants and brutal assimilation of Indigenous peoples offer extreme examples of how the making of home can unfold through illiberal repression and violence. However, for many people home connotes daily struggle rather than stability, particularly those who do not come from an economically successful, middle- or upper-class background, showing a need to follow socially diverse ways of reanimating home through cycling.

The second domestic lesson driving offers cycling involves the environmental nuances of making home and managing moral friction between urban home and wild nature. The good roads, touring cars, and familial driving experiences of early twentieth-century North America envisioned a nature whose wildness (e.g., Indigenous hunting for subsistence) deeply offended white male colonial sensibilities, demanding domestication through an imperial process of ordering, taming, and civilizing (Elias 2000). A need to colonize and bring order

to nature still thrives across Canadian yards, parks, cities, and countrysides, generating friction with nature's spontaneous agency (and
growing "rewilding" movements). However, beyond human orderings,
domestic mobilities contain other ecological nuances that embolden
more progressive linkages between making home *with* nonhuman
beings, linkages that resonate with Indigenous ways of knowing the
more-than-human environment. Both domestic and ecological ways
of moving cultivate people's familiarity with their surroundings and
animate translocal, traditional knowledge through play, adventure,
and relations of care. This progressive association between different
moral assemblages shows the potential for expanding domestic cycling
by overgrowing the anthropocentric walls of the common good. To
examine how these lessons can guide the assembly of domestic cycling,
I offer three case studies: 1) a comparative case of mothers cycling with
their children in Vancouver; 2) an atypical case study of Celestina
cycling with memories of her family's history along Vancouver's first
local bikeway; and 3) Helena in Winnipeg, who cycles into the heart
of the North American continent. Each case features unique routines
of flowing home-on-the-move, traffic-calmed routes, and translocal
roots. As a set, these cases show a wide range of domestically worthy
practices, infrastructures, and relations with the past.

Flowing Families: Cycling with Children in Vancouver

One particularly tangible way by which home and familial roots flow
through cycling entails parents and children becoming co-mobile
through shared cycling routines. Like the more familiar process of car
"passengering," wherein people travel as "a together" (Laurier et al.
2008), becoming *vélomobile* under conditions of co-presence similarly
affords a domestically rich, if less understood, form of dwellingness on
the move. My focus here lies in how parents routinely "co-cycle" with
their young children using cargo or carrier bikes (both self-propelled
and electric). Composing one domestic form within a range of shared
"social cycling" practices—which also include, for example, family rides
with children using their own bikes and school bike tours (McIlvenny

2015)—carrier cycling offers a compelling form of domestic mobility. This form of cycling together helps conduct traffic, conveys a compact entourage of familial furnishings, and generates an intimate sense of co-presence as parents and young children together become familiar with their larger local environment. Canada's carrier bike scene is itself in its infancy compared to, for example, European Nordic countries. Yet this is quickly changing, particularly in places like Vancouver, not because of its temperate weather as much as because of the city's extensive and expanding network of traffic-calmed bike routes, its wealthy population who can afford to purchase and maintain expensive cargo bike equipment, and its morally supportive local communities that are enticing families out of their cars. This new growth in domestic mobility is all the more remarkable considering having children and starting a family has been the one life-cycle event that could compel even the most die-hard cyclist in Canada to capitulate and buy a car.

Always ready for rain in Vancouver, Catherine wrangles a "muddy buddy" rain suit onto her eighteen-month-old son, coaxes her four-year-old daughter into putting on her rain jacket, dons her own rain skirt (an image of which she nicely posted on Facebook to show a family cycling group), and gathers all the mittens, helmets, lunches, and other supplies for the day before shepherding her kids out the door to "Mama's minivan." Not your typical Canadian minivan, mind you. Catherine hoists her kin onto "Poppy," one of the lightest long-tail self-propelled cargo bikes on the market, named affectionally by her daughter for its red finish. Less tippy and easier to accelerate than Catherine's last cargo bike, Poppy, despite the joy it brings her children, is a workhorse. "It is not like we are going with the family for fun family biking. It's for transport," Catherine says. "I don't go out on bike rides just for fun on Poppy." Critically, "In the morning we need to get going." Catherine and her kids rely on Poppy to go both to and from her son's day care and her daughter's Irish dance academy (see photo 8) and, in a uniquely frenetic convergence of domestic flows, school—a private school, with little car parking options to which chaperoning parents arrive rushing and late from all over the city. One of Poppy's secret weapons is slowness. Like her husband Catherine is skilled at speedy individual cycling, through which they both have endured perilous collisions with cars. On Poppy, however, "I'm going so slow with the kids it is a completely different experience because I have ample time. It is quite rare that a car surprises me." Poppy's bulkiness and special cargo trailer afford a slowness with which Catherine safely rolls her young family to their engagements faster than her car-driving neighbors—even when they are heading to the same school.

Having cut her cycling teeth in the chaotic, fast-moving traffic of Montréal, Catherine evokes a kind of French Canadian "tiger cyclist" who never shies away from occupying the street and controlling traffic to protect her cubs. She builds buffers around her family by taking up the lane, which avoids car doors and also renders her party more visible: "There is no reason to be tight against the car. I want cars coming in the other direction to see me long in advance and to realize that they can't just blast through us." While smiling at drivers and making eye contact, Catherine, avoiding the use of earbuds, listens to her children and talks about the things they encounter. She "feels" when they become irked by a speed bump or a dog and when they become excited by a bus or the sight of donuts. She also hears and acts upon drivers' signs of indecision and impatience and effectively influences the behavior of car drivers around her:

> There are so many drivers who are not sure about what speed they are going, what speed you are going, what is going on, what exactly am I supposed to do when there is that red sign there. So I find that I can boss them around basically and they'd rather listen to me than try to guess it for themselves. Whenever there is a car that looks like they don't know what they are doing I will give them hand signals with the most common being the extended hand, stop thing. Especially if I'm going downhill. I will always make the motion "no thanks, like stay there" and they do it, like they will not start crossing if they have seen you and you have done that. I most of the time say "thank you!" (Interview 2017)

8. Catherine transports her children. Photo by Sharlie Clelland-Eicker.

Politely saying "thank you!" and "sorry!" also facilitates riding illegally on sidewalks, where aside from understandably not wanting cyclists in their space, "pedestrians are harder to communicate with." Such unconventional bits of routes pay off where Poppy bypasses fast cars, skirts construction detours, and seamlessly rolls between yards, parking lots, and city streets. Besides, oftentimes, "I don't have a choice," Catherine says.

Without downplaying Catherine's determination, what really moves her party along on Poppy involves something with which less confident cycling parents can relate. While cycling with children, "there are actually more interactions with cars, but they are different in nature and less confrontational. Having the kids on the back of my bike creates a protection in an odd way." It creates an invisible buffer, one that motorists are less likely to pass, "less likely to go oh, I'll just take a chance. They just kind of sit back more." Therefore, it is not just Poppy's slowness that allows Catherine and company to control the streets; it

is also their capacity to elicit slowness in others. Poppy has another
secret weapon up her handlebar. She opens passages where none exist:
"If I have to cross at an intersection where there is no stop sign or
what not, there is a much higher likeliness that the cars will stop and
let us go." By building her own buffers and exploiting the buffering
power of her party (like a little bike gang), Catherine shows one strong
way of routinely creating road space for practicing—and domestically
equipping—family cycling and flowing home on two wheels.

Furnishing family cycling for Catherine—making the bicycle feel
habitable—goes beyond finding the right bike and fitting onto it
multiple-sized human bodies. It gathers an entourage of lights, helmets, and baskets full of domestic things like Bluetooth water bottle
music players and heavy-duty locks, whose significant costs convey
the privilege related to riding with children. Lights help control the
unpredictable nature of traffic. As Catherine says, "You got to have
lights to really think ahead of what the drivers are doing." Helmets,
through their agency, create a safe atmosphere. "We always wear them,"
but she quickly adds, "sometimes I wish I didn't. I'm not a helmet
advocate. I think they are discouraging people from riding." And she's
right. The risks of cycling, which are around the same levels associated
with walking ("Cycling in Cities," UBC 2017), are overstated in Canada
(and outweighed by cycling's physical benefits), making mandatory
helmet laws and "danger discourse" unproductive. But parents with
kids face high expectations for cycling safely and guarding their children against the car's epidemic violence. So while Catherine does
not follow most Canadian parents who treat the helmet as a natural
piece of cycling attire, she always wears one when with her children
"as a rule, so as not to confuse them." By contrast, a very real danger
that frequently evaporates family cycling is theft, not just of lights
and seats—though this is "another pain in the ass"—but the whole
cargo bike, whose high cost puts a target on its back. Poppy, then, is
another being Catherine looks out for: "I keep thinking what asshole
would steal a bike with kid helmets on it? But I know it happens all
the time. I'm seldom away from the bike long." In high-risk areas she

raises her care, using multiple locks and, when indoors, checking for Poppy out the window.

Beyond social practices and domestic equipment, cycling home depends critically on building good roads. Good roads for cycling often align diverse infrastructures into composite bike routes, affectively united by their lack of fast-moving cars and multi-sensorial sense of calm. If Catherine is the tiger cyclist who takes command of the street, Li (more like the rest of us) is the occasional, fair-weather cyclist deterred by busy intersections, large hills, cold rain, and swarms of pedestrians; both mothers cite traffic-calmed bike routes as the *sine qua non* reason for biking routinely with their young children. Riding with her one-year-old son nestled between her and a milk crate on the back of their basic electric carrier bike, Li relies almost exclusively on such bike routes, especially Adanac Street—Vancouver's first local bikeway (constructed in 1994). Unlike Catherine, who "conquered the world" as soon as she "was able to put [her] son and daughter on a cargo bike," Li requires a wider, heterogeneous array of supports. Pricey electric bike technology is pivotal (once again affirming the class privileges associated with familial co-cycling): Li tired of walking her self-propelled bike up Vancouver's prodigious hills when she was pregnant. Also salient are social supports. A lifelong leisure cyclist, Li only recently started bike commuting because of Vancouver's new local street bikeways. Yet with help from supportive cycling colleagues at work, a local community organization called HUB, a family cycling Facebook group, and informal support from her partner, she has overcome the skepticism of her friends with young children who avoid cycling. Through this constellation of material (Adanac) and social (familial, community, digital) actor-networks, Li, like thousands of Vancouver families, started mapping her home's routines onto bike routes. Now Union-Adanac, a full-blown bike corridor and lynchpin of the city's cycling network, forms part of her familial infrastructure.

Through its nation-leading assembly of traffic-calmed bike routes, Vancouver is not only altering how home flows in the city but also changing how people justify and critique the domestic worth of urban mobility. Simple technical interventions—speed bumps, traffic circles, curbs, and traffic diverters—by slowing the speed and reducing the volume of cars on residential streets near schools and parks, are creating safer cycling places that parents and local communities are becoming quick to own and keen to defend. Some rather sharp domestic judgments come from parents' own mouths while in the midst of riding these routes, many of whom have a story about an aggressive driver coming into their new home and disrespecting the rules. Catherine just recently judged

> a lady who was going a lot faster than 30 kilometres per hour [speed limit] on the bike route. I motioned to her to slow down with my arm and she got quite offended. So I stopped next to her and said perhaps you would rather be using different roads so you can be part of the solution instead of being part of the problem. (Interview 2017)

Li recently faced a slew of expletives from a driver after criticizing him for illegally parking in her bike lane. While far from unique, these negative assessments are outnumbered by affirmative judgments parents enjoy while riding with children. Cargo bikes and kids are mutually reinforcing conversation starters, observes Catherine, "like a puppy. We stop at a light, there is a car next to us and someone rolls down their window and says wow, that is such a cool bike." More often there are happy, bell-ringing exchanges with other local families who are cycling together: "It creates community." As both criticism on the street and validating judgments add up across the city, they feed a novel road-building movement mobilizing a different flowing of home.

Families cycling together do not simply defend new bike routes through "social traffic control" and everyday judgment; they bring good roads to life through both political and emotional domestic work. Although they may not think of themselves this way, Catherine and Li are active members of the new good roads movement. As an extension of street critiques and local community-making, they build good roads for their families by lobbying their city government—Li, for example, recently persuaded the city to fix a shoddy pedestrian crossing on her local bike route (which for her doubles as a deterrent to speeding cars and a safe crossing for carrier bikes), while Catherine reported a dangerous bus driver. Furthermore both mothers work with emotional intelligence behind the scenes to carry out arguably more difficult forms of "family judgment work." Catherine works to convince her husband to publicly report the dangerous and illegal things that motorists sometimes do to (or around) him as he cycles, rather than him staying quiet. Sometimes he gets embarrassed in public when she talks to dangerous drivers. And on occasion they argue about the individualistic value of helmets—him as a medical doctor who draws strong moral support from his father. Li's judgment work is even more delicate than this. Part of a traditional Chinese family, she says: "My mother does not see my cycling as very proper. Safety issues. She does not think that any of our family should be cycling because it's too dangerous" (Interview 2017). Consequently Li takes her mother, who cares for her grandson twice a week, out of the cycling loop, shuttling him there by car. Her judgment call seems less like a domestic disconnection than a careful ironing of a generational wrinkle. Both their hearts are in the right place.

Like an earthquake striking the West Coast, Vancouver's local bike route expansion is bound to trigger further domestic tremors that travel into other moral assemblages of mobility. While striving for the good domestic life in Canada without a car, Catherine and Li's co-cycling experiences, and the substantial social and monetary resources they depend on, point to domestic troubles brewing over the meaning of home—troubles fueled by larger market-civic frictions. Canada was once a leader in enabling women to participate in the workforce. Since 2007, however, it has stalled (around 70 percent of Canadian women are employed), while countries like Germany—by expanding subsidized child care, equal parental leave for men and women, and workplace reintegration resources—have caught up. Without enough public "support from above" (Saunders 2017), many families face logistically and financially daunting child-care scenarios that end up limiting their capacity to cycle together, particularly for women, whose unpaid domestic labor tends to be higher than men's and daily travel tends to be more complex.[2] Li, for instance, relies on her mother for child care. Aside from disapproving of Li's cycling, her mother lives in a far-flung part of town (further incentivizing the car), whereas Catherine's family can afford the high cost of day care (plus private school and extracurriculars) in their neighborhood. In neoliberal urban Canada, a lack of public social policies for parenting on the move, such as affordable and accessible day care and family-friendly work hours, ushers market competition and inequality further into domestic life. Wealthy Vancouver families like Catherine's enjoy increasingly more time and space for animating home through co-cycling. They also require disproportionate capital for securing coveted housing in neighborhoods with good bike routes in the first place.

Herein lies a growing market-civic storm hanging over Vancouver's noble new domestic roads movement. Vancouver is arguably doing more than any other city in Canada to support domestic cycling, building on the Union-Adanac cycling corridor as a foundation for growing local cycling communities. It is also, through developer-friendly city politics (explored in chapter 3 through cycling gentrification), fomenting a hypercommodified real-estate market that places its housing among the priciest on the planet, out of reach for all but the wealthy and connected. This does not necessarily cripple domestic cycling—after all, Vancouver's mansion districts and old-money enclaves are beginning to embrace new bike routes. However, it damages prospects for cycling putting down roots through which more diverse homes and families can flow and thrive together. The prohibitive cost of housing in Vancouver, an enshrining of home's market value ahead of its civic worth, does not curb domestic cycling so much as threaten to constrain its flow to an elite few who can afford to dwell and grow there—financially banishing families and millennials who cannot. In short, possibilities for reassembling domestic mobility via family cycling to an extent hang, in Canada's wealthiest urban quarters, on the growth of civic cycling. Meaningful growth in domestic cycling depends on governments and citizens fostering more equitable relationships between cycling and domestic work, paid labor and affordable housing, particularly for non-wealthy mothers cycling with kids. Where civic cycling withers, domestic cycling will ossify into a summer toy for tourists and a ride for the rich.

Celestina Flowing: Cycling as "Memory-Making Machine"

On any given day along Vancouver's seminal Union-Adanac cycling corridor (hereafter, simply "Adanac"), you might cross paths with parents biking with kids like Li, teenagers cycling, or commuter athletes zipping by in colorful spandex—or maybe an impromptu group of folks with their dogs running beside them in the street (within which, while zipping by, I once became trapped). Adanac invites a wide cross section of society to cycle. Equally important, Adanac quilts with unusual depth the ups and downs, to's-and-fros of some people's families and homes.

Take Celestina. You might cross paths with her on Adanac because she regularly cycles home there. She describes herself as "a memory-making machine. I'm nostalgic for things that happened yesterday." For her Adanac's rolling hills, oceanic skies, and mountain vistas bring to life home's still sacred, quasi-religious environment, behind which "stands Nature—maternal if not uterine" (Lefebvre 1991, 120–21). Celestina offers an "atypical" case study, whose layers of domestic mobility are worth excavating.[3] Her Adanac cycling—the memories it affords, the roots it remembers, the places and people it resurrects—offers fleeting glimpses, not just of physical places that Celestina has called home but of the historico-poetic life of her "House." As much cosmic as human, nostalgia as everyday life, Celestina's House flows from its roots in her childhood home and twists its way around Adanac like the moss creeping below and the crows barreling overhead, who contravene any linear, straightforward notion of time, birth, or decay. Cycling back home on Adanac, she says, feels like "slowly digging into deeper recesses of my mind" (Interview 2018).

One gray April afternoon, I caught up with Celestina cycling home along one of Adanac's sweeping little valleys. How she cycles Adanac hinges sharply on direction. Riding (east) back home means cycling against gravity, where steep climbs present her with physical challenges that quickly become internal battles. The rhythmic rocking of her hips and the burning sensation in her thighs draw her inward, where all she sees is pavement as her struggling body opens up a powerful thinking space for remembering. She describes it as a "rattling in my inner space." That rattling, a "frenetic ping-ponging back and forth" is how "everything that has ever caused me pain becomes wrapped up in this little ball of energy." Within this dense little energy ball lies long-term fallout from family trauma: "Frankly, my childhood was chaotic, painful, violent and unsafe." Today, while cycling up Adanac, she feels "confidence in physical frustration [making a rattling motion] . . . I feel like I'm six again. I'm little, but I feel mightier than I ought to." Yet the whole time Celestina climbs she knows with growing kinaesthetic awareness that she's heading toward "*that* House." Part of her wants to ride back down the hill "and get as far away from my home as I can get."

In sharp contrast, riding (west) away from home means cycling with gravity, where the same hills whisk Celestina toward an expanding Pacific Ocean panorama. While cruising down Adanac at sunset she feels like she's "returning to the cosmic womb." She could pick a point in the middle of the sun and, like "E.T., suddenly levitate, but instead of the moon it's a blood red orb." So in either direction on Adanac, Celestina checks out from her immediate vicinity. Taking full advantage of traffic calming, she instead draws inward, letting her memories wander around this place and grapple with her history here—especially last fall. Last fall Celestina moved back home into her House after being gone for fourteen years. At this time she was cycling often to an emotionally abusive now-ex-lover's flat in Vancouver's West End—the neighborhood where as an adult she had re-created some of the same trauma as her youth—and back home again. Essentially: "It was really hard. I felt that in either direction there was no safe place." Her cycling along Adanac became a temporary revolving refuge between dangerous origins and destinations, a mobile dwelling with either a bloodred orb or shadows dancing on the pavement.

It was at that House where Celestina's father raised her to be a sporty, "proper little boy." Down the street at the family business, Celestina created fantasy landscapes with her sister and brother and learned how to bicycle on a dusty warehouse track around pallets of tile and grout. At six, "my dad took off my training wheels and said, figure it out. That was my childhood, it was always, you're smart, figure it out. Go." Cycling didn't become part of Celestina's everyday life until her early twenties. Living on her own she became enthralled with the way cycling makes her feel like a part of, rather than apart from, the world. Now, retracing the places along Adanac where her House tacks and folds into the city, her House hails her attention through her cycling body. Her working muscles, she says, "have a way of bringing to my attention demands of my thinking mind and a pattern of remembrances that accords with its own agenda." The past stalks Celestina on her bike. As we ride on Adanac she recalls high school sleepovers with a Filipino friend whose mother would caution them not to sleep on their stomachs: "I remember, lying on our bellies outside tanning—my Guidette phase—her mom coming out and saying, 'girls, what are you doing? You don't want to flatten your ladies!' "

It is not merely memories of her own life that hail Celestina's thinking mind through her cycling body along Adanac. There's an entire familial history that she was not a part of that she imagines while riding. Before her father and her aunt and uncle moved there, her *nonno* and *nonna* bought their first house on Adanac. Her nonna tells her stories about walking from that first house a couple blocks over to work in one of the factories in Chinatown. With "barely any English and grade five education," her nonna "worked in factories her whole life," like many in the Italian diaspora that landed in East Vancouver and North Burnaby. Celestina finds herself there, imagining what it was like for them in the late 1950s and early 1960s. She knows "from their stories there was a culture of sitting in front of your home, drinking espresso and playing cards, and you know, the ladies walking past." Celestina's memory-making links together generations under conditions of absence: "I've never actually seen that [1950s and 1960s scene] in my hometown, but it feels to me as real as my own childhood memories of being on Hastings and going to fucking fast food restaurants."[4] Decades ago gentrification started swallowing East Vancouver, and Nonno wanted out, so he bought a plot in Burnaby of what was farmland. There he built that House.

Celestina has always felt connected to that House. Officially she lived there from ages six to fourteen. But "because of everything that was going on with my mom—who was in rehab while breastfeeding me"—she skipped around a lot, living with her dad in Coquitlam as a toddler and again as a late teen before leaving the family den. Since she was a young girl Celestina has suffered recurring nightmares, terrors, and sleep paralysis, "all of which took place in that House." Brought up strictly Roman Catholic, there was "mass on the TV every morning and mass [in person] twice a week, one catechism, the other worship." She was "raised to believe in demons and Satan, as well as God and angels and the power of Mary as someone to intercede on your behalf." Throughout her childhood, because of the trauma experienced with her mother, there was a lot of chaos. It was "just constant screaming and . . . just constant fear. I had a lot of paranormal experiences as a kid in that House," like awakening to her bed shaking and the intense presence of shadows. Celestina came to think these experiences were nonsense. Then she moved back into that House at twenty-seven, "and the same shit happened again, and it was terrifying."

Celestina only ever knew her mom as an addict who could not stay clean. In and out of rehab, "as true addiction does, it destroyed [her] family for a while." At some point after her mother was gone for a long time, "we thought she was dead. I lived a lot of my childhood think-ing she was dead." Then one day her mom returned. "She came back, pregnant with some guy from the street's kid, who is my half-sister and whom I love dearly." After watching her mother overdose in front of her new child, Celestina cut off contact. She was sixteen. The last time Celestina saw her mom, she says, "I was with my brother. We were on the Skytrain. She was high. She looked right at my brother and didn't recognize him. She didn't see me, fortunately." The last time Celestina talked to her mother was on her nineteenth birthday. Her mom had called to wish her happy birthday, and Celestina said, "Thanks, but I don't want to hear from you." Soon thereafter her mom died, "over-dosed, finally fatally." It was Celestina's first year of law school, and her world was rapidly spinning and expanding.

It took some time for Celestina to return to that House from which all of her nightmares have been about fleeing. It took her mom's death, the realization that she is an addict herself, and ultimately, she says, "a kind of softening to my own family's shit" and "finding compassion for her"—her mom. A few months after her mom died, Celestina bought herself a new bike. She still adores it. "Biking," she says, "is all me. That's part of why I love it. It's like my father saying, go!" Her family dislikes her cycling; "They think I'm going to die, get hit by a car." Anytime she leaves the House, Nonna "says the sign of the cross, telling me to do the same." Nonna sinks her "little claws" into Celestina's shoulders, calling upon Jesus to provide her safe passage. But by the time Celestina shuts the door, rides up the street, turns, and starts cruising down Adanac, she feels a sense of freedom and joy. She says, "I feel like I'm a little girl, and the world's fucked up and scary but I'm okay. I've got the sun that I'm riding toward, and this chaos is not mine." Now, she can almost deal with her House. However, she never thought she'd stay so long (or that it would be so hard), and for the past few months she's been gearing up to leave again. Everything is coming to an end.

The family business is closing, Nonno is dying with Alzheimer's, and soon that House itself will be gone, sold. As Celestina puts it, "As my Nonna likes to say, it's done. It's ending. It's all finished. It's broken, done." She feels like she's come back home "to watch the curtains close." She finds herself frantically trying to remember how everything was, where that chair was placed, how the light changed the room at a certain time, and "really, really remember the sound of my Nonna cooking in the kitchen. And Nonno farting in his lounge chair, and my Dad coming home from work everyday and making himself a panini with cheese, eating it and saying 'I wish I didn't eat it.' " For a long time Celestina was embarrassed of her working-class immigrant family who mostly went out to fast-food joints. She begrudged her family's "vampiric quality" of finding their suffering and "because it's

so familiar, holding onto it." But since coming home it has occurred
to her that "my family has just done the best they can with what they
have." Celestina tears up knowing she has "an anchor," that she belongs.
And while her nonna is the closest thing to a mother she's ever had,
Celestina is starting to wonder if she herself might actually be more
like her nonno.

As Celestina's nonno retreats on his lounge chair into his oldest
memories, like his mother's voice, Celestina, up and down Adanac's
hills, backward and forward in time, agonizes over how to leave. She
remembers how he met her nonna. Smoking, working, and boxing at
eight, her nonno comes from a small, rough-and-tumble town in Italy.
With one pair of pants and a bicycle, he was delivering bread to prisons
and neighboring towns when he first saw her, looking beautiful up on
a balcony. They had only been dating a little while before her family
would uproot and move to Canada for a better life, and she asked if
he would come. He sailed after her—a year later—leaving his family
behind. Luckily the priest in Vancouver gave them an extension on
getting married so they could date a while longer. Watching her nonno
on his final days, as the family business, his legacy, crumbles away,
she knows for her own sake she needs to move away from this House
where so much trauma took place. She can't help but think, just like
her nonno, that "maybe it's okay to leave home behind, knowing that
I'll never really leave it."

Sometimes while cycling down Adanac during twilight Celestina
crosses paths with little gangs of crows, like "pepper in the sky," all
quickly converging into an aerial black river heading for their roost.
They help guide her inward, conspiring with Adanac's hills, vistas, and
calming protection from the noisy, violent velocity of cars—without
which, "the meditative state I'm in wouldn't be possible." In this state of
cycling Celestina feels "like tapping, like playing an instrument you're
really familiar with" and at the end of the day creating something that
"has no purpose. There's no record of it. All I'm left with is this feeling
of fluidity." The moss and the grass growing up through cracks in the
street and thousands and thousands of crows flying overhead reassure

her "that it's all a bit of a joke anyway. Collapse and renewal are part of the same circle." In turn Celestina's meditation on that little rattling ball of energy conspires with Adanac's sheltering of her memories by allowing her to imagine other familial futures—like her own "strong desire to have a daughter. I like the idea of teaching her to cycle along Adanac. It's fun, it's safe, there are so many other cyclists. I think I would be a really great mom." If she had to guess what the crows were doing flying up over Adanac, she'd say, "Going home."

Cycling into the Heart of the Continent

Part garden and nature park full of native species, part historic site, entertainment complex, and human rights museum, the Forks, broadly speaking, is the junction of the Red and Assiniboine Rivers in downtown Winnipeg. This place entwines water highways that have been drawing people here for over six millennia: "Early Aboriginal peoples traded at the Forks, followed by European fur traders, Métis buffalo hunters, Scottish settlers, riverboat workers, railway pioneers and tens of thousands of immigrants" (Forks North Portage Corporation 2018). Geographically, and in a spiritual way to many people who dwell in Winnipeg, the Forks, with its ever-freezing and -flooding rivers, feels like the pulsing heart of the continent. It is to this ancestral city intersection that Helena regularly experiences a sense of what Phillip Vannini (2012) calls the "pull of remove." She feels pulled to the Forks because it removes her from the noise of daily life and reconnects her with a wider, older nature, of which Winnipeg is but one piece. A lively tourist destination, she says the Forks represents a small dose, "an interim measure," of the nature she needs in order to cope with life in the city. Yet the Forks lies handily in the city center, so she reaches it all the time. Often there are a lot of folks there, "but people when they're at the Forks are in a different head space. It's a lot about the feeling and energy when I go there, it's more contemplative and relaxed" (Interview 2015). Helena's routine cycling to the Forks, not unlike Celestina's riding along Adanac, removes her from the cacophony of the city and the car. However, it also unfolds a sense of refuge and domestic atmosphere from her apartment into an ancient gathering place at which point her own wandering home gets in touch with the city's ancestral roots.

As a West Coast Gen Xer raised by a single working mom, Helena in many ways is emblematic of the mobile subject thought to define our drifting and distanciated times. From Kelowna to Vancouver and Halifax to Winnipeg, as her home unfolds it contravenes urban, rural, and continental divides. Far from itinerant, Helena's biography betrays a sense of direction whose arc can be gleaned in a single bicycle. Helena's face lights up and overflows with joy when she remembers a green Miyata mountain bike. "I love that I had it for so long. I love that my mom gave it to me." Her Miyata took her all the way from high school, where cycling with friends for adventure became less important to her freedom than borrowing her mother's car, to university in Vancouver, which led to a completely different relationship with cycling, one in which cycling was no longer simply for play and riding down mountains but also for everyday travel. It was here, in her early twenties, when "probably not in my head, but somewhere in my heart, I had the realization that the bicycle is actually a really great portal to freedom." Later, while living in Halifax and teaching environmental education, her relationship with cycling evolved yet again, politically this time, "towards cycling as a statement of my values. Not that I lord it over people." For twenty years, from long-distance tours in Quebec to inner-city rides across Vancouver, Halifax, and Winnipeg, Helena's Miyata connected her to her mom and her past. After affording adventure and freedom it eventually led her to community by way of lessening her impact on the environment. Helena's home may not be contained by any one house (or city), but rather than pulling up her roots and leaving them behind, Helena's cycling carries them with her. Her roots flow in a rhizomatic way across Canada.

En route to the Forks Helena stitches together the eclectic, personalized kind of route that tends to animate domestic infrastructures. On a new road bike—she finally let go of her beloved Miyata while moving to Winnipeg—Helena easily plies familiar side streets and sidewalks over bridges, safe spaces to which she feels she deserves access around her

9. Helena rides to the Forks on Winnipeg's first cycle track. Photo by author.

home. Part of her route includes Assiniboine Avenue (see photo 9), which magnifies the moral significance of Helena's domestic cycling. It composes Winnipeg's first cycle track and "complete street" that also caters to pedestrians. Built in 2010, Assiniboine Avenue teems with civic capacity. It invites generations of people to cycle, including families with children, reinforcing the cycle track's domestic power. Like most people Helena says she feels less isolated from others while cycling compared to being in a car, and her feeling of local connection grows stronger over time on safe, tranquil infrastructure near her home, like Assiniboine. Here she can take her helmet protection off and "feel more like a part of my moving community. There's more opportunity to say, hi so-and-so! Oh hi so-and-so!" The longer she lives in a place, such opportunities seem to snowball to the point where she finds herself "bike-ganging it home with other people, a completely different experience of cycling, one with more empowerment and sense of entitlement." Along Assiniboine and Winnipeg's other multiuse cycling routes by the rivers, the moral valence or combining power of Helena's domestic-civic cycling starts to swell.

10. Helena circles the Forks. Photo by author.

Helena's route to the Forks features a range of moral complexities owing to its eclectic nature, but its strongest moral valence emerges from domestic-ecological connectivity. Domestic friction does arise with industrial and financial forces when, farther along Assiniboine Avenue, condominium construction sunders Assiniboine's seamless cycling flow, throwing Helena from the cycle track onto the street. This same friction again builds when Helena penetrates the Forks through a backlot loading zone, where motor tourists looking for places to park their cars mingle with delivery trucks and the industrial supply chains that feed, and feed off of, the profitable complex. However, as an entire voyage Helena's domestic route opens most compellingly onto a riparian ecological infrastructure, which unrolls her meandering home all the way into the city's ancestral dwelling place on two rivers. After bypassing the shopping and dining part of the Forks, she reaches and revolves around the Oodena Celebration Circle (see photo 10), a natural amphitheater developed by the city in the early 1990s "to demonstrate our reverence for the long cultural history of the site, and to put us back in touch with the natural elements of earth, fire, water and sky" (Hilderman et al. 2015). Around the Circle, eight steel armatures curl up into the sky, pointing at night to constellations, while the monoliths upon which the steel arms sit align at solstice and equinox with sunrises and sunsets. Ojibwe for "heart of the community," Oodena "pays homage to the 6,000 years of Aboriginal peoples in the area" (Forks North Portage Corporation 2018). Helena is well aware that more than homage and public historical park education is required to heal Canada's relationship with Indigenous communities, and Oodena offers an inspiring reminder of this sacred gathering place's Indigenous roots.

Helena's domestic cycling comes closest to ecological mobility when she finds the riverside and soaks up the quiet, reflective atmosphere. What really draws Helena to the Forks and the city cycling pathways and unofficial routes (see photo 11) with which the Forks intertwines, is the water. When I asked her why she keeps cycling there, she dwells on it:

> In the city there's a few places that are green, and there's a sense of removal from traffic, and then quiet, or like a different noise. And so the Forks is one of those. And, it's just really close. And there's spots, like the bridge I love, and the place where you can stand in the middle and make noise echo [in the middle of the Circle of Celebration], and, like, by the river there's spots where you can kind of get away, I guess . . . even around other people. . . . For me, I have a real connection with water. Water feels . . . soothing. It feels grounding. It feels quiet. It feels like I can stand on that bridge and watch. And it feels like I get in more contemplative space. I've always been drawn to water. (Interview 2015)

The passionate, deeply familiar way that cycling draws Helena to the rivers reflects the value and agency she attributes to rivers themselves as sources of home and life in a more-than-human world. Her cycling generates a way of practicing a kind of wilderness (Vannini and Vannini 2016) that unfolds home in the city. Helena's domestic cycling routes and routines, converging with her fluid and rhizomatic roots, weave home like a patchwork quilt with nature and act as a "moving community" that includes human and nonhuman beings. I interpret

11. Helena rides home along the Assiniboine River. Photo by author.

this quilt as foretelling how cycling becomes a subversively good home in a neoliberal capitalist world.

Entitled to Cycle: Domestic Mobility Futures

This chapter on domestic mobilities focuses on familial co-cycling, memory-making, and cycling home within a more-than-human environment to examine how different homes and families are assembling *their* roots, routes, and routines around cycling. I emphasize "their" because Canada needs more humans (especially civically engaged parents) who feel sufficiently entitled to claim good roads for cycling—not unlike the explosive good roads movement that claimed space for driving cars in the 1920s. "Cycling entitlement" is often sneered at by the media and opinion leaders (see Quinn 2017), who conflate it with incivility or blatant disregard for rules of the road. But this caricature misses the larger, positive potential for feelings of entitlement—as a sense of actually enjoying the right to belong on the road in the first place—to help people cycling together foster long-standing relations among families, dwellings, roads, animals, plants, and affective atmospheres of home. The moral worth of these relations comprises the connecting principle for the cases presented in this chapter. Catherine, Li, Celestina, and Helena show a range of domestic ways in which cycling puts down translocal roots that embrace familiarity, care, and making memories with human and nonhuman beings. They also illustrate how domestic mobilities might learn from the history of the car by constructing a less-violent, less-colonializing way that people can assemble home together attuned with environmental repair.

Cycling excels at domestic mobility because people riding outside together tend to experience, remember, and care for their translocal environments much differently and more intimately than those who stay inside their motor vehicles. Cycling's domestic capacity to put home and tradition into action through a slower but deeper engagement with place offers an alternative political grammar and infrastructure for policymakers, transport planners, and advocates seeking to justify the expansion of cycling beyond the dominant economic frames of efficiency and profit. Of course domestic moralities do not always support forward-thinking politics, fueling, for example, not-in-my-backyard-style attacks against change, like appeals to "heritage homes" that shield single-family housing tracts and outdated zoning in central cities from modest urban intensification that could help expand cycling while also easing housing crises. But this chapter shows how cycling could expand domestic mobilities in a more positive yes-in-my-backyard direction by helping transport planners bolster public support for building traffic-calmed bikeways like Vancouver's Adanac-Union corridor. The everyday domestic judgments of many parents and local communities of what constitutes a safe road for cycling add further social support for building bikeways. Compared to fast roads for cars, there are very few bikeways whose history and heritage planners can appeal to, planners who will always be tempted to instead appeal to efficiency and the bottom line. But Adanac is getting older every day. Building popular bikeway networks, and linking them up with cycle tracks in high traffic areas and wilder pathways closer to nature, offers a concrete urban policy for domestic cycling.

Looking to the future, domestic cycling hinges on two challenges. First, a key political and practical hurdle lies in whether cycling can live up to higher ideals of home and place by putting down roots and "good roads," not by displacing and sundering the roots of others but rather by recognizing and honoring those who have been uprooted, and reassembling the city through new roots and roads wherein multiple traditions of home can flourish. The second challenge relates to how cycling deals with external moral crises beyond the domestic world. On the horizon a market-civic storm is brewing. Looming over domestic cycling are complex, deepening socio-spatial inequalities surrounding paid and unpaid work, housing, and urban wealth accumulation. Dim are domestic futures where only the privileged few are entitled to cycle home. Not unlike the inclement weather at which many Canadians casually point as a reason for not leaving their cars, exposure to this market-civic storm may keep domestic cycling out of reach for many. If cycling is to play a larger role in building the good domestic life in liberal democratic societies, its domestic assembly will require moral valence with civic and ecological mobilities.

12. Cycling into Huron Line, Windsor. Photo by author.

13. Huron Line from the Ambassador Bridge, Windsor. Photo by author.

2. Industrial Mobilities

Road Engineering, Urban Planning,
and Infrastructuring Efficiency

What makes mobilities industrially good? What makes a bike lane good for cycling efficiently? What industrial lessons might cycling take from driving? These questions illuminate a unique moral assemblage of mobility built on technical standards, generic solutions, productivity, growth forecasting, and the rationalization of flow. With deep philosophical roots that run from the Enlightenment via the Industrial Revolution into the apex of high modernism and top-down urban renewal, this powerful moral assemblage had by the mid-twentieth century come to dominate the built environment by reconfiguring it as an object of engineering and scientific planning. In spite of, and owing to, prolific success in assembling complex systems for the car, industrial automobilities carry ambivalent lessons for the expansion of cycling.

Industrial assemblages of mobility, held up against the domestic mobilities examined in chapter 1, strike a sharp contrast. Unlike the value invested in place and traditional hierarchy that embeds domestic mobilities in local knowledge, the modus operandi of industrial mobilities entails the extensive dis-embedding of local relations in order to control, scale, and generalize abstract solutions independent of locale. Efficiency, often at odds with tradition, is for industrial mobilities an end unto itself. However, industrial mobilities share an important quality with domestic mobilities: industrial mobilities project space but also time, and herein lies an important source of continuity between dissimilar moral assemblages. Unlike other assemblages (with the exception of ecology), both domestic and industrial mobilities situate worthy people and things within an expansive temporality—in opposite directions: whereas domestic mobilities look deeply into the past, industrial mobilities gaze just as far into the future. Coupling a panoramic conception of time-space with a drive to scientifically control nature and manufacture the city according to abstract "representations of space" (Lefebvre 1991), industrial mobilities have turned the car into the quintessential manufactured object of the twentieth century (Sheller and Urry 2000). The rise and domination of automobility is inextricably tied to its becoming an open-ended industrial assemblage. This formidable assemblage, so evocatively painted in panoramas by Diego Rivera, hints at how cycling can unleash its own impulse to order, plan, and engineer roads across the twenty-first century.

The dismantling of modern industrial automobility presents an opportunity and inspiration for rethinking urban space. Consider the twin altars of high automobility that, for now, bookend urban Canada: Vancouver's Georgia Street Viaduct and Halifax's Cogswell Interchange. Erected over a half century ago as concrete pieces of flyover highways, these infrastructures face imminent demolition, with Vancouver and Halifax seeking to repair urban social spaces sundered by automobility. These modern roads, built with an unwavering faith in scientific progress during the late 1960s and early 1970s, have a lot to say about mobilities as they unravel, if we let them speak (Jensen 2012). They find themselves isolated and out of place, stillborn monuments to free-flowing superhighways that never came to fruition. One was meant to usher the Trans-Canada Highway into downtown Vancouver, the other a new highway, Harbour Drive, into downtown Halifax. Both modern planning experiments failed but not before demolishing Vancouver's only historic black neighborhood and a large swath of heritage homes in Halifax. Ironically the Viaduct's westbound lane now affords one of Vancouver's most prolific cycling highways, the imminent loss of which raises the question of whether, and how, cities should engineer new highways for cycling (Cogswell, which never adopted a bike lane, is as unfriendly to cycling as the day it was conceived).

The rise and fall of the Georgia Street Viaduct and Cogswell Interchange traces an arc of infrastructural (dis)connection along which "historical futures" (Harvey and Knox 2015) of automobility—past longings for modernity—are erased from the cities they helped reconfigure. This crumpling of car futures begs the questions: What sort of industrial cycling futures might rise in their stead? Which urban objects and principles of time-space might cycling use to manufacture new ways of living together?

Infrastructuring Efficiency

Industrial mobilities thrive on judgments, practices, and infrastructures that optimize efficiency and facilitate planning for the future (Thévenot 2002). At the crux of industrial worth the principle of efficiency demands the construction and maintenance of infrastructures that more or less *work*. When mobility infrastructure works it technically functions as intended and can be counted on to afford the smooth flow of persons and things. At the same time, the actors and complex socio-technical relations upon which continuous flow and smooth displacement depend are hidden and easily taken for granted—at least until infrastructure inevitably breaks, revealing, if only for an extraordinary moment, the heterogenous "mediators" that make it work (Latour 2007).

Infrastructuring efficiency entails coordinating material space for moving objects smoothly across time, from point A to point B, but also social and political space for the industrial experts who keep things running. These are the engineers and planners who model and apply "essential aspects of the physics of organized bodies" (Boltanski and Thévenot 2006[1991], 119). Such experts are worthy assemblers of industrial mobilities. In the dizzying heights of the Industrial Revolution, it was thought that they might reorder all of nature and cure society of such vices as feudalism and inept governance. For example, in the nineteenth century Henri de Saint-Simon believed strongly that science and technology could fortify humanity with a healthier administration, because "political economy, legislation, public morality, and everything that constitutes the administration of the general interests of society are only a collection of rules of hygiene" (cited in Boltanski and Thévenot 2006[1991], 119). By discovering the objective and universal "rules of hygiene" that make people function well and by generalizing them using new scientific techniques of economic production, early industrial experts thought they might manufacture society itself to run as efficiently as a well-oiled machine. From bold beginnings city engineering and planning officials erected a rational modern system of knowledge against which other ways of knowing and valuing the world were collectively judged.

Contemporary experts of industrial mobilities are no less removed from the world or deeply entangled with its unpredictable social tumult. The social lives of roads for motor vehicles (Hall 2015) are not lost on engineers, although it may seem that way, given their compulsion to build infrastructures, and to hold them together, by continually measuring, modeling, and predicting actions in a time-space conceived as Cartesian, homogeneous, and universal. Despite this "God-trick" (Haraway 1991), sometimes the best-laid plans of industrial experts (e.g., highways for uninterrupted flow) go sideways, which experts themselves acknowledge. As anthropologists Penny Harvey and Hannah Knox (2015, 5) have closely documented, engineers' "intentions always run up against the intrinsic multiplicity of infrastructural systems." Engineers and quantitative planners may see themselves as objectively ordering the world over and above local knowledge through generalizable solutions, cloaking their own political assumptions about correct social relations in scientific neutrality. However, some industrial experts also step outside their generic solutions, aware that unpredictable things happen. For example, Harvey and Knox (2015, 6) identify "engineer-bricoleurs" who pragmatically appreciate the social dynamics of highways, approaching them as calculable outputs but also as "open-ended structural forms" that combine contradictory aspirations. Cycling engineers and planners who deploy a range of knowledge and multiple notions of socially worthy roads, I contend, also run up against, and help create, the multiplicity of infrastructure.

They are not only helping cities learn from the infrastructural mistakes of modern automobility but also reorienting industrial expertise itself "after the car" (Dennis and Urry 2009). To avoid erecting ill-fated altars for modernist mobilities like the Georgia Street Viaduct and Cogswell Interchange, engineers and planners must find a better way of infrastructuring efficiency for cycling.

The rising popularity and political power of cycling in Canada render it susceptible to, and generative of, industrial judgment, practice, and infrastructure. By the turn of the millennium, cycling expansion had jumped from fringe policy to political priority in cities across Canada. As municipal governments strive to replace modernist roads for cars with "complete streets," they seek scientific means, not only for controlling and rationalizing the movement of a growing number of cyclists but also for dealing with long-standing "bike battles" over cycling's public legitimacy (Longhurst 2015). This political shift has unleashed a wave of new cycling standards and regulatory frameworks by empowering a growing number of experts to track, quantify, model, and predict the flows of cycling. However, translating the emerging science of cycling into material reality by overriding preexisting city relations and power dynamics that favor automobility is elusive. Despite a prolific flow of "traveling ideas" (Tait and Jensen 2007) for cycling expansion between the Danish and Canadian capitals since the early 2000s, for example, local incongruity in Canada's cycling infrastructures remains pronounced—as Ruth's commute home from work in Ottawa demonstrates in this book's introduction. However, there are growing signs of cycling becoming an industrial force capable of generating its own conceptual terrain, or what Henri Lefebvre calls "abstract space":

> Abstract space functions "objectally," as a set of things/signs and their formal relationships: glass and stone, concrete and steel, angles and curves, full and empty. Formal and quantitative, it erases distinctions, as much those which derive from nature and (historical) time as those which originate in the body (age, sex, ethnicity). (Lefebvre 1991, 49)

The production of abstract cycling space is seen most vividly across Canada in the diffusion of urban policies and infrastructural standards via formal cycling plans, plans that animate public judgments of cycling's industrial worth. In a postmodern age weary of totalizing blueprints, the first cycling plans of the twenty-first century have adopted a humbler tone compared to postwar master plans, clearly aware of the need for public engagement. However, contemporary cycling plans nevertheless deploy a quantitative "objectal" focus similar to their modernist forebears—projecting conceptual models and representations of mobility that transcend nature, history, and the body.

The techno-scientific practices of industrial experts, together with formal cycling plans and their material products, outline a city-scale infrastructuring of cycling efficiency. While this powerful approach to cycling expansion, like that of automobility before it, takes on variable forms and intensities across contexts, it resonates strongly with cycling planning and engineering that emerged in North America during the first decade of the twenty-first century. I refer to this loosely demarcated, wavelike swelling of policy and engineering activity as "first-wave cycling planning." Carried throughout this chapter, first-wave cycling planning repositions cycling as a product and producer of industrial mobilities, the socio-technical assembling of which deeply embroils cycling with the ambivalent industrial legacies of automobility. In the industrial world cycling is on the car's home turf.

Driving Lessons

Imagine yourself in the mid-1950s motoring down North America's first divided superhighway, the Queen Elizabeth Way (QEW), inside a new top-of-the-line 1953 Chrysler Imperial sedan. When it opened for car traffic in 1939, the QEW was North America's first divided interurban highway, one of the most successful cases of technological infrastructure in Canadian history, and the longest lighted corridor in the world (van Nostrand 1983). The luxurious Imperial sedan, whisking you along the well-lit QEW, matches the power and colonial trappings of the modernist highway itself. Among the first mass-produced cars to feature power steering, the Chrysler Imperial allows your hand to rest lazily atop its steering wheel as you effortlessly guide the hefty car down a linear superhighway at sixty miles per hour (in pre-metric Canada). You are somewhere between Buffalo and Toronto—it's hard to tell since all the underpasses, service roads, and colonial landscaping flying by outside your window look the same—and you are driving in style. Power brakes and power windows reduce the need for physical exertion. Air-conditioning keeps the muggy summer atmosphere at bay. To the envy of Americans driving by on vacation, a stylized eagle hood ornament captures the freedom of your Imperial on the QEW, where "motorists were known to travel hundreds of miles out of their way to enjoy a Sunday's outing along it" (van Nostrand 1983, 11).

The 1950s Queen Elizabeth Way is not your father's highway. To get ahead of the rising number of drivers owning cars (spiking in Ontario from 4,230 in 1910 to 470,000 in 1934), the QEW boasts a 132-foot-wide right-of-way, with room for two double-lane roads, a central median, gravel shoulders, and ample ditches (van Nostrand 1983). Moreover, following the new science of engineering traffic for the free circulation of automobiles (Brown 2006), the QEW is divided and flanked by service roads and grade-separated crossings to restrict access to the highway. Cloverleaf interchanges steer cars seamlessly onto intersecting highways. However, to your chagrin, the promise of uninterrupted flow—for both Imperial sedans and lowlier vehicles—soon ends in bumper-to-bumper traffic. Ironically the congestion is generated by the superhighway itself. The QEW is ever widening, not only through its right-of-way but also via adjacent lands: housing tracts, shopping plazas, and industrial parks trace a "golden horseshoe" around Lake Ontario, from Toronto all the way to the eastern tip of Lake Erie. Making matters worse, all the high-speed driving fed by the suburban sprawl around the QEW has turned the superhighway into a "death trap," where it is "as dangerous to stop as not" (van Nostrand 1983, 11). As you drive your Imperial down the QEW, the traffic takes you in like an accordion, breathing in space between you and the other cars before collapsing you back into bumper-to-bumper formation. As the great accordion expands and collapses, your custom-padded dash brings you comfort (in the age before seat belts).

The mass production of automobility in twentieth-century North America, capped off by outsized vehicles and superhighway sprawl, offers three broad industrial lessons for expanding twenty-first-century cycling. The first lesson is to resist privatizing, monetizing, and selling infrastructure to the highest bidder by essentially instrumentalizing long-term urban planning and road engineering for short-term profit. Long before Margaret Thatcher, Ronald Reagan, and the rise of Canadian neoliberalism, the QEW tightly coupled its material and social life to private highway-driven development, channeling its upgrading from a four- to a six-, an eight-, and in some areas now, a ten-lane superhighway, locking engineers and planners into an ever-elusive chase for uninterrupted car flow. Under the guise of scientific progress and modernization, highway-driven development—"the City on the Highway" (Hall 2002)—coupled with oligopic car production helped transform automobility into a self-organizing, autopoietic system that "generates the preconditions for its own self-expansion" (Urry 2004, 27). With experts now contemplating cycling's transformation into its own self-organizing, ever-assembling system of mobility (Watson 2013), the friction between short-term market-driven cycling development and building efficient cycling infrastructure for the long haul will only grow.

The second lesson for cycling expansion, less to do with moral assemblages outside industrial mobilities than with living up to industrial principles themselves, entails preventing an all-knowing scientific epistemology from looking down at the city "like a God" or with a "solar Eye" (de Certeau 1988). A totalizing, all-knowing dynamic characterizes modernist planning in the postwar period that led infamously to sweeping urban renewal schemes, destructive mega-projects, and hierarchical, functionally segregated systems of highways and collector roads engineered for uninterrupted flow of traffic (Brown 2006). This modernist system, owing to its socio-technical momentum (Hughes 1983), remains largely unbuilt. In fact its expansion across Canada is still touted as progress. The lesson here, lurking in the limits of techno-scientific expertise, speaks to the importance of promoting scientific planning that not only grapples with infrastructure's multiplicity but also acknowledges spatial practices and lived mobilities outside the formal conceived boundaries of plans themselves. Additionally it suggests new cycling systems should aim to live up to the principle of efficiency, broadly speaking, by affording smooth flow for people cycling without compromising their long-term health and safety through epidemic danger on the roads, "death traps," or hubristic schemes to tear down and revitalize urbanity.

The third industrial lesson from automobility for cycling expansion is distinctly positive: engineers and planners, as industrial experts, excel at transforming disparate materials, knowledge, and environments into surpassingly functional, long-lasting roads. The expansion of cycling depends on, to an important extent, scientific plans for materializing cycling infrastructure—putting it on the road—so that it furnishes and optimizes future cycling. This positive industrial lesson, alongside warnings about the excesses of modernism and capitalism, suggests cycling ought to adopt a nuanced and ambivalent perspective of engineering and planning. In what follows I analyze the assembling of industrial mobility by cycling in the least likely of contexts, Motor City, with its full-throttled embrace of industrial automobility. Here I include an in-depth look at the cycling engineer-bricoleur. I then follow cycling's industrial assembling in the most likely of contexts, Ottawa, with its long-standing penchant for ambitious urban planning. The chapter concludes with an ethnographic vignette to illustrate the everyday practice of cycling through industrial infrastructure in Dartmouth, Nova Scotia. The vignette shows that, while industrial spaces for driving and cycling can be analytically separated, in Canadian practice they are usually experienced together.

Reengineering Motor City for Cycling

Among the least likely cities one would expect cycling to take hold of in North America, Motor City, the car's eponymous metropolis, takes the cake. Motor City refers to two cities, Windsor in Canada and Detroit in the United States.[1] Detroit is much larger and better known for its prolific depopulation, "ruin porn" (Herscher 2012), and economic collapse, but similar urban transformations, on a smaller scale, echo across the Detroit River into Windsor. Together Windsor and Detroit form the core of North America's twentieth-century car-industrial complex. Like nowhere else these cities funneled their long-term worth and urban development into the industrial production and consumption of automobility. Motor City built a sprawling laboratory for assembling motor vehicles and launching global titans of corporate automobility; it also tried to engineer urban time-space outside the factory for continuous car flow. This time-space is a paradoxical place, searching for never-ending flow along the assembly line through the corporate showroom onto the ever-expanding freeway. The socioeconomic contradictions of industrial car flow, clearly visible when GM started moving plants and jobs to more profitable pastures in the 1980s, were laid bare by the 2008 financial crisis when it became obvious that Motor City had long privileged automobiles over people, who left Windsor and Detroit en masse. Yet Windsor's economic lifeblood flows on through the production of Chrysler minivans, and Detroit's corporate power still pulses through General Motors (with Ford headquartered next door in Dearborn MI), and as Clint Eastwood puts it, echoing some academics (Tabb 2015), Motor City is ready for a comeback. In short, Motor City presents formidable spatial, political, and cultural hurdles to cycling's expansion. It also offers a "critical case study" (Flyvbjerg 2006) that highlights cycling's generalizability. If it can take hold of Motor City, cycling can take hold of just about anywhere in North America.

Early cycling planning and engineering for Motor City in the new millennium stepped into a veritable infrastructural vacuum. Still getting into the "on-street" game after spending decades in the wilderness, cycling planning for the city was starting from the ground up, or as Detroit's "Nonmotorized Urban Transportation Master Plan" (the Nonmotorized Plan 2005, 4) puts it: "Currently, neither the Traffic

Engineering Division nor the recently revised City of Detroit Zoning Ordinance outlines standards or requirements for non-motorized facilities."[2] Notably, the Nonmotorized Plan's name, besides failing to mention cycling, takes motorized transport as its frame of reference. It sets the tone for conservative cycling planning, such as lacking targeted goals to increase cycling rates and arguing that "bike lanes can be completed by re-striping the roadway to provide the needed extra space. Adequate space generally exists to allow for bike lanes without impacting existing traffic patterns" (2005, 31). Not impacting existing traffic, or reducing capacity by taking away road space for driving, is an explicit goal of planning nonmotorized mobility in Motor City. So is cost effectiveness. The Nonmotorized Plan warns that its primary goal to install "nearly 400 miles of bicycle facility improvements is no easy challenge to undertake, given budget constraints" (2005, 41). The Plan, an unobtrusive, relatively inexpensive road re-striping operation, failed to win over Detroit City Council for over three years.

In the absence of government leadership, cycling urban planning in Motor City has grown more dynamically in the nonprofit and private sectors. The Detroit Greenways Coalition (DGC), for example, acting as Detroit's unofficial cycling department, has been funded by the Kellogg Foundation, one of the biggest philanthropic groups in North America. The DGC has slowly assembled one of the most influential cycling projects in Detroit to date, the Inner Circle Greenway (26 miles; 42 kilometers), by converting disused industrial rail infrastructure into a citywide passageway that has helped trigger further cycling planning and development. The DGC's founder and executive director, Todd Scott, judges it to be the "mother of all non-motorized projects, because almost every other project connects into it" (Interview 2014). The Inner Circle Greenway inspires imitation across the Detroit River in Canada.

Windsor's contemporary "Bicycle Use Master Plan" (2001), or BUMP, is a twenty-year plan with ideas and political challenges comparable to Detroit's Nonmotorized Plan. BUMP envisions cycling expansion through a similar boutique of "bicycle facility improvements," entailing off-road trails, on-street signed routes, shared parking and curb lanes, paved shoulders, and, where feasible, bike lanes. Through these facility improvements, BUMP aims to double cycling trips and increase Windsor's modest cycling modal share (the proportion of all person-trips) from 2 percent to 4 percent within a decade. For BUMP (City of Windsor 2001, 53): "Bike lanes on urban roads consist of a designated space between the edge of the vehicular lane and the curb. Pavement markings, symbols and signage are used to designate this space for exclusive bicycle use." In other words, as in Detroit's Nonmotorized Plan, bike lanes for BUMP do not entail physically separated cycle tracks on streets—the only infrastructure that resolves the issue of safety, without which many people say they will not cycle (Horton 2007). Rather they are striped and marked as symbolic (see photo 14). BUMP was formally adopted by Windsor City Council in 2001, but it, too, has faced significant difficulties in winning government support or changing existing road-building practices.

Windsor's most touted cycling project to date, outlined in BUMP and assembled with the help of technically savvy cycling advocates, traces a circle around the city of Windsor. Like Detroit's Inner Circle Greenway, the Windsor Loop (42.5 kilometers; 26 miles) is nothing to sneeze at. A diversity of neighborhoods and nascent cycling facilities connect to, and derive connectivity from, the Loop. However, the Loop is lacking critical pieces. A vital yet highly contested link, Cabana Road, just barely came into being after Bike Windsor Essex (a registered nonprofit organization), under the leadership of Lori Newton, lobbied for a dedicated bike lane on Cabana. After participating in the environmental assessment Bike Windsor Essex failed to persuade the city to build a dedicated cycle track but successfully nudged it toward a "buffered bike lane" removed from cars with more than the usual (0.3 meter; 12 inch) painted space. This went against the wishes of municipal traffic engineers, local property owners, and some politicians who argued that because of all the driveways along the road, bike lanes separated from car traffic on the street would not be possible. Like the Detroit Greenways Coalition, which relied on traffic studies conducted by

14. Bike lane, Riverside Drive, Windsor, Ontario. Photo by author.

transport experts at Wayne State University, Bike Windsor Essex, with support from City of Windsor urban planners, successfully deployed industrial arguments to positively judge the scientific efficiency of cycling for mass mobility and public health.

Windsor's BUMP and Detroit's Nonmotorized Plan typify first-wave cycling planning: an emphasis on painted, in-traffic (nondedicated) lanes located on underused roadways (low-hanging fruit), circumferential off-road greenways, and low (or nonexistent) modal split objectives. Politically first-wave cycling planning suffers from a lack of high-level support from government and never stops running up against recalcitrant policymakers and engineers. On the ground first-wave planning merely consists of a loose collection of painted lines and sharrows (shared lane markings), route signs on utility poles, and repurposed railroad tracks. However, it has established a baseline for publicly evaluating cycling as an industrially legitimate form of mobility, and in abstract, conceptual space first-wave cycling planning catalyzed an upswing of engineering imagination. In this fluid planning context there emerged the "engineer-bricoleur" (Harvey and Knox 2015) for cycling, a versatile industrial expert who thinks of the road outside the dominant "technological frame" (Bijker 1997) of automobility.

What defines a "good road" to an engineer? "A lot of them, their first answer would be a smooth surface. Nice and straight. Reasonably fast." This is according to Thomas, a highway engineer who worked for twenty years at the county road agency in suburban Detroit before entering private development, specializing in cycling expansion (Interview 2014). For Thomas many engineers are hamstrung by the technical "vernacular" of automobility: "You've got whole sections of highway engineers who say, this is a highway, this is a road, it is for cars. Cyclists should be on the sidewalk." For example, "levels of service" entail a powerful technical means to evaluate roads, ranking, as in school, from A ("free" car flow at or above speed limits) to F (car flow breakdown, congestion). Such highway standards, institutionalized in transportation departments across North America, continually block opportunities for building bike lanes. Yet in the city, where dwelling and access, not just smooth, straight flow, is highly desirable, these standards themselves break down. Thomas continues: "It's not quite like grading for a class, where A is fabulous, and you really want to strive for the A. With road level[s] of service you probably don't want an A." Engineers like Thomas understand this politics of standards—"It's gone to the point where the numbers became the driving force"—which renders difficult any deviation from existing industrial practices for building roads. He also plays off this politics to advance engineering beyond the car by stretching and reframing industrial knowledge.

To make cycling infrastructure work, the engineer-bricoleur moves between multiple ways of knowing the road and rendering it functional. Thomas uses the vernacular of automobility alongside emerging standards for nonmotor travel, including discussions of providing complete streets that promote safe and efficient passage for cyclists. "Having the highway background became a natural way into the non-motor, because I could play the non-motor game on the highway basis. You have to play on their own turf to get the stuff to work." For example, after completing some of Detroit's earliest on-street bike lanes and signed routes in the city's southwest, Thomas's firm has worked on reengineering one-way roads back to their original two-way configurations and taking away some of the lanes for cars on roads with seven-plus lanes, so-called road diets. These projects, crucially, make space for bike lanes without compromising levels of service for cars and so, from a purely physical standpoint, seem easy. "You almost couldn't get them not to work," says Thomas. "It was just paint, for the most part." However, Thomas faces strong push back from, he says, "road engineering people who follow national standards to the letter that try to preempt cycling." These road diets nearly never left the ground when state-level standards threatened to penalize Detroit: on the books bike lanes reduced "travel-lane miles" for cars, so the city stood to lose federal gas tax monies. Facing unprecedented urban depopulation and excess road capacity, Michigan revised the books, and the transformation of Detroit's roads began. Thomas's tactic, giving space to cycling without reducing levels of service for motorists, paid off. The city instituted painted bike lanes "into their normal pavement marking program on roads that have excess lane-age," quickly striping hundreds of cycling travel-lane miles.

With operational bike lanes to work with, the cycling engineer-bricoleur proceeds to generalize and scale this novel way of judging and infrastructuring urban space. Once bike lanes publicly qualify as financially legitimate spaces of travel, engineers and planners coordinate where, across the city, they can most efficiently expand. Not all parts of the city want cycling infrastructure, and not all complete streets need them. While searching for optimal places to paint new bike lanes, and with any luck building dedicated tracks, the cycling engineer-bricoleur leaves the strictly technical sphere along multiple avenues for the social production of cycling. To scale up cycling space Thomas appeals to competing publics and contradictory aspirations for roads. "How we frame a cycle track pitch depends on audience: if it's a study or engineering plan, we frame the arguments differently." In dense-enough urban areas, like in Detroit proper, "it's a lot more of

15. Bike lane, Wyandotte Street, Windsor, Ontario. Photo by author.

a stripped transportation, social equity, economics discussion." In the
suburbs, "where social justice may not be the thing, we push economic
development as the bigger issue." Moreover, in conservative suburbs,
equity issues and environmental aspects of cycling infrastructure do
not sell at all, because people think it's "just you greenies trying to do
something." Ultimately "the business case there is crucial, and some
unique suburban areas are getting it." Much of the public still complains
that road dollars should be spent on filling potholes instead of building
bike lanes. Businesses and property owners still publicly criticize new
bike lanes for disrupting long-standing car parking arrangements. But,
"I haven't heard anybody saying it's not good for business," says Thomas.

Motor City presents unique opportunities for the industrial assembling of cycling, but these opportunities are not equally distributed
between Windsor and Detroit. With about four times fewer people,
South Detroit—as Windsor is affectionately known—also faces extensive
long-term depopulation and a glut of road capacity. But it has strug-
gled to institute bike lanes into the city's normal paving procedures,
complete nascent cycling networks like the Loop, and remove heavy
obstacles in the city's urban core, like the never-ending procession of
car carriers from Chrysler rumbling toward Ambassador Bridge down
Wyandotte Street, where the city, in a rare win, striped a bike lane
in 2014 (see photo 15). To help explain Windsor's auto-inertia, Alan
Halberstadt, city councilor from 1997 to 2014 and cycling advocate,
takes the long view:

> What's really been frustrating is major road rehab work on arteries. I
> always get on my high horse and ask engineering, why don't you put
> in separated bike lanes while you're doing this? Well, they say, it's not
> in BUMP. We spend tens of millions of dollars on roads that would
> be the logical ones for separated bike lanes, yet "it's too expensive."
> But if you're going to spend sixteen million to redo this road, why
> don't you spend seventeen million and do the right thing? They're
> trying to keep the cost down, but it doesn't make sense in the long
> term to do those roads without putting in separated bike lanes. This
> is the way the world is going. Yet it'll be another generation before
> they have a need to redo those roads. (Interview 2014)

The right way to engineer future arteries, by Alan's public judgment,
includes cycle tracks that protect cyclists from fast-moving motor
vehicles—which in Motor City include ceaseless streams of 18-wheelers
transporting automobiles. Alan's political work, like Thomas's, betrays
a long-term industrial vision of the road at odds with the vision of
many Motor City engineers. "Our engineers are sort of black and
white, straight line people," he says. "Their main goal is to move traffic
quickly and efficiently." Unfortunately they still equate traffic with the

car. "That's the mantra, that's been their discipline. To get them out of that narrow hole, it's a battle."

Building on Alan's industrial vision from seventeen years as an icon-oclastic city councilor, cycling advocates in Windsor increasingly look across the Detroit River for inspiration. In 2015 on Jefferson Avenue in Detroit's downtown eastside, after years of study and a road diet, Motor City opened its first dedicated cycle track. With more road diets, cycle tracks, and one- to two-way road conversions to come, Detroit is supported now by high-level city politicians, planners, and the dogged DGC. The city is extending on-street lanes and greenway networks, and managing industrial-domestic friction by making infrastructural com-promises with long-standing local businesses to advance cycle tracks. To the envy of businesses in Windsor, Detroit is manufacturing bicycles and testing a forty-three-station public bike share. In short, Detroit is actively seeking ways to use cycling to drive economic development in the city and capitalize on cycling's advantages. The most obvious, lucrative case of "cycling-oriented development" in Motor City is Orle-ans Landing, a $61-million retail and residential complex along the Dequindre Cut. The Cut, a two-mile (3-kilometer) greenway close to downtown and beachhead for the Inner Circle Greenway, converted part of an old Grand Trunk Railroad line into a wide passageway for cycling and walking, a protected passageway that helped spur urban development after it became a magnet for leisure mobilities and public art (Jarvis 2016). The Inner Circle Greenway, according to DGC exec-utive director Todd Scott, was framed from the start as cycling infra-structure that could lessen urban blight and stimulate higher property values (Interview 2014).

Windsor cycling advocates, including a few recently elected city councilors, are increasingly optimistic about transforming their own road-building practices. To be sure, the dominance of the car seeps deep into the industrial culture of Canada's Motor City. As Alan Halberstadt distills it, "There's a lot of motorheads in Windsor. A lot of guys with garages who tinker with cars. People love their cars here. It's hard to knock that. Politically, very hard." At the same time, Windsor is on the verge of updating BUMP, at last incorporating dedicated cycle tracks into the city's future blueprint for persuading straight-line engineers. Windsor can—even in the absence of strong political leadership, as Detroit has shown—effect socio-technical change in Motor City without compromising the car's road capacity or reducing its level of service. Whether cycling can blaze a new development pattern and approach to urban blight is another, deeply industrial, question.

At the end of the day, despite the unique opportunity presented by Motor City's depopulation and excess road capacity for writing cycling onto the built environment, "sprawl" (see photo 16), as Thomas puts it, "makes it hard to actually convert motorists into cyclists." The golden horseshoe across southern Ontario triggered by the QEW tightly couples industrial automobility with sprawling car-oriented development— infrastructure that continues to undercut nonmotor mobilities and pull the faraway, long-term horizons of planners and engineers into short-term growth cycles driven by real-estate investors, private developers, and economic boosters. A puzzle for Motor City moving forward is whether cycling, too, will be co-opted on an industrial level by global market forces beyond its control through the financialization of urban growth and gentrification. Long-view cycling planning, where it fails to produce a fast profit or a strong business case, hangs in the balance.

Forecasting Progress: Cycling as Modern Mobility?

Among the most likely cities one would expect cycling to take hold of in North America, Canada's capital city tops the list: Ottawa currently enjoys the highest proportion of cycling commuters (along with walking and public transit commuters) among large metropolitan areas in Canada (Statistics Canada 2017b). Ottawa started assembling off-road, multiuse pathways for cycling and walking in the 1970s, decades earlier than its peers, as part of a century-long mission to project itself through ambitious urban planning as a beautiful and functional city for the nation.[3] Ottawa's present form took shape through a totalizing blueprint, what one prominent planning historian, David Gordon, calls "the most important Canadian plan of the mid-twentieth century"

16. Suburban sprawl, Windsor, Ontario. Photo by author.

(Gordon 2001, 57). A strange quality distinguishes this master plan from other modernist visions of the day: "It was widely acclaimed and well received by an almost total majority of the population and by many (though not all) professional peers at the time, and for decades afterward" (Miguelez 2015, 254). Ottawa continues to engage in bold, long-range planning on a variety of mobility fronts, such as building an extensive light rail system, that help promote cycling. Canada's capital city, in short, offers enticing spatial, political, and cultural openings for cycling expansion. It also offers a "critical case study" (Flyvbjerg 2006) that highlights the limited generalizability of cycling. If it can't take hold in Ottawa, cycling might fail anywhere in North America.

Under the surface of Ottawa's bureaucratic, well-organized city image lies a story on the limits of planning mobilities, one that flows from that most important twentieth-century blueprint for Canada's capital. If Robert Moses is America's master builder after the Great Depression, architect Jacques Gréber is Canada's master planner. Both industrial experts sought to write automobility onto the city as if the city were tabula rasa. But unlike Moses, Gréber cloaked the car in Beaux-Arts credentials, Garden City flourishes, and above all, scientific principles of modern planning as articulated by Swiss architect Le Corbusier and the 1943 Athens Charter: "land use segregation, expressways, decentralization, reduced densities, urban renewal, open space and the neighbourhood unit" (Gordon 2001, 49). Gréber unveiled his master plan for Ottawa in the lobby of Parliament on a tapestry woven in silk and wool using the colors of leaves he gathered in Gatineau Park. The tapestry's naturalistic renderings, a poignant counterpoint to the raw machinic power of Rivera's *Detroit Industry Murals*, concealed Gréber's modernist plan to remake the capital according to functionalist representations of flow.

Gréber's plan proceeded by demolishing rail infrastructure, dismantling streetcar lines, and straightening out the street grid to make room for a new hierarchical road system crowned by an expressway, "slicing through space like a great knife" (Lefebvre 1991, 164–65). Faster roads for cars would soon whisk workers away from decentralized office parks to low-density suburbs. While this city plan had many benefits, like cleaning up polluting rail yards in the city's core (Gordon 2001), Gréber failed to organize what he called the "rational circulation of constantly increasing automobile traffic" (Gréber 1950, 79). Ultimately the urban expressway, around itself, made worse the very industrial problems Gréber set out to fix—traffic bottlenecks, dead-end streets, and downward pressure on adjacent property values (Miguelez 2015). The unbridled confidence in objective scientific planning with which Gréber sought to comprehensively design the city around future (auto) mobility, should act as a cautionary tale for industrial cycling expansion.

The expansion of cycling through urban planning embroils cycling in the production of growth forecasts that predict population growth and future needs based on existing propensities for transport and housing. Mobility forecasts, representations of future time and space, hide blind spots that reflect the prerogatives and ideological judgments of their creators. For example, according to historians, Gréber's plan's "Achilles' heel" (Gordon 2001, 55) lay in its gross underestimation of population growth, which set up central components of Gréber's plan for failure, including road capacity, housing needs, and a greenbelt designed to stop urban sprawl.[4] However, this assessment overlooks the specific way in which Gréber's objectives were undermined by his failure to anticipate and plan for growth. The 1950 plan (poorly) projected a population not like the existing one, dependent on streetcar transit and everyday walking, but rather a more modern population of future automobile drivers who were weary of city life and preferred to live in open spaces close to the countryside. Consequently when the greenbelt burst, it was an unprecedented sea of car-dependent sprawl that spilled out. Contemporary forecasting has sought to correct these projection problems and ideological blinders of postwar planning. As Ottawa's longtime chief forecaster, Tom (a pseudonym), explains, population projections no longer merely extend existing conditions of space and mobility as a static, uniform reality, but rather anticipate how existing conditions will evolve and continue to change over time:

> Historically, including the update we did in the mid-90s, we just took the most recent housing propensities and applied them forward. What we did after 2001 is put a great deal of work into looking at historical trends and a lot of thought into how those patterns might continue to change over time. In other words, we projected changes forward. So we anticipate an ongoing significant shift away from lower density to higher density housing. (Interview 2010)

Instead of projecting, say, single detached housing propensities for the 75-feet-wide and 120-feet-deep lots leapfrogging Ottawa's greenbelt in the 1960s, the city now extrapolates smarter, transit-oriented growth to plan for an increasingly compact future city. Statistical projections of urban socio-technical change rooted in Canadian census data point to the potential of population-level forecasting to promote cycling, one that may go well beyond imagining future propensities for denser housing and shorter blocks that underlie nonmotor mobilities.[5] At the same time, "projecting changes forward" for cycling has only just begun to reshape infrastructure.

The City of Ottawa formally judged cycling as a publicly qualified industrial good for the first time in the postmodernist era in 2008. The 2008 *Ottawa Cycling Plan* (OCP), a long-term, twenty-year strategy, bears all the hallmarks of first-wave cycling planning, comparable to that seen in Motor City. The plan focuses on the expansion of in-traffic, nondedicated cycling facilities, including painted lanes, paved shoulders, and wide curb lanes as well as off-road multiuse pathways. A central objective of the plan is to increase cycling's modal share from 1.7 percent in 2001 to 3 percent by 2021 (City of Ottawa, OCP 2008, 7). In practice this entails re-striping and re-signing operations under-taken as roads come up for prescheduled repair, dubbed a "following the pavers" approach widely criticized for leaving gaps between cycling lanes, or building "bike lanes to nowhere" (Corfu 2017). Compared to Motor City, however, Ottawa envisioned a much larger nondedicated cycling network of over 2,500 kilometers (1,550 miles), planning for a long-term shift toward cycling by painting bike lanes evenly across the sprawling capital region—regardless of whether spatial conditions supported cycling expansion or not. The nature of this nondedicated network shows an elaboration of first-wave cycling planning through a quantitative, objectal focus on formal, homogenous relations between urban space and cycling, a totalizing, objectal lens that aims to transcend place and the body (age, sex, ethnicity) by casting cycling uniformly across the city. Ottawa's longest-serving cycling planner, Damien (a pseudonym), reflecting on the limitations of the OCP, carefully words it this way:

> We tried to make the entire city cycling friendly, and that created a new set of challenges. A lot of resources have spilled out to sub-urban and rural areas, and that has hurt cycling, where the biggest problems are. The greatest potential is in the central part. It has been a little bit left out, because of this need to include all of the city. (Interview 2011)

This generic blanket approach, in Lefebvrian terms, conceives of the city as a geometric, passive space, waiting to be filled up by cyclists represented as undifferentiated users; it conflates what is lived and perceived with what is planned and conceived. First-wave cycling planning in Canada's capital failed to grapple with the social complexity of cycling infrastructure, generating industrial-civic friction by effectively excluding women, older folks, and children who prefer to take short trips on continuous, dedicated bike lanes (Aldred et al. 2017). However, as in Motor City, this early industrial planning and moral friction unleashed a flurry of infrastructural imaginings that pushed the industrial boundaries of what efficiency might mean for cycling.

Ottawa leaped forward in a revised 2013 "Cycling Plan" (City of Ottawa, OCP 2013), learning relatively quickly from the industrial deficiencies of the original OCP by collating more diverse data and using these data to project more diverse infrastructure targeted to different spaces, bodies, and traffic.[6] Owing to quicker than expected progress toward the 2008 plan's goal for increasing cycling levels, the 2013 OCP raises the citywide modal share target (for 2031) from 3 to 5 percent. The target further rises to 8 percent inside the greenbelt, where increasingly dense, connected, and mixed-use space contains the highest potential for cycling growth. To reach these targets the 2013 OCP draws functional distinctions for an "ultimate cycling network" between "continuous, higher capacity spine routes for direct, longer distance travel," "smaller scale local routes for local access," and "the City's and National Capital Commission's off-road pathway network" (OCP 2013, 53). Overlaying and combining these spines, routes, and pathways are functionally separated crosstown bikeways for inter-neighborhood connectivity and neighborhood bikeways that offer "comfortable cycling routes for residents within their local communities . . . on quiet, low traffic volume local roads" (OCP 2013, 65–66). Yet another functional distinction separates facility types: "on-street bike lanes, shared lanes with mixed traffic, multi-use pathways and cycle tracks (separated bike lanes)" (OCP 2013, 39). Translating all this conceptual infrastructure into material bike lanes entails a data-intensive process based on "the number, tim-

17. Bidirectional cycle track, Ottawa, Ontario. Photo by author.

ing, location, length and purpose of cycling trips in Ottawa, as well as the demographics of cyclists" (OCP 2013, i). Drawing from the census, origin-destination surveys, and biannual screen-line data, but also on an expanding array of automated bike counters, cycling indices, and Bixi (bike share) usage data, public evaluation of cycling infrastructure has turned the bike lane into both a product and producer of mobility techno-science.

As the bike lane elaborates its own conceptual representations of time-space, often fraught and politicized judgments over bike lane construction turn into neutral-sounding outputs from an opaque, ever-blacker box. For example, the choice between controversial cycle tracks (see photo 17), which frequently remove car parking, and other configurations has since the 2013 OCP become a product of a Cycling Facility Selection Decision Support Tool, called a nomograph, that judges the most appropriate facility based on average daily traffic volumes and motor vehicle operating speeds. Another quantitative tool, echoing the standards of automobile flow, establishes "a level of service for cycling . . . to assess the quality of different cycling facilities" (OCP 2013, 44). Based on "Level of Traffic Stress" methodology, levels of service for cycling use vehicle speed, the number of lanes, and the presence of parked cars to calculate the actual and perceived safety of cycling facilities. Safety and stress form, as one might imagine, an inverse relationship: if perceived safety is high, say, while riding next to the river along an off-road pathway, then traffic stress is low; if perceived safety is low, say, while cycling in fast-moving traffic, then traffic stress is high, helping publicly justify the need for dedicated infrastructure. While levels of service for cycling have a long way to go before they, like those of the car, not only technically inform but politically dictate road engineering—the point where the numbers become the driving force—the parallel language shows the power of calculating standards in scientific plans for judging efficiency.

The new cycling techno-science provides tangible benefits to cycling planning and, in light of the impacts of twentieth-century high modernism, a cautionary tale. Using a more objective Facility Selection Tool may reduce the political precarity of cycle tracks, plans for which have been all too easily stymied by businesses protesting from Ottawa to Copenhagen against removing public road space where people can freely take off their cars. A common theme that repeatedly came up in my interviews with industrial experts is that wielding a scientific plan, having some kind of technical judgment at hand, is indispensable for persuading bureaucrats, politicians, and publics alike of the legitimacy of new cycling facilities. Moreover, cycling standards that model the qualitative experience of cycling, particularly where they differentiate cycling stress and safety by socio-demographic data, bodes well for cycling systems living up broadly to the industrial principle of efficiency by advancing public health and economic productivity instead of undermining them. However, through its animation of urban planning and road engineering, cycling is fast crystallizing its own hierarchical way of ordering everyday mobility. Like automobile techno-science developing after the Great Depression, emerging industrial standards of cycling carry the potential to obscure the lived experience of mobility, homogenizing and confusing this socially diverse experience for conceptual models of cycling efficiently.

Furthermore the new cycling techno-science, by collating better data with which to project more diverse and targeted infrastructure, paradoxically, narrows the multiplicity of the bike lane by fixating its functionality. To paraphrase Gréber (1950, 79), coordinating the rational circulation of constantly increasing cycling traffic entails modeling and materializing the appropriate functional structure of bike lanes. This structure can be seen now taking shape through the functional distinctions drawn between spine and route and neighborhood and crosstown bikeways that work to segregate "through cycling" from "local cycling"—a segregation that echoes how the Gréber plan, following the new science of traffic engineering, sought to rationalize postwar automobility:

> Where the roadway system of a town has not been rationally conceived and adapted to the demands of traffic circulation, the resulting conditions must be that public highways often have contradictory functions, embarrassing to traffic circulation, and causing delay to local movements of vehicles, with consequent loss of time and money. It is incontestable that a public highway, serving in common through interurban traffic and the traffic demands of abutting commercial and industrial activities, cannot ensure the effective fulfillment of both or either of these functions. (Gréber 1950, 176)

Given the slower speeds and greater sensorial powers of cycling, it is worth wondering if it is similarly "incontestable" that a good bike lane, serving in common *through* inter-neighborhood traffic and the demands of *abutting* neighborhood activities, cannot effectively fulfill both or either of these functions. After all, the top-down functional segregation of cycling space by high-speed "through" and slower "local" traffic lanes rationalizes and stratifies space and flow by speed, generating more efficient circulation at the cost of defining and controlling what kind of cycling a bike lane is for. This, in turn, places pressure on people to cycle along roads with bike lanes rather than roads without them (whether they wish to or not). In this sense the segregation of flow and speed via cycling techno-science narrows the multiplicity of a bike lane, and roads in general, for the common industrial good of the overall system.

Modernism may be passé, but cycling is immune neither from techno-scientific hubris nor from myopic planning-for-profit—two hallmarks of modern mobility—and the two interlink. As the infrastructure for a hierarchical mobility system falls into place and starts igniting the transformation of its surroundings, automobility shows us that industrial expertise has the potential to generate a totalizing, all-comprehending dynamic in which mobility is rationalized according to ever-finer functional distinctions and is assembled regardless of preexisting practice and lived experience. Industrial mobilities tend to spur further differentiation and interventions that keep users in line, "locking in" trajectories of urban growth and economic development. For example, a hierarchical cycling system must constrain access to speedy cycling spines, elaborate intersection controls, and physical barriers for regulating flow, and contain complex safety problems generated by cyclists mingling with each other and other road users across different speeds. As this system grows in scale and connectivity, safe and stress-free cycle tracks along major desire lines define new commuting and leisure routes but also circuits of consumption and cycling-oriented development, from trendy shops, coffeehouses, and restaurants to luxury condos. Clearly the dense, centripetal urban development triggered by emerging cycling flows (e.g., Dequindre Cut) differs from the centrifugal suburbs and commercial parks (e.g., Golden Horseshoe) generated by modern systems of automobility. But the industrial morality is the same, even though capitalism is changing. Complex mobility systems generate the spatial conditions for their own self-expansion, in the neoliberal city, by bending the flows of international investment. The farther abstract cycling space leaves the ground, looking down at the city like a solar eye, the higher the chance that cycling infrastructure will flow with the turbulent currents of capital—a fate more certain if cycling reaches the point where the numbers become its driving force.

Cycling to the "Mall on a Highway," Dartmouth, Nova Scotia

As the car drives east of Ottawa 1,440 kilometers (895 miles), Liam cycles to Dartmouth Crossing, a $280-million, 207-hectare (510-acre) retail mecca in the city for which it is named. Opening in 2007 in a decommissioned quarry near the junction of two major highways, Dartmouth Crossing epitomizes car-based development, steering business from a struggling urban core to the outskirts of town with a collection of big-box stores, fashion outlets, restaurants, and entertainment that could stand in for just about anywhere (IKEA recently moved in, to the joy of Halifax's economic boosters and ready-to-assemble furniture lovers).[7] When this mall on a highway sells itself as "a prime location that offers consumers value and convenience in an exciting and unique environment," it is talking to motorists.[8] For Liam, who lives on the opposite side of that highway junction, reaching this "prime location" entails cycling beside, under, over, and around the often impenetrable infrastructure built for a seamless flow of automobiles. His nonlinear voyage shows but one evocative way in which the everyday assembly of industrial mobilities deeply embroils cycling with the infrastructural legacies and historical futures of automobility.

Luckily Liam has help from a set of passages loosely united under the mother of all Canadian nonmotor projects, the Trans Canada Trail. After leaving his house Liam rides along the Lake Banook Trail (see photo 18), a popular multiuse route and enrolee into the new Trans Canada. For Liam pathways removed from car traffic are not merely an aesthetic addition to his commute but an obligatory point of passage. At sixteen, while cycling to work in Halifax, he was sideswiped at high speed by a car when the driver, shoulder-checking his opposite blind spot ahead of changing lanes, suddenly swerved into his path. A month later, just as he began to regain his confidence, Liam hit the pavement again after a motorist flung open her door. Since then, defensive and a little skittish, Liam has continued cycling but with less

18. Lake Banook Trail, Dartmouth, Nova Scotia. Photo by author.

of the speed and occasional reckless abandon that used to animate his commute. He bucks the stereotype that roads in low-cycling contexts like Dartmouth cater to athletic, spandex-clad men. Liam happens to be a highly competitive, spandex-wearing athlete, but prioritizing his safety—riding on sidewalks, breaking down hills, and taking the long way—has become second nature.

So Liam welcomed the construction of the Lake Banook Pedestrian Bridge. Now, instead of riding up a sidewalk into a partial cloverleaf interchange before awkwardly crossing onto a busy arterial road with an on-again, off-again painted bike lane (a chronic problem in Dartmouth and Halifax), he crosses the lake before the expressway. The pedestrian bridge was planned in the 1990s before it lapsed for lack of funds. When it finally materialized more than two decades later, it closed an important gap for nonmotor mobilities with a nudge and financial support from the Trans Canada Trail Foundation, becoming part of the Trail. Canada's macro-scale cycling infrastructure, the

19. Dartmouth Crossing on the left. Photo by author.

Trans Canada Trail is a volunteer, donor-driven, community-based project. Yet like the Trans-Canada Highway, it affords national circulation, spanning 24,000 kilometers (14,913 miles) and all thirteen Canadian provinces and territories. One hundred percent connected in 2017, the Trans Canada Trail has drawn mixed reviews (CBC News 2017). Some of its rural parts comprise not so much trails as risky shoulders on highways, ATV routes, and waterways. Like local urban cycling systems, the new Trans Canada makes space for cycling out of a diverse range of passages. After crossing Lake Banook, in short order Liam's experience ranges from side streets and off-road pathways to arterial roads and park trails, much of which hold together through sidewalk detours and parking lots (not to mention civil interaction with pedestrians and dogs).

As Liam emerges from the woods he spies Dartmouth Crossing on the horizon (far left in photo 19). From this vantage a remarkable juxtaposition of highways comes into view. Between Liam and the mall lies the expressway for the car, whose impenetrability to persons without cars has from the beginning textured his voyage—from the circuitous route to the speedy motorists Liam faces at intersections (either anticipating or coming off superhighways). Beside the expressway in front of Liam lies an unimpeded stretch of unpaved park trail, the newest highway on the block. And to his right Liam sees Lake Mic Mac, part of the Shubenacadie Canal water highway between Halifax Harbour and the Bay of Fundy, used by the Mi'kmaq for at least four thousand years (and source of inspiration for the name, Dartmouth Crossing). Some engineers would see in these highways, side by side, a clean evolutionary model graduating all the way from meandering, slow, and inefficient to linear, fast, and functional. Other industrial experts might see a different typology moving in the opposite direction, from least to most sustainable in the long run. For Liam, however, while visually it appears as if these highways form neat separate lines, on the ground his experience is totally different. He feels the wind pick up off the lake, filling his nostrils with its organic particles, while his whole body trembles with the machinic drum of traffic on the expressway. In multi-sensorial cycling practice, the highways spill into one another.

Before long Liam finds a rare point of access up the great wall of automobility (see photo 20). Between a mall eager to portray itself as an environmental steward and a Trans Canada Trail seeking to attract corporate donors by "stimulating tourism and creating jobs," a path was constructed for cyclists and pedestrians that lifts Liam safely up and over the expressway.[9] Dartmouth Crossing's nonmotor connections, bike parking, and other nods to the environment, such as restoring two brooks and resurrecting trout on the property (Markan 2016), are nothing to sneeze at. But the long-term impact of ramping up car-based consumption on the Shubenacadie waterway through runoff worries many in the community, including Liam, whose family has for decades relied on Dartmouth's lakes for work, recreation, and respite. Because of the mall the expressway became even wider, elbowing its way farther into an ecologically and archeologically important city park through a new highway ramp. The top of the ramp is what launches Liam's path

20. Liam rides over the highway. Photo by author.

over the highway, the geometry of which recalls Lefebvre's (1991, 49) idea of abstract space "as a set of things/signs and their formal relationships: glass and stone, concrete and steel, angles and curves, full and empty. . . . eras[ing] distinctions . . . from nature and (historical) time." When Liam finally rolls into the mall, he finds only a trace of historical urban space, called the Village Shops (see photo 21). The Village Shops mimics a traditional nonmotorized place, but for the car-borne shopper. It also shows how ambitious cycling infrastructure, try as it might to engineer its own economic spin-offs, settles for the spoils of automobility.

Re-Infrastructuring Efficiency: Industrial Mobility Futures

This chapter on industrial mobilities focuses on road engineering, urban planning, and the lived experience of biking through industrial space to examine how different cities are assembling functional infrastructure for cycling. Between Motor City and Canada's capital, Liam's house and

21. The Village Shops, Dartmouth Crossing. Photo by author.

Dartmouth Crossing—and all across the vast nation between Vancouver's Georgia Street Viaduct and Halifax's Cogswell Interchange—lies a bricolage of cycling infrastructures slowly developing into larger-scale systems. The guiding principle behind the industrial assembly of these infrastructural systems is to render cycling more efficient. According to this forceful industrial morality, mobilities are good insofar as they advance the safe, rational, and productive circulation of people through the city over long-term horizons. To create efficient circulation, cycling relies on many of the same materials (asphalt, steel, and paint), practices (road building, route formation, everyday commuting), and public judgments (city plans, levels of service) as the car. Further echoing the history of automobility, cycling is tempted to treat the city as tabula rasa and judge its infrastructure on economic results and profitable urban growth, as evidenced by first-wave cycling planning and cycling-oriented development.

However, across the same urban contexts cycling expansion shows signs of potential for resisting the financial excesses of capitalism and the techno-scientific hubris of modernism. From bricoleur-engineers who leverage multiple ways of assembling bike lanes to the modeling of the qualitative complexity of cycling across different urban contexts, the industrial worth of cycling is itself evolving and diverging from the muscular modernism that characterized the formative postwar growth of mass automobility. Moreover, nascent national networks like the Trans Canada Trail may yet gain industrial and governmental support. They might become better by following city cycling systems and the lead of the national capital—technically an urban model for the nation. All these new developments point to how transport planners and engineers, as relatively powerful brokers of cycling's moral worth, can reinvent industrial mobilities for cycling in the twenty-first-century city.

To what distant futures do industrial mobilities beckon? Even if cycling can handle market pressures (a topic examined more closely in chapter 4) and live up to its own industrial principles, stormy moral seas lie ahead. Because cycling is not unfolding across tabula rasa, its expansion will continue to contest traditional knowledge and relationships with place, from long-standing car-parking arrangements to indigenous ways of assembling the environment. Further moral friction flickering inside the industrial assembly of cycling relates to the social exclusion associated with merely painting bike lanes on the street. While inviting a small number of Canadians to cycle with traffic (i.e., mostly middle-aged men), this symbolic marking effectively excludes many people who, like Liam, prefer to cycle with physical protection from fast-moving automobiles and increasingly distracted drivers. Exacerbating industrial-civic friction, cycling models often treat people as undifferentiated users and inputs for functionalist, abstract representations of flow, ignoring, *inter alia*, differences between bodies and uneven access to mobility (a topic examined more closely in the next chapter). If governments used only this homogenous way of infrastructuring efficiency for cycling, bike lanes might never serve marginalized populations.

Fortunately industrial approaches to cycling expansion are moving beyond first-wave cycling planning in ways that may reduce this moral friction, notably in a shift toward building cycle tracks and conceptual models of cycling that respond to the perceived stress of riding in traffic. The result is the production of increasingly hierarchical, functional cycling infrastructure. Of course how far functional differentiation will ultimately go in channeling cycling flows across ever-more specialized passageways is an open industrial problem.

22. Tweed Ride, Windsor. Photo by author.

3. Civic Mobilities

Dedicated Bike Lanes, Cycling Social Movements, and Cycling Justice

What makes mobilities civically good? What makes a bike lane good for cycling equitably? What civic lessons can cycling learn from driving? These questions open up a moral assemblage of mobility predicated on democratic freedoms and citizenship, the creation of solidarity, and the amelioration of inequality. Enjoying explosive growth in the twentieth century as nations united citizens for war, and peace united nations toward the pursuit of universal human rights and a new multilateral world order, civic worth gained further momentum through postwar social movements to expand civil and political rights and the redistribution of wealth through the social welfare state. While the neoliberal turn of the 1980s and 1990s in Canada undercut its advancement, civic worth remains a critical, widely institutionalized common good for judging fairness and equality among humans and their political and material arrangements—one notably enshrined in the *Canadian Charter of Rights and Freedoms* (1982). Critically, civic worth provides the preeminent moral counterweight to the ongoing marketization of public space and excesses of industrial, fossil fuel–driven capitalism. At the same time, as with industrial worth, civic worth has played a critical role in expanding automobility and likewise poses profoundly ambivalent lessons for the growth of cycling.

Civic assemblages of mobility transcend the moral worth embodied over time in particular families, traditions, and local communities—demarcated as domestic worth—into a wider, disembodied common good forged through the convergence of all individual wills that are explicitly placed above private interests. For civic worth "the common good" takes on a precise meaning. It encompasses a Rousseauian general will as that which transcends the egos, vainglories, and hyper-partisanships of individuals and groups that prevent humans from pursuing the common interests of a nation, polity, or society. In practice the gap between domestic and civic worth is not always clear. Some actors and objects cross between these worlds of worth. Ghost bikes (see photo 23), for instance, are a compelling cross-world thing. On one hand, these roadside memorials in honor of cyclists killed by motorists, cared for by friends and family members of the victims for months, sometimes years, afterward, offer a poignant domestic account of death by car. In the fall of 2015 the City of Ottawa faced public backlash for proposing to limit the display of ghost bikes to ninety days. One man (whose sister was killed after getting doored and knocked into the path of an oncoming car, as memorialized by the ghost bike in photo 23) argued: "The ghost bike ended up allowing us to focus our energy, to channel our grief, [it was] a place to congregate, a place to drive anger and a place to raise awareness. There's no way that 90 days would be adequate" (Crawford and Britneff 2015). On the other hand, ghost bikes express another judgment of industrial-scale death by automobility. As the grieving man said, they "raise awareness," pointing to a systemic inequity between motorists and cyclists, regarding not so much their memory as their right to live in the first place. Although this criticism flows from a local memorial, it transcends the particular histories and communities of those involved in the pursuit of justice—moving us squarely into civic territory.

While it may be tempting to dwell on the history of inequities, violence, and unequal power relations that unfold between motorists and cyclists on the road every day, an even more interesting civic analysis lies in what cycling can learn from the car. The fact is that both cycling and driving have their democratic deficits. From the colonizing "good roads movement" of early twentieth-century Canada to postwar urban renewal schemes and freeway building that tried to erase black communities from Vancouver to Halifax, the car carries a sordid history

23. Ghost bike on Queen Street, Ottawa. Photo by author.

of perpetuating racialized social exclusion (Bullard et al. 2004). The continuing rise of neoliberal urbanism and gentrification in the twenty-first century, especially in "global cities" (e.g., Vancouver), begs the question: Will cycling planning and urban practice simply carry on with this exclusionary history or cut a more equitable and inclusive path?

Toward an Expansive Cycling Justice

Aaron Golub, Melody L. Hoffman, Adonia E. Lugo, and Gerardo F. Sandoval, in their groundbreaking book *Bicycle Justice and Urban Transformation* (2016, 9), define "bicycle justice" as "an inclusionary social movement and practice based on furthering material equity and recognizing that a diverse range of qualitative experiences should influence public investment in transportation." They link bicycle justice directly to social justice, weighing justice on whether cycling planning and development in the United States can check its white, upwardly mobile privilege; draw on the experiences of marginal "invisible cyclists"; and stop cycling from fueling inequity through gentrification (Lubitow 2016). This approach to bicycle justice resonates with Canada's uneven mobility landscape, where cycling planning and development is similarly tied to gentrification. However, the data show that people cycling in Canada are less economically marginalized overall than their American counterparts (Statistics Canada 2011), and while white privilege may bias cycling advocacy in Canada as well, many cities in the country also support cycling organizations connecting with women, immigrants, and other low-cycling groups (Savan et al. 2017). Therefore building on the idea of bicycle justice, I offer a more expansive concept of "cycling justice" (so named because cycling is more than two-wheelers) that includes social justice while moving beyond it in three salient ways. First, what is *just* generally aligns with what is *good*, and social justice with civic worth. Thus domestic, industrial, market, and ecological worths offer four other ways of making cycling just—although for consistency I follow the liberal-egalitarian tradition (Rawls 1971) and reserve "justice" specifically for civic worth and social equity. Second, in the edifice of a larger "mobility justice" (Sheller 2018), cycling justice is not simply about civically unequal power relations and social exclusion but also about distributions of capabilities (Martens et al. 2016)—including capabilities for citizenship.

Third, and most crucially, a more expansive cycling justice *qua* civic worth must not only attend to unequal power relations and distributional fairness but also to the sociopolitical conditions and practices that underlie and legitimate the procedures and institutions of justice in the first place. Without asking what social unity and political legitimacy require beyond a shared commitment to higher principles, cycling justice ignores "one of the great unresolved questions of political philosophy" (Kymlicka 2001, 257). I return to this problem, around which the book slowly revolves, at the very end. Under the weight of stock market crime, exploding inequality, voter apathy, and long-term declines in social trust and civic engagement (Putnam 2000), liberal democracy was creaking well before Russian meddling in the 2016 American election of President Donald Trump, social media silos, and the most recent wave of authoritarian populism washing over the world. To legitimate liberal democracy and bolster commitment to social justice, civic worth appeals to good citizenship and a shared sense of national or multinational belonging. Some philosophies (communitarianism) and states (say, Hungary and Poland) go further and promote one official shared way of life—undermining the plurality of the common good and courting illiberal democracy. More promising from a liberal democratic perspective is cultivating a sense of belonging through a cosmopolitan sense of nationhood and teaching civic virtues like civility, public reasonableness (i.e., the ability to give a public justification for something that appeals to the common good, rather than a narrow one based on creed or the interests of one class bracket), and willingness to dialogue with those with whom we disagree through democratic public education (Kymlicka 2001; Gutmann 1987). Jean-Jacques Rousseau's classic ideal of civic worth as renouncing selfish interests for the "general will" remains remarkably relevant here. By "general" Rousseau refers to a nobler state of association reachable by "each person when, shedding his or her singularity and sacrificing all particular interests, he or she comes to know what is good in general, and succeeds in desiring the common good" (Boltanski and Thévenot 2006[1991], 110). In short, cycling justice needs ways of educating and equipping citizens to serve common causes that transcend their own interests.

The sociopolitical and material contexts within which ideals of cycling's civic worth confront reality are not exactly the same in Canada as they are in the United States. Golub, Hoffman, Lugo, and Sandoval frame their book's examination of (mainly) American bicycle justice through the following disconnect:

> A new profile of urban cycling has emerged, one associated with the middle class whiteness that was once more at home in suburbs and suvs, but is now venturing, mostly by choice, back into the city riding buses, trains, and bicycles. But this mediated profile of the upwardly mobile bicyclist is misleading. The greatest share of bicycle commuters in the U.S. fall into the lowest U.S. Census income bracket. (Golub et al. 2016, 1)

The greatest share of cycling commuters in Canada, by contrast, does not qualify as low income. Rather they distribute fairly evenly across income deciles (Statistics Canada 2011). Canadians, moreover, are more concentrated in major cities and cycle more than Americans, owing in part to Canada's greater urban densities, mixed-use neighborhoods, shorter trip distances, and safer conditions for cycling underpinned by more extensive cycling infrastructure (Pucher et al. 2006). These social and material differences between national contexts have not prevented the transnational diffusion of cycling's new urban profile as part of a consumptive, hipster lifestyle, especially for white men with bushy beards that hark back to racist 1890s lumberjacks. Canada, too, suffers from this view of seeing cycling as a hipster lifestyle (see Brown 2015) and the tendency of using cycling infrastructure to rebrand city spaces for impending real-estate investment. However, Canada's is clearly a different distributional puzzle. American-Canadian comparisons show the need for a heuristic approach to cycling justice attuned to the power of context.

Cycling justice, I propose, requires a heuristic, intersectional approach to understanding complex inequalities (Scott and Siltanen 2016). This means rather than assume a priori what axes of inequality (gender, class, ethnicity, ability, etc.) will be significant in any given context (neighborhood, city, province, year, etc.), their "relevance for the configuration of inequality under analysis needs to be a question, not an assumption, of the research" (Scott and Siltanen 2016, 3). It is not simply that each axis of inequality is not always everywhere relevant. How each axis relates to one another depends on, and interacts with, context. For example, the association of higher cycling rates among men in Canada (Ramage-Morin 2017) interacts with infrastructure (Winters and Zanotto 2017) as well as neighborhood cycling levels: where cycling levels are high (e.g., Trinity-Bellwoods, Toronto), the gender gap dissipates (as cycling safety rises), but not everywhere (Aldred et al. 2017), because high cycling levels are not the only important factor. Or consider gentrification: in some contexts it poses a colossal challenge to cycling justice (Vancouver); in others it is less pressing (Ottawa). Liberal-egalitarian models of justice focusing on equity, without also considering the sociopolitical conditions and practices that underpin justice, ignore this power of context. Karel Martens, Daniel Piatkowski, Kevin J. Krizek, and Kara Luckey (2016, 90), for instance, pose the compelling question: When is it "justifiable to ask one individual to sacrifice so another can cycle?" Their answer: only when a bike lane or cycling policy enhances the "levels of accessibility of persons 'disadvantaged' in terms of sub-standard accessibility levels." Even cycling investments for millennials should "be critically scrutinized" (2016, 94) because of their privileged capacity to choose cycling over driving. This ledger for social cycling justice is too simple for the expansion of civic cycling. It makes strong civic sense to target cycling investment at groups (and also neighborhoods) with low accessibility. But cycling justice cannot stop there. It makes equally strong civic sense to simultaneously expand cycling for everyone as a communal way of practicing a more civil, publicly reasonable, and less violent form of mobility citizenship on the road—one that can bolster collective commitment to cycling justice in the first place.

Driving Lessons

Imagine yourself as an eighteen-year-old in the summer of 1972 hitch-hiking across the North American continent, East Coast to West Coast, on the new, nearly finished Trans-Canada Highway—because it prom-ises you nothing less than freedom. With fourteen dollars in your pocket, you slowly start learning the ropes in the company of an old friend. The first day, standing on the wrong side of the highway inter-change, you waste six hours sweating bullets in the hot sun.

You finally get a knack for hitchhiking though, and escaping mos-quitoes: tuck in your shirt, no sunglasses, have a clear sign, and know where (highway merges, ramps) and when (under lights at night) to beat the crowd (it seems everyone is hitchhiking). Rides vary: skunky Volkswagen vans or Corvettes; room for one, two, or three; drunk or sober passengers or drivers. You try to focus on sober rides with more than one spot, but supply is tight. You soon have to leave your friend—you'll meet again in the next city—and rely on inebriated driv-ers. Lodgings vary: missions, hostels, parks. A fugitive from Dorches-ter penitentiary triggers a regional hitchhiking blackout, from which you can only Greyhound your way out. A nice-seeming man driving a Cadillac becomes belligerent after you reject his advances, a fright-ening situation that heightens your sense of situational awareness. Hitchhikers tilt at a ratio of about 3:1 men, but both women and men carry Buck Knives, which makes things interesting in Quebec among francophones and anglophones piling onto the Trans-Canada, where it's not yet finished, and you lose your way for a time on provincial roads. In Thunder Bay Aboriginals throw objects at you, making you question how they have been treated by the community and the government. Farther south, in the United States, you watch out for police as they intensely surveil interstate highways of impressive scale (in Canada, east-west is the only game in town). You gain a new respect for the draft dodgers hitchhiking north of the border. In Alberta, shortly after climbing by yourself into a hippy van of questionable direction, you spend a night in jail with your new driving party in Banff (a town of which you remain suspicious to this day). Your party draws straws for who takes the blame for drug paraphernalia and leaves on bail (you escape the short straw). So after some life-altering detours around prison breaks, dangerous drivers, French lessons, and jail in Banff, at long last you reach Vancouver, Terminal City, and feel far more attached to Canada. The country is more diverse than you thought. You camp for a month in a Terminal City park by the ocean. Someone takes your rolled-up tent from beneath your sleeping head, you find a substitute in Chinatown, and after experiencing the countercultural and psycho-geographic limits of Canadian freedom, you hitchhike your way back home.

The civic assembly of national roads for automobility and the spontaneous car-sharing practices of the late 1960s and early 1970s carry two core civic lessons for cycling. The first civic lesson is to mandate civility, public reasonableness, and good citizenship into national mobilities through democratic design and practice, including practices for sharing the road. This lesson is really about fostering the socio-spatial and political conditions of mobility justice. The completion of the Trans-Canada Highway and subsequent explosion of hitchhiking helped put together the nation, not simply by circulating people in cars through every province and territory of Canada and creating a shared culture of automobility but also by remolding the nation's civic imaginary—transforming how and with whom (and at what speed) Canadians could imagine themselves relating, belonging, and rebelling. However, universal automobility in Canada did not exactly pan out as such; it instead created new forms of incivility and inequality. Hitchhiking the Trans-Canada is often fondly remembered as a universal rite of passage, while in practice it was disproportionately a white middle-class movement by young baby boomers, with higher social and physical risks falling on women (Mahood 2018). Moreover, the universal automobility of the Trans-Canada Highway suffers from "design-determinism" (Golub et al. 2016, 7): expecting ostensibly common infrastructure through sheer speed and scale to somehow correct histories of social exclusion and unite the nation. The Trans-Canada's slow fall from grace, from an agent of democracy to a site of restricted access, everyday accidents and violence, and socio-spatial segregation, underscores the need for cycling to carry democracy through both equitable design and civic practice.

The second core civic lesson is to break from the car's history of perpetuating racialized social exclusion (Bullard et al. 2004) and foster mobility justice through complex forms of equity that respond to sociopolitical context. In many cases cycling justice is expressed as expanding access and democratic design through dedicated bike lanes, easing moral friction between civic and industrial cycling. In other cases cycling justice focuses less on design and more on "embodied deliberation" (Johansson and Liou 2017) and civic participation, trying to advance "bicycle justice as an inclusionary social movement" (Golub et al. 2016, 9) outside the cycling planning establishment, easing friction between civic and domestic cycling. In still other cases community organizations advance cycling justice by fighting gentrification, a growing source of market-civic friction increasingly intertwined with city cycling. As in domestic and industrial assemblages of cycling, civic cycling—and indeed cycling justice—takes on a surprising level of multiplicity across different urban contexts.

The emergence of more inclusive cycling plans featuring dedicated bike lanes characterizes a civic swelling of cycling design, advocacy, and practice around the end of the twenty-first century's first decade in Canada, which I call "second-wave cycling planning." Critical of first-wave, industrial approaches to cycling planning that cast a homogenizing, quantitative gaze over the city and ignore socio-spatial differences between people and contexts, second-wave cycling planning invites women, seniors, and children to participate in cycling on dedicated bike lanes. This civic paradigm shift has faced criticism, however, for ignoring or failing to address new, often-racialized forms of socio-spatial exclusion flowing from some dedicated bike infrastructure. An intersectionality-based approach to cycling equity that explicitly problematizes cycling gentrification (Lubitow 2016), design determinism, and complex inequality already shows signs of an emerging "third-wave cycling planning." Whether a third wave will coalesce into a pan-Canadian movement is an open question. Tensions between these second and third waves of planning for cycling justice figure into each of the following case studies.

Laurier Avenue and Cycling's Democratic Turn

July 17, 2013, marks a major milestone for city cycling in Canada: Ottawa City Council approved the permanent installation of the capital's first segregated bike lane on Laurier Avenue (see photo 24). While there were historical precedents and contemporaneous projects in Montréal and Vancouver for dedicated bike infrastructure, Laurier Avenue is one of the earliest European-style cycle tracks in Canada and the first one whose worth, owing to Ottawa's need as a capital city to project an entire country through its urban planning and design, is publicly connected to the worth of the Canadian nation. Its permanent installation following two years as a pilot project represents not simply a change in infrastructural design. Offering an implicit public acknowledgment of the limitations of industrial approaches to cycling expansion, Laurier Avenue materialized a social and political movement toward greater cycling democracy.

The socio-technical limits of industrial cycling—what I call first-wave cycling planning—were already painfully obvious by 2008, the year Ottawa passed its first official "Cycling Plan." That is why Ottawa snuck into its "Cycling Plan" an approval of a future pilot project for a segregated bike lane separated from traffic by a median somewhere downtown (pending public consultation). Recall that the "Plan" (see chapter 2) was preoccupied mainly with painting a uniform, abstract network of on-street lanes across the city that would more or less only be used by middle-aged men and sports enthusiasts, as women, children, and older folks often view cycling in car traffic as unsafe (Aldred et al. 2017; Winters and Zanotto 2017). Persistent cases of cycling-death-by-motor-vehicle, like Melanie Harris's in 2009 (who was struck down by a bus on

24. Laurier Avenue, Ottawa. Photo by author.

Sussex Drive in front of the Department of Foreign Affairs and memorialized by a long-lasting ghost bike), had become so intolerable to the
public that in October 2011 the Ontario government, reacting to a spate
of cycling fatalities, announced its chief coroner would undertake a public review. This "Cycling Death Review" found that cycling deaths are
both predictable and preventable, and offered a number of recommen-
dations: mandatory helmet laws, new provincial planning and legislation, policing changes, and new cycling networks of "connected cycling
lanes, separated bike lanes, bike paths and other models appropriate to
the community" (Office of the Chief Coroner for Ontario 2012, 28). This
plan to prevent cycling death, like other first-wave cycling planning,
appeals to dispassionate, scientific models that manage individual risk
and optimize cycling's efficiency—largely without re-dedicating urban
rights-of-way to cycling. Chafing under this technocratic approach,
cycling planning took a liberal democratic turn, one in which a "future
pilot project" suddenly acquired wider moral significance.

After some progressive planners in Ottawa spiced up the city's "Cycling Plan" with a segregated-lane pilot project, something unexpected happened that launched the idea into global jet streams of cycling design. The National Capital Commission (NCC)—the federal planning agency that helps develop and project the city of Ottawa as a capital to Canadian citizens and nations around the world—became enamored with the idea and led a delegation of Ottawa leaders on a fact-finding mission of world-class cycling facilities in Northern Europe, culminating in the Velo-City 2010 conference in Copenhagen. Inspired by the Danish capital, the delegation returned with an ambitious agenda to "Copenhagenize" Ottawa by building segregated bike lanes across the city. It was quite a civic turn for the NCC's approach to city cycling. The NCC was originally assembled to implement Ottawa's car-dominated Gréber plan (Gréber 1950), which perfunctorily relegated cycling to a beneficial form of recreation in nature. On an innovative streak in the 1970s, the NCC started building multiuse, riparian pathways in Ottawa for walking and cycling but was late getting into the "on-street game" for cycling (following a similar trajectory as the mountain biking founders of the Detroit Greenways Coalition, whose work I explore in chapter 2). Ultimately the NCC failed to foment a Copenhagen-scale vélo-revolution but did help cement segregated bike lanes in the national imaginary as an internationally progressive urban intervention and continues to slowly assemble new segregated cycling infrastructure (CBC News 2018). Together the City of Ottawa, the NCC, and community advocacy groups like Citizens for Safe Cycling have helped coalesce a general will to assemble rights-of-way dedicated to cycling.

The "segregated bike lane," also called a separated lane or cycle track, represents a critical infrastructuring of civic worth. In much the same way that traffic-calmed bikeways express domestic worth and multiuse pathways in urban nature embody ecological worth, the segregated bike lane qualifies or composes cycling for civic judgment through relations of moral equivalence among diverse beings. While segregated lanes can provide access to nature and familial riding, their strongest moral worth relates to cycling justice and social inclusion. Segregated bike lanes are more civically just and socially inclusive than on-street (painted) lanes and sharrows because in many high-cycling contexts, they invite women, children, and older folks to cycle safely in busy urban areas they otherwise may avoid (Aldred et al. 2017; Winters and Teschke 2010). While trip characteristics and societal norms also figure into the large gender gaps observed across low-cycling anglophone contexts like Canada and the United States (Garrard et al. 2012), infrastructural preferences play a significant role. Shrouding this civic worth, Ottawa, reading the prevailing moral winds, notably rolled out its first pilot program for segregated lanes under an industrial veil, stressing its selection of Laurier Avenue in February 2011 as a result of an objective technical evaluation of all possible east-west downtown corridors. However, by the time Laurier's segregated lanes were opened on July 10, 2011, it was clear, given the public's denunciations, that Ottawa's pilot project was in fact a "paradigmatic case" (Flyvbjerg 2006) aiming to establish a new, more equitable mode of arranging rights-of-way.

Despite the City of Ottawa's best efforts to sneak in a seminal transformation of existing rights to the road as a neutral-sounding industrial output, the mobility paradigm shift was not lost on the public. Public criticism of the pilot project varied, revolving around the loss of car parking spaces and access for delivery trucks (which the city redistributed to other streets). Local residents decried the loss of parking, judging the segregated lane as domestically destructive of long-standing arrangements for visitors to the city. The moral tenor of most denunciations, however, quickly became a matter of market worth. "It's hurting everyone's business," said one owner of a café along the route (Clarke 2012): "If you have a delivery or if someone wants to quickly buy something[,] they can't because there is no parking." This complaint echoed as a media talking point, and business improvement area associations (who lobby for local commercial districts) fanned the flames until the city felt publicly compelled to justify Laurier's new lanes through its profitability. Wielding market research showing how cyclists stop more frequently and spend more money at local businesses than motorists

(Sztabinski 2009), the city took pains to qualify segregated bike lanes as good for business. I talked with Ottawa's deputy city manager, Lynn (a pseudonym), about the controversy. As an engineer-turned-top-city-bureaucrat, with a nuanced perspective of industrial-civic friction, she argues that "once it takes off," like previous cycling projects in the capital against which many folks were dead set, the public will embrace its advantages and overcome

> push back coming from the businesses because of the loss of parking. Some of my staff were in Copenhagen for that [Velo-City] conference and came back and said that's not unusual, wherever you implement it. So, it's that first one. We have to get to a point where people go, "oh yeah," and really get why we want to do it. And yes, people will use it. (Interview 2011)

It turns out her optimism was warranted—and clearly related, in retrospect, to her leadership in helping reorganize the city bureaucracy to better plan and engineer cycling.

The Laurier Avenue Segregated Bike Lane, as this project is called, was, and is, a resounding civic success. After the local business revolt the city temporarily tempered plans for expanding segregated bike lanes, quietly removing extensions of Laurier from some planning proposals (Reevely 2013). But the city was not abandoning dedicated cycling infrastructure, only fine-tuning its strategy to implement it. Laurier Avenue tripled cycling volumes and greatly enhanced the safety of cyclists (City of Ottawa 2013), two of the most important variables for closing the cycling gender and age gaps in North America. Once it became permanent on July 17, 2013, the Laurier Avenue Segregated Bike Lane won the 2015 Sustainable Communities Award in Transportation from the Federation of Canadian Municipalities. In the words of Farah, a female city planner for the City of Ottawa, who works on Ottawa's cycling infrastructure:

> We have lots of people who cycle for recreation, but very few who cycle for commuting. One of the main reasons is that the people who

cycle for their commute and cycle in traffic are really committed, while the majority who cycle for recreation like being away from traffic. They like to be segregated, they don't feel or perceive being safe on the road. I am one of them! (Interview 2011)

Farah argues that segregated bike lanes can open safe cycling networks in congested downtown areas and facilitate recreation-commuter transitions (perhaps also showing that if there were more women in city planning roles, there may be more and better dedicated cycling infrastructures, encouraging more women cyclists and closing that gender gap). Laurier Avenue in Ottawa, along with earlier dedicated bike lanes in Montréal and contemporaneous infrastructure unfolding in Vancouver (Toronto was a notable holdout), sparked a second wave of more inclusive cycling planning, one presently diffusing dedicated bike lanes across the urban nation.

Though this project is a success, the architects of the Laurier Avenue Segregated Bike Lane are uncomfortable with its name. The thought of "segregating" cyclists raises a thorny civic issue with separated bike infrastructure. Although they called the pilot a "segregated" bike lane, Damien, Ottawa's longest-serving cycling planner, says that "not long after that, we thought it was a bad word for a number of reasons. But it stuck" (Interview 2011). They regret the name for its connotation with racial segregation. This misstep points to a larger problem with second-wave cycling planning, just as it takes flight across Canada, whereby the planners are confronting problems with their plans just as they roll out. First-wave cycling planning's philosophy was about motorists and cyclists sharing the road as a common right-of-way. The second wave depends on separating cyclists from motorized traffic. While this "civic design" approach may be appropriate in some contexts, particularly where motor vehicles move at high speeds and in high numbers, it may not be appropriate in others, like quiet neighborhood streets and pathways by the river. Additionally, learning how to cycle while sharing city streets with both motorists and pedestrians may be vital to learning how to live together—for integrating the city.

Expecting infrastructural segregation alone to produce cycling justice breeds design determinism. Factors other than infrastructural preferences (e.g., cultural norms, trip complexity, division of domestic labor) engender cycling inequity, including wider neighborhood inequalities whereby core gentrifying neighborhoods enjoy a preponderance of dedicated bike lanes.

Pushing the planning envelope, Ottawa—a "most likely" case (Flyvbjerg 2006) of developing mass cycling in North America, with strong institutional support and the highest proportion of cycling commuters among large cities in Canada (Statistics Canada 2017b)—is sowing seeds for a different approach. Laurier Avenue's paradigmatic case shows both the civic power and the limitations of relying on segregated infrastructure. While Ottawa's most recent cycling plan (2013), as discussed in chapter 2, expands on previously industrial approaches, similar to its 2008 plan, it also introduces new civically promising tools (e.g., "Level of Traffic Stress" methodology for selecting types of bike lanes, which incorporates the stress people feel while riding in car traffic) that respond to the experiences of low cycling groups, including women and children. Moreover Ottawa's 2013 plan imagines a more complex ecosystem of dedicated and nondedicated cycling routes that accounts for evolving neighborhood-level conditions—including crosstown and neighborhood bikeways and light-rail connections that are poised to expand cycling access to relatively marginalized neighborhoods (e.g., Bayshore, an inner suburb relatively excluded from all the cycling lanes being built downtown). From out of the first- and second-wave cycling planning battles in Ottawa there is already emerging a "third wave" of cycling planning with the potential to address complex cycling inequalities in order to create cycling opportunities for everyone. Such an approach will be critical for urban contexts beyond Ottawa that lack high-level institutional support or face a higher threat of gentrification.

"Bike Gangs" of Motor City

Another avenue for expanding city cycling as civic mobility pertains less to design and democratic infrastructure than to political deliberation and embodied practice. In recent years cities around the world have seen an explosion of mass city cycling events. They range from contentious protest rides that directly challenge city authorities by occupying streets normally monopolized by motorists, to family-friendly events with sanctioned routes, if not police escorts, that engender an organized, unthreatening atmosphere. The Critical Mass ride is the archetypical case in the former camp, with its use of "corking"—using some riders to block traffic from side roads so the mass can flow uninterrupted through red lights—and its slogan, "We aren't blocking traffic, we are traffic!" In the latter, family-friendly camp are neighborhood- or city-led car-free days, memorial Rides of Silence events to honor cyclists killed in traffic, and bike carnivals and parties—like Vancouver's "Bike the Night," one of Canada's largest open-streets (fully permitted) night rides featuring a "pre-party with live music, free bike tune-ups and decorating, food trucks, a kids' zone and tons of awesome prizes" (HUB 2018). While these mass cycling events diverge in level of contention and organization, they mutually and collectively construct cycling as an embodied political practice (Furness 2010; Spinney 2015; 2016; Stehlin 2014; Lugo 2013), one that both contests dominant systems of power and creates novel "public spheres on the move" (Johansson and Liou 2017, 59). They challenge hegemonic automobility and mobilize public spheres by harnessing the physical and political power of cycling as a vital activity done "together," a social practice that, given the laws and spatial constraints of streets designed for cars, for small groups is often difficult to do—at least without a driver rolling down their window and chiding, "Single file, please; safer for everyone!" or "Get off the road!"

In low-cycling contexts, mass cycling rides act like "bike gangs" negotiating the right to move and dwell in urban public spaces to which they supposedly do not belong. I borrow this phrase from women and mothers cycling with children (see chapter 1), who describe exhilarating moments of "bike ganging" through the city when they ride with others in groups, leveraging their numbers for laying claim to their right to appear in the street. Similar to the way in which actual gangs exploit weak institutional oversight, in low-cycling contexts in places like Motor City—a "least likely" case of mass cycling, with economic and cultural dependence on industrial automobility—mass rides step in where public authorities have largely failed to give people a way to cycle. In such contexts, up against deep car cultures, mass rides play a larger role in facilitating the community-led participation in cycling shown to be integral for making cycling advocacy more inclusive (Golub et al. 2016). Like Pernilla Johansson and Stacy Liou (2017), I understand mass rides as a form of political deliberation, whose embodied affective experience mobilizes people cycling together as a community that feels it has a stake in the city. While public deliberation, following the Habermasian tradition of focusing on communicative rationality, is often tied to verbal discourse, it can also be found in the way people "talk" with their bodies just by collectively traveling as a group together. By refusing to conform to a city's car culture, mass rides illuminate hierarchies between city mobilities, and politically challenge the car-driving majority to rethink what a street is for. At the same time, in their push for cycling equity mass rides also inscribe new hierarchies as cyclists negotiate boundaries between each other and their changing positions vis-à-vis different urban contexts on their rides.

While various mass cycling events periodically take over the streets in Canada's Motor City, including Critical Mass rides and Rides of Silence, Windsor's largest mass ride is the Tweed Ride. It started in the fall of 2011, when the owners of City Cyclery, a local bike shop known for its community outreach and advocacy of city cycling, borrowed a movement that began in London in 2009. As co-owner of City Cyclery and 2014 Tweed Ride organizer Stephen describes:

> You use vintage bikes or vintage-inspired bikes, and you go for a bike ride, stop at some restaurants and bars, and go and enjoy riding a bike with other people. But you dress up as if it was the turn of the century. The positive thing about it I find, unlike Critical Mass rides of the past, you're assembling upwards of 700 people on bicycles, they're dressed up funny and smiling and waving at cars, and there

is this positivity attached to it. It's not a cars versus bicycles dichotomy, but a much friendlier approach. (Interview 2014)

With its festive, playful, and "cycle chic" (Colville-Andersen 2012) atmosphere, the Tweed Ride thus falls into the second, family-friendly, camp of mass cycling rides. It secures permits from the city to sanction the event and generates a wider sense of political and social legitimacy by incorporating cycling-friendly local restaurants, bars, and other businesses. Moreover, tactics acceptable on Critical Mass rides, from speeding and ignoring traffic signals to physically challenging motorists and police, stand in contrast to the peace-loving, genial practices encouraged on the Tweed Ride. While Johansson and Liou (2017) emphasize how such nonconfrontational mass rides can encourage their participants to create an "orderly" political constituency palatable to government (Stehlin 2014), for example, by mandating helmets, this does not reflect my firsthand experience of the Tweed Ride. While a friendlier approach especially vis-à-vis motorists was encouraged, few people wore body armor, and folks I talked and cycled with demonstrated there was ample room on the ride for unruliness (particularly after stopping at the pub). The Tweed Ride's more formal organization may lessen its level of political contentiousness, but it simultaneously opens up a more socially inclusive space for mass riding and a more civil form of political deliberation in Canada than the Critical Mass ride—which, in my firsthand experience in Motor City (and Ottawa, Vancouver, and Halifax), overwhelmingly appeals to men and young adults.

The Tweed Ride, versions of which were quickly copied after London's inaugural 2009 event in cities around the world, came about through the transnational diffusion of a repertoire of collective action (Tarrow 2011) geared toward cycling equity. Beneath the beer, costumes, and mobile sense of "collective effervescence" (Durkheim 1965 [1912]) uniting the mass ride lies a movement toward better urban mobility. As Stephen describes, Tweed Riders are

predominantly people who are interested in cycling as a form of transportation, not as a sport, or a necessity [e.g., after having their license revoked, many of whom reside in Windsor and Detroit]. It's people who often think progressively, they are thinking about health and the environment, and they're thinking about a more intimate relationship with their city. (Interview 2014)

In this same observation by Stephen we can see where the mass ride's emancipatory and "egalitarian potential" (Stehlin 2014, 21), like many of the Tweed Riders' vintage suits, starts to fray. While many socially marginalized, blue-collar folks regularly cycle out of necessity down Windsor's main drags, they are notably absent from the Tweed Ride. Like invisible cyclists in other cities, "their practical knowledge is often devalued relative to imported European models of mobility—even though the latter are based on completely different city structures and contexts" (Johansson and Liou 2017, 68). And while the Tweed Ride does well at including women, older folks, and children, with a vintage British aesthetic that smacks of "stuff white people like," it does less well at including non-European Canadians (e.g., Windsor's large Arab community). Finer points of civic friction arose on the Tweed Ride during my participation, for example, when we skirted an Iraqi part of town and it suddenly became obvious to some riders how white the group was, and when on the final stop at a fashionable restaurant, not everyone was socially comfortable or able to afford the refreshments. Like formal cycling advocacy, social cycling movements, too, despite their passion for cycling equity, are often delineated as white, middle-class spaces.

In a civic counterpoint to the Tweed Ride, an even bigger Motor City mass ride called Slow Roll winds its way around Detroit every Monday night from May through October. Established in 2010 by a pair of locals "as an excuse to get together with friends, cruise through the city, and have a glass of wine halfway through the trip," by 2014 Slow Roll was drawing an average of two thousand people with a peak of four thousand riders on cool summer nights (Waraniak 2015). It had

grown into Michigan's largest weekly bike ride and has expanded to 8 cities so far. Slow Roll is for everyone, all ages and types of bikes, with a slow pace that's geared to keep everyone together and safe. A welcoming group of Detroiters provide for lots of positive energy and an amazing community. (Detroit Slow Roll 2014)

While participating in one of the larger 2014 rides, I was struck by the ways in which Slow Roll converges and diverges from the Tweed Ride and other mass rides I've joined across Canada. Like the Tweed Ride, Slow Roll falls into the family-friendly camp of mass cycling events, seeking out local businesses for sponsors and watering holes en route and, since 2015, relying on city police to help block off streets. However, Slow Roll is more diverse than the Tweed Ride. Its infectious chant, "Sloooow Roll Deeeetroit!" is "recited by everyone from black teens on lowriders and white hipsters on fixed gears to senior citizens on road bikes and suburban families who've come downtown for an evening cruise" (Waraniak 2015). A more collective cycling-for-everyone mentality than "poor-touring" (Johansson and Liou 2017, 69) suffuses the LED lights, boom boxes, and barbecue grills attached to flashy frames that suggest participants want to be seen on Motown's streets more than they want to move fast. Moreover, Slow Roll takes its civic community-building mission further by frequently visiting marginalized, forgotten neighborhoods in depopulated Detroit that are without access to city services and new bike infrastructure—places where many of the ride's participants would have no reason to otherwise enter.

Slow Roll, like the Tweed Ride, is part of a larger transnational movement encouraging slowness and deceleration "to act and move differently, to experience the social and ecological environment in ways that run counter to the logic of speed" (Vannini 2013, 117). The virtues of slowness, from slow food and tourism to slow professing (Dickinson and Lumsdon 2010; Berg and Seeber 2016), take on an explicitly civic dimension for collective cycling where "slowing down is an inventive tactic of resistance against an overwhelming strategy of speed," one "which oppose[s] at every step the strategies for fast mobilities concealed in the designs and regulations of road space" (Popan 2018). Riding slow with others makes time for conversation (see photo 25) among people who do not always connect, for dwelling among and taking in unfamiliar surroundings, and, of course, for play. Slow Roll's carnivalesque sociability and situationist-like performativity—sometimes reminiscent of Le Monde à Bicyclette, a 1970s movement in Montréal that united francophone nationalists and anglophone anarchists behind cycling advocacy through similar tactics (Morissette 2009)—fuels its popularity among locals and growing throngs of tourists. After 2014, when Slow Roll cofounder Jason Hall appeared in an Apple commercial showing his orchestration of routes and riders with the stroke of an iPad, Slow Roll has grown ever larger, inspiring versions in Chicago and London and taking Hall from TEDx conferences to Esquire Television. Slow Roll's growth and diffusion to other cities, along with its high-powered advertising and local luxury-goods sponsors (such as Shinola), foreshadows market friction with the mass ride's self-professed virtues of slow citizenship. However, like the Tweed Ride with its ties to businesses and moments of consumption, Slow Roll has managed thus far to limit this friction from damaging its inclusive brand.

The "bike gangs" of Motor City point to productive possibilities of market-civic cross-pollination for cycling in car-hegemonic contexts desperate for economic diversification—possibilities made all the more significant given strong market friction surrounding dedicated bike lanes and, as I take up in the following section, gentrification. The throes of pre- (Windsor) and early (Detroit) gentrification in which Motor City finds itself, at least in relation to contexts like Toronto and Vancouver, raises the morally intriguing question: How might mass rides as cycling social movements intervene to prevent the problems in response to which third-wave cycling planning is arising from even transpiring in the first place? While this question garners no simple answers, one clear strength of the mass rides explored in this section lies in their twin rebuke of the design determinism of dedicated bike lanes and the socially exclusive nature of mainstream cycling advocacy movements such as Complete Streets, a very large, well-known planning movement to include non-car modes of travel on streets (Zavestoski and Agyeman 2015). Based on my own participant observation I would

25. Slow Rollers dwell in Detroit, Michigan. Photo by author.

by and large corroborate the perspective of Stephen, the Tweed Ride organizer, when he says that

> you don't feel you need to be a certain type of person to be involved. You don't need to be rich, you don't need to have a certain level of fitness, if you basically know how to ride a bike, you'll be able to do it. It's slow, it's accessible. It's like Slow Roll in Detroit. (Interview 2014)

Whether successful mass rides ultimately end up keeping and expanding their (relatively) inclusive character, or simply end up selling out mass rides as a cycling commodity feeding the same gentrification processes as dedicated bike infrastructure, is worth exploring in future research.

Cycling Gentrification in Chinatown

Vancouver is renowned for its extensive neighborhood bikeway system (see chapter 1) but over the last decade has invested heavily in other kinds of cycling routes. The surge began in 2009 with the implementation of separated, or what Vancouver calls "protected," bike lanes on Burrard Bridge, putting to bed an acrimonious political debate spanning decades over transferring bridge space from driving to cycling (Siemiatycki et al. 2016). A year earlier the city elected Gregor Robertson as mayor, awarding his Vision Vancouver Party a strong social and environmental mandate, with which it has constructed protected bike lanes in high traffic areas that have contributed to a significant rise in cycling uptake, including a 40 percent jump in trips by bike from 2008 to 2011. Cycling has become the fastest growing transport mode—its share of all trips rising from 4 percent in 2013 to 7 percent in 2016 (City of Vancouver 2016)—and Burrard Bridge, according to automated bike counters, is now the busiest cycling route in North America (Perkins 2018). Elected mayor twice more, Robertson has linked cycling investment to Vancouver's audacious goal to become "the world's greenest city" by 2020 (City of Vancouver 2017). Cycling has also become an important tool for "Vancouverism," a global brand of urban development based on slim residential towers atop commercial podiums that promote density and street life, expansive views of coastal mountains, sundry parks, and sustainable mobilities (Kiger 2014).

Vancouver is also renowned, of course, for being one of the world's most unaffordable places to live. At least as often as Robertson is praised for his pro-cycling policies, he is also criticized for his cozy relations with private real-estate developers who, in top-down fashion, dictate the city's economic growth while pricing socially marginalized groups, families, and younger generations (from millennials on down) out of the city. While cycling's role as a tool for attracting affluent white newcomers to Vancouver may not be as explicit as in, say, Portland or Chicago (Lubitow 2016), some racialized residents are making the connection between cycling lanes and neighborhood displacement via material and symbolic forms of gentrification. While it is transforming the entire Lower Mainland, nowhere in Canada are the effects of gentrification more visible and keenly felt than in Chinatown and Vancouver's Downtown Eastside. Walk but ten minutes between Chinatown, East Hastings Street, and Vancouver's historic Gastown neighborhood and you encounter some of the poorest and the richest urban quarters in Canada, in what may be the urban nation's sharpest socioeconomic edge. Like Celestina in chapter 1, Chinatown offers an "atypical" or extreme case study that activates an unusual number of actors and mechanisms in the problem at hand (Flyvbjerg 2006). Here Canada's own "white lanes of gentrification" (Lubitow 2016) highlight the need for third-wave cycling planning to ameliorate complex social inequalities.

Located in the oldest part of colonial Vancouver, Chinatown has endured social and political upheaval wrought by revolutions in mobility since its inception. Once the Canadian Pacific Railway was completed in the late 1880s, railway workers settled there only decades after the Musqueam, Tsleil-Waututh, and Squamish peoples were dispossessed from the land without a treaty. In the early years Chinatown faced outright white supremacy, from the 1885 Chinese head tax and a 1907 mobbing by the Asiatic Exclusion League that ransacked Chinatown to the 1923 Chinese Exclusion Act. It would not be until April 22, 2018, that the Chinese community finally received an apology from Vancouver delivered by Mayor Robertson for the city's "dehumanizing" and "stigmatizing" polices from 1886 to 1949. After coming together to fight a common enemy, life improved for Chinese Canadians in the postwar period. The Chinese Exclusion Act was then repealed, reopening the door to citizenship, and in 1957 the first Chinese Canadian was elected to Canadian Parliament for the Vancouver Centre district encompassing Chinatown. However, the area was soon again under assault. The city planned to bulldoze part of the neighborhood for a freeway and started by demolishing Hogan's Alley, the city's sole black neighborhood connected with the south side of Chinatown. Before it could raze Chinatown, local residents rose up and helped protestors kill the project. In 1971 Chinatown won provincial protection as a historic district. Over the 1980s and 1990s it expanded, welcoming an influx of Chinese immigrants from Hong Kong (prompted by the impending 1997 "Handover" of Hong Kong's sovereignty from the UK to China) and building the Chinese Cultural Centre, Dr. Sun Yat-Sen Classical Garden, and other important community spaces.

After the overtly racist railway era and the specter of freeway-driven removal of neighborhoods, Chinatown now faces in the twenty-first century perhaps its greatest existential threat. Once again expressed through changing patterns and politics of mobility, this threat may take the form of a white, upwardly mobile man on a bicycle, a trendy barbershop, or a taxidermy-dotted restaurant that, in an ironic arc, hark all the way back to the frontiersmen and settler aesthetics of the 1890s when Chinatown faced off with British Columbia's colonial pioneers (Brown 2015).

This new specter, gentrification, keeps Doris up at night. With deep multigenerational ties to Chinatown, like her parents and grandparents before her, she finds home, work, and a sense of communal belonging here. Her career entwines this place, jumping between food security and other social enterprises that hire local workers from the neighborhood. At United We Can, a bottle depot offering people in poverty a way out through recycling jobs, Doris used to work with Vancouver's "binners," many of whom are Chinese, following and improving the diverse ways in which they use bikes, buggies, trailers, and "traplines" (territorial routes through the city). Binners still warmly greet her on the street (see photo 26). Even her (bare-bones) bike comes from a social enterprise that refurbishes stolen bikes and parts donated by the police after they fail to find a home. It is thus with deep ambivalence that Doris watches hipsters ride by on new bike lanes, lanes that directly preceded the new condo towers, renovictions, and rent hikes that are pushing out an aging Chinese population and other socially marginalized people in Chinatown: "I cannot think of a bike route that has not been gentrified" (Interview 2018).

With Chinese migrants now moving mainly to Richmond and other suburbs around Vancouver, Chinatown's Chinese population is aging and struggling to deal with immense redevelopment pressures on the area. In this context Doris cofounded the Youth Collaborative for Chinatown (YCC), intent on flipping public stereotypes of Chinatown as impoverished, irrelevant, and bereft of Chinese people and culture on their head, and showcasing it as "more than a place where people

26. Doris converses with a binner in Chinatown, Vancouver. Photo by author.

buy their soy sauce." Doris says the YCC is trying to be "political with a little *p*" and change Chinatown's trajectory by turning young people into stakeholders, challenging old boys' clubs (e.g., clan societies with no succession plans), and mobilizing Chinatown's rich historical and cultural resources to help it politically articulate its own needs. After the YCC organized popular night markets and a mahjong day in May 2015, to which 150 people showed up, politicians started paying attention and the YCC began pushing more directly against insulting urban redevelopment, which included a proposed condo on 105 Keefer Street consisting mainly of unaffordable market units (and, at one point, a Versace Home store) aiming to tower over Chinatown's war and railway worker memorial and Sun Yat-Sen Garden. For Doris neither the new bike lane running by 105 Keefer nor the idea of condos are really the problem as much as the city's and real-estate industry's top-down way of imposing development ignorant of neighborhood needs. While the root cause of displacement, as in contexts like Portland (Golub et al. 2016), is probably market-oriented condo growth rather than cycling infrastructure, the two are nevertheless correlated, and failing Chinatown together.

Chinatown illuminates how cycling can be at once emancipatory for some and oppressive to others (Golub et al. 2016). It is not the Chinese Canadian senior citizen in subsidized housing (or the Indigenous working poor next door), whose income depends on bicycle binning, that the city is targeting by coupling new cycling infrastructure with multiple condo towers, luxury shops, and trendy restaurants. This upwardly mobile cycling-oriented development courts white privilege, when Chinese seniors struggling financially to live and access Chinatown can no longer bike or even walk safely without feeling bullied by fast traffic and even quicker cyclists. The Chinese senior–cycling disconnect is worsened by a developer-driven condo boom that has long ignored multigenerational (i.e., more than one bedroom) housing. This disconnect grows wider yet when prominent white developers portray themselves as rescuing non-white neighborhoods. When I asked Doris if she ever saw what Lindsay Brown (2015) calls a "heritage hipster," she laughed and said: "Bob Rennie." Canada's "Condo King" and controversial art collector, Rennie is the ultimate heritage hipster. He owns and preserves Chinatown's oldest building, and grows poppies to pay homage to the opium trade. He doesn't so much "appropriate" Chinese culture, says Doris, as try to "own it." The aesthetic pretension Rennie's condo marketing shows for Chinese heritage forms the high-end version of a white 1890s-style lumberjack leisurely riding his bike through Chinatown between cold brew coffee and craft beer. This multilevel symbolic gentrification, wherein white men act as saviors of wild, unclean places, worries residents in American immigrant neighborhoods as well (Lubitow 2016). One has to wonder whether in Vancouver a similar pattern of racialized social exclusion as happened last century, one that helped define Chinatown in the first place, is occurring again (or else continues) through cycling gentrification—in the very same neighborhood.

Doris grapples with a self-described "inner personal politics" that many Chinese people and women in general face while publicly interacting with a white male biking majority. Vancouver justifies bike lane investments in part because cycling "supports connected communities.

People travelling on foot and bike are more likely to engage in a friendly interaction during their trip than people travelling by transit or vehicle" (City of Vancouver 2016). While friendly civil engagement often occurs between cyclists—especially on local bikeways with children (see chapter 1), where Doris prefers to cycle—this is not everywhere the case. Many women and seniors also share stories of hostile, uncivil encounters with other cyclists (many of whom are white males) who blow by and startle them without so much as an "on your left," or make sexual come-ons at busy intersections followed by pretentious explanations for how to cycle correctly. This fleeting incivility may be less deadly than the road rage that occurs between motorists at higher velocities, but it corrodes cycling citizenship and cycling's civic worth. Additionally it contributes to a structural context of "multiple jeopardy" in Chinatown, where perceptions of a dirty, dying, yet somehow authentic neighborhood in need of saving feed into, and become reinforced by, images and performances of cycling as both a status symbol and a hot commodity for upwardly mobile architects, game designers, tech workers, and other entrepreneurial "influencers." Sometimes it all makes Doris wish (jokingly) that Vancouver "looked more like Asia, with all its rusty bikes and fucked up seats." How cycling pretense interacts with luxury and masculinity in Chinatown creates a daily source of market-civic friction for Doris and many longtime residents—who believe cycling should be a mobility right, not a (white male) privilege.

The future of Canada's largest historic Chinatown seems, as it has in the past, up in the air. Through the civic work of the YCC and the city's efforts to support "legacy businesses," Chinatown continues to strengthen its political ability to articulate and defend its needs. But the sheer onslaught of condo towers, commercial development, and new cycling infrastructure, coupled with an aging Chinese population, is ominous. It shows that while creating *economic* opportunities for residents in some immigrant neighborhoods may help make cycling-oriented development more equitable (Lubitow 2016), this development must also, if it is to reduce displacement in places like Chinatown, tailor to and prioritize *cultural* identities and *historical* spaces as they continue to evolve. Additionally this tailoring must address pernicious, everyday forms of incivility that undermine cycling as a common and liberal democratic good. Ultimately protected bike lanes are a necessary yet insufficient condition of civility and cycling justice. Even as these lanes expose the sometimes more aggressive male biking majority to women, older folks, and children, who may cycle differently and bring with them different needs, they simultaneously propagate wider webs of racist, classist, and sexist urban development. Dedicated cycling infrastructure, therefore, needs to be reassembled through meaningful public engagement with marginalized communities and cycling social movements that bring people into these lanes under playful, noncompetitive conditions who otherwise might avoid them. These cycling movements might take a grassroots form, like those in Motor City, or a more formal structure, like Vancouver's HUB, a nonprofit organization aiming to make cycling more accessible through family-friendly night rides, cycling training programs that help women and immigrants, and other educational and community-led events. In the end if cycling inequities are to be seriously addressed, so must be the inequities of market-driven housing with which, through gentrification, cycling is increasingly co-constructed.

Fight for Cycling Justice: Civic Mobility Futures

This chapter on civic mobilities focuses on dedicated bike lanes, mass rides in low-cycling contexts, and the process of cycling gentrification to show how city planners, cycling social movements, and community organizations are assembling an expansive cycling justice. I define such an expansive cycling justice as cycling equity, which includes the social and political conditions, such as good citizenship practices, that underlie cycling equity as well. This approach offers a wider perspective of civic struggles as citizens lift up city cycling to higher standards of social inclusion through liberal democratic principles, design, and practice.

Among moral frictions, tensions building between civic and industrial as well as market moralities are emerging as pivotal forces transforming the nature of cycling in Canada. These frictions include a politically provocative move by planners away from industrial-dominated cycling planning toward embracing civic infrastructure, including "segregated" or dedicated bike lanes that offer policymakers and activists a concrete transport tool for expanding the cycling franchise. Cycling leaders in cities like Ottawa, not wanting to repeat the same civic sins as the car by heavily restricting access to infrastructure through a deterministic design lens, are instead guiding cycling development through infrastructural diversity that responds to urban social diversity. This chapter follows a "third-wave cycling planning" emerging through these subtle moves in Ottawa and, more performatively, across the big "bike gangs" of Motor City as they help break down the socially exclusive walls of organized cycling advocacy (Golub et al. 2016). It remains to be seen whether this third wave can come together in a coherent or united way across Canada over the next decade. As cities across North America illustrate, dedicating increasingly coveted urban space to cycling in a way that meaningfully advances equity takes tremendous political courage and capital.

Beyond city or transport planning, social cycling movements carry extra moral weight and potential because of their cross-pollination with market worth. Yet in a point of strong moral friction, local businesses and business improvement area associations in many cities across the world (even in cycling-friendly Copenhagen) brand dedicated bike lanes as bad for business. Further inflaming civic-market frictions, gentrification exacerbates racialized, neighborhood-level cycling inequalities, especially in global cities such as Vancouver where, as we saw in chapter 1, a housing affordability crisis is already constricting domestic cycling to the wealthy people who can afford to stay in the city. Cycling gentrification is particularly worrisome from a civic perspective (quite the opposite view exists from a market perspective, as we will see in the next chapter), because it effectively co-opts dedicated bike infrastructures of high civic and industrial value into the competitive circuits of market-oriented urban development. As industrial cycling planning and infrastructure falls further into the orbit of this market development through gentrification, tourism, and the global financialization of urban growth, civic mobility futures point to an increasingly ferocious moral clash between cycling justice and cycling capitalism.

In the coming fight for cycling justice and cycling solidarity, urban planners, social movements, community groups, and policymakers ought to appeal to nothing less than a more civil, sociably connected humanity. Inspiring examples of civic justifications for cycling are emerging across diverse urban contexts, from Motor City to the Canadian capital. For example, Colin, the driving public force at the City of Ottawa for the Laurier Avenue Segregated Bike Lane, says of persuading a car-dependent population of the need for better cycling lanes:

> You look at it at a very high level, and hammer home the benefits of having a more healthy cycling community. You talk about the health aspects and the community aspects of bringing people together, the pedestrian or cyclist, rather than being anonymous in our car, in a more lively street scene where people see each other eye to eye, and acknowledge each other, versus what they do in their tinted window cars that are pretty much anonymous. (Interview 2012)

Similarly, this emphasis on acknowledging and "seeing" rather than looking through each other is shared by Slow Roll cofounder Jason Hall:

> We've created these barriers like Eight Mile and the suburbs, but our people have always wanted to see what's on the other side. When we started Slow Roll, that's where it came from. It came from everybody finally being able to see what's on the other side. (cited in Waraniak 2015)

What these and many other inspiring agents of civic change share in common is the frank assessment of cycling justice as an exodus from our comfort zone through a whole new way of bringing people together after the car (Golub et al. 2016).

27. A woman ponders urban Amazonia in Seattle, Washington. Photo by author.

4. Market Mobilities

Neoliberal Urbanism, Bike Share, and
the Commodification of Cycling

What makes mobilities good for commerce? What makes a bike lane good for cycling profitably? What market lessons can cycling learn from driving? These questions open a door into an unusually powerful and morally invasive assemblage of mobility. Turning families, communities, experts, and citizens into consumers and agents of enterprise, market mobilities connect the common good to the power of a shared marketplace within which people earn their worth by competing for inalienable ownership over rare things and coveted experiences. With a philosophical pedigree dating back to Adam Smith's *Theory of Moral Sentiments* (2011[1759]), market mobilities imagine human flourishing through the prism of profit and consumption. This way of measuring worth had, by the Great Depression in North America, suffused industrial expertise through automobility, fleshing out modern capitalism via Fordist manufacturing, unionization, and mass consumption (Norton 2008; Paterson 2007). By the end of the twentieth century, market worth was threatening to eclipse industrial worth through neoliberalism and its reformation of the city (Fanelli 2016; Hackworth 2007). The ascension and diversification of market worth from industrial capitalism to neoliberal capitalism and more recently through divergent forms of urban neoliberalism (Walks 2009; 2015)—with automobility intertwining each of these political constellations as Fordism and post-Fordism's most iconic and profitable concern (Sheller and Urry 2000)—shows that market automobilities at once hold very high stakes and equivocal lessons for the expansion of cycling.

If I could nominate a memorial to the old, industrial car capitalism—
that is, the steel and glass, fossil fuel–devouring automobility that
started mushrooming early in the twentieth century—I would choose
Motor City's eighty-seven-year-old Ambassador Bridge. I introduced
in chapter 2 the Ambassador and its economic power an example,
not because the creaky old expanse sits on the brink of demise like
other industrial monuments to automobility, but because it is the
most profitable and economically important crossing in the whole of
Canada. The Ambassador handles more than a quarter of all Canada-
U.S. trade per year (30 percent of which is carried by truck), about
$120 billion in annual trade (2.5 million trucks; 4.2 million vehicle
crossings), and about $60 million in annual tolls for billionaire busi-
nessman Matty Moroun (Gollom 2017). When it opened in 1929 the
international span was an industrial marvel linked broadly to the
futures of these two countries—close allies and trading partners.
Today, after buying up shares in the 1970s on the New York Stock
Exchange (competing with Warren Buffet), Moroun, ninety-one years
old at this writing, privately owns and effectively monopolizes the
crossing—the industrial and civic awkwardness of which is not lost
on the good people of Motor City.

Moroun has long made plain that the bridge, anomalously, is neither
for long-term efficiency nor for the health of communities around
the crossing but rather for making him money, be it through tolls and
profits reaped from duty-free gasoline and diesel his company sells
on-site cheaper than at nearby stations (Associated Press 2011), or,
more recently, from a years-long legal battle to prevent the Canadian
government from building a more efficient crossing downriver that
would cut into his profits. Instead Moroun wants to build his own new
span beside his old one. He has already bought out and boarded up
about 120 houses in Windsor's historic Sandwich Town neighborhood
near the Ambassador that he wants to demolish, refusing Windsor's
request to repair them and turning "a once vibrant neighbourhood
into an area full of dilapidated buildings" (Gollom 2017). While some
of Windsor's residents view Moroun as a robber baron from whose

bridge flows an unending procession of heavy trucks trembling their homes and city streets, others take a different view. Business experts portray a wily, successful billionaire who "outmanoeuvred everybody" (Gollom 2017). After years of litigation Moroun recently secured a permit from Canada for his new bridge with the condition of tearing down the old Ambassador. His risky strategy of what we might call "attritional automobility" seems to have worked, winning more market value, but at the cost of building better infrastructure for the future.

The rise and (possible) fall of the Ambassador (Moroun is still fighting to keep it so he can own two bridges) traces a historical arc of market growth and development at the expense of industrial and other ways of morally assembling urban mobilities. It begs the questions: What kinds of market growth lay in store for twenty-first-century cycling? By what forms of consumption and capital might cycling monetize profitable new ways of living and competing with one another for sought-after objects and experiences? Is cycling expansion via a neoliberal market order destined to gobble up "moral shares" held by other assemblages of mobility?

Neoliberal Urbanisms and Cycling Capital

In a world assembled through the market, the possibility of resolving disagreement and strife rests on a vision of human nature as innately drawn toward competition and exchange in the pursuit of one's personal interests. For Adam Smith a refined division of labor was not some magical source of market reciprocity so much as a gradual outcome of "the natural propensity to truck, barter, and exchange one thing for another. It is common to all men, and to be found in no other race of animals, which seem to know neither this nor any other species of contracts" (cited in Boltanski and Thévenot 2006[1991], 47). A shared natural capacity for reaching a deal makes it possible for all individuals to come together through, and create social conventions around, their common passion for rare and coveted goods—objects that articulate the wants of others. This "orchestration of acquisitive desires" (Boltanski and Thévenot 2006[1991], 49) via the invisible hand of Smith's competitive marketplace both governs and justifies differential access to wealth. As in other moral assemblages,

> the worthy are the ones who, by means of their worth, maintain the possibility of a reference to the *higher common principle*. In striking their bargains, the wealthy maintain competition in a marketplace. It is in this sense that luxury benefits everyone, rather than by virtue of the industry it spawns. Unlike patrimonies, wealth that supports market exchanges is profitable to the polity. (Boltanski and Thévenot 2006[1991], 79; italics in the original)

In this way markets—in direct contradistinction to the general interest of civic worth and with disdain for the chains of personal dependence that define domestic worth—ground the common good in the personal "appetites" or interests of individuals.

The way in which classical ideals of market worth rely on individual interests must be distinguished from the way neoliberal governmentality today defines this interest as self-regulation and enterprise where individuals embrace responsibility for their own choices (Rose 1999). In Adam Smith's conception—before a new "science" of economics had sundered "objective" from "subjective" value, retooling humans as rational calculators of utility (Schumpeter 2008[1942])—humans have the capacity to sympathize with others in an impartial enough way to both want and respect the rare goods commanded by others, as long as the winners maintain a competitive marketplace. Where their acquisitive desires orchestrate human flourishing, individuals, in the classic market sense, are not mere atoms but rather "as metaphysical as the collective beings of sociology" (Boltanski and Thévenot 2006[1991], 44).

This market-driven notion of a common humanity must seem alien today, after Margaret Thatcher declared there is no such thing as society. Her famous dictum resonates in Canada, as when former leader and neoconservative economist Stephen Harper implored his political opponents not to "commit sociology" on matters of carrying out justice for terrorist threats and missing and murdered Indigenous women (Kaye and Béland 2014). The "neo-liberal eclipse of the Canadian welfare state unfolded tentatively and incrementally" compared to that in the United States and the UK (Brodie 2002, 387). But by 1995, with a pivotal slash-and-burn budget (Dobbin 2003), Canada had sharply reoriented the role of government toward facilitating business growth and market choices, economic freedom, and other basic tenets of postwar neoliberalism (Peck 2010; 2011). Today Canada exhibits some advanced hallmarks of this utopic ideology (Harvey 2005): "a reliance on market solutions to public policy problems, privileging the actions of the wealthy and the 'talented', the privatization of state assets and functions, and an attack on welfare state provisions" (Walks 2009, 346). In these neoliberal times, individual consumer choices drive an uneven, expansionary market whose "solutions" grow ever more disconnected from the common good.

The growing role of markets for solving complex sociological problems and the privileging of individual choice over collective decision-making have complex effects on urban mobilities. This political ideology, neoliberalism, made material by the system of automobility, is unevenly applied and takes on a range of forms across geopolitical, historical, and urban contexts (Hackworth 2007; Brenner and Theodore 2002). The seeds for a market-dominated approach to mass mobilities were planted in 1920s North America as diverse automotive interests challenged the industrial expertise of traffic engineers. The first gasoline taxes and parking meters, whereby motorists began to pay for roads and curb space, reconfigured the road itself as a "commodity purchased by individual users," where "road capacity was not a question for public debate but a matter of supplying a commodity to those who paid for it" (Norton 2008, 200). After the car and its infrastructure became commoditized, and a recession and an OPEC embargo in the 1970s triggered the deregulation of labor and financial flows, divergent forms of neoliberal urbanism sprouted that strongly affect where and how cycling can now expand. On one hand, neoliberal urbanism ranges from "secessionist automobilities" in the racialized growth of some American cities (Henderson 2006) to fascist-like, authoritarian populism seeking to protect the car and its system from Communist "cycling pinkos" in tony downtown Toronto (Walks 2015; Robinson and Barrera 2012). On the other hand, downtown brands of neoliberal urbanism, like Vancouverism (see chapter 3), contest Fordist auto-mobility, or accumulation built on scientific management, unionized labor, and standardized production and consumption (Paterson 2007), through transit and cycling-oriented gentrification and the financial-ization of cosmopolitan urban intensification.

Blurring these extremes on a national level, sitting Canadian prime minister Justin Trudeau rhetorically strikes a new eco-fiscal "third way" beyond the war between the economy and the environment. This entails quelling authoritarian, pro-car populism by aggressively supporting and subsidizing Canada's automotive sector and oil and gas industries while somehow warmly embracing urban sustainability and a "new deal" for cities. In practice Trudeau's third way extends the neoliberal drift of his center-left predecessors by failing to seriously address either the chronic underfunding of housing and transit and sky-high infrastructure deficits or their root causes, namely, a sys-temic downloading of service provision from federal to provincial to municipal governments and the nonprofit sector—often without the authority to make decisions—and a constitutional lack of political representation for cities (Fanelli 2016; Walks 2009). While Trudeau once stated his support for "highway bike lanes for the middle class" ("Trudeau Announces Bike-Only Lanes for Trans-Canada Highway" 2015), his government maintains a long-standing pattern in Canada of virtually ignoring cycling as a national transport strategy for the highly urbanized country. Unlike in the UK—which for a period acted like a "cycling state" with a National Cycling Strategy before it "rolled back" cycling to its historical status as a nonstate issue tied to respon-sible choices by individuals for healthy lifestyles and the environment (Aldred 2012)—Canada never had the opportunity to outsource and "roll back" cycling because it was never a state priority in the first place.[1] Like the United States, where cycling has also failed to coalesce into a meaningful national transport policy, city cycling in Canada thus faces multiple neoliberal urbanisms at national and local political scales that simultaneously valorize and attack cycling as a sign of market success and failure.

Cycling's chances for international market success are entwined with the sort of neoliberal urbanism championed by global cities such as Toronto and Vancouver, not a "roll back" but a "roll out" neoliberalism (Peck and Tickell 2002), ushering private-public partnerships, global finance, and cosmopolitan, condo-dwelling gentrifiers into upscale neighborhoods around downtown (Walks 2015). I envision this sort of cycling market potential as "cycling capital." By cycling capital I mean the peculiar "network capital" (Elliott and Urry 2010) commanded by "cycling globals," or wealthy, kinetic elites who use cycling to facilitate their super-mobile, affluent lifestyles. Such capital includes the capacity to work anywhere and access data at a distance, use and combine multiple kinds of vehicles (bikes, boats, cars, planes, trains) and their infrastructures, and spend large sums of money on luxury rides, communication devices, and tourism. This cycling capital resonates with the particular "connexionist" spirit of neoliberal market capitalism (Boltanski and Chiapello 2005[1999]), a spirit that drives "a world of networked and globalized firms, organized around transient project-work, and one in which flexibility, creativity and mobility have been elevated to the highest common good" (Blok 2013, 502).

Connexionist cyclists abound in Canadian cities. You might see them ride by you in colorful spandex suits chatting into Apple earpieces about real estate on their lunchtime ride, hitching mountain bikes onto their SUV for a heli-biking excursion, or simply using bike share to shop and tour the downtown area. Or you might spot them shifting seamlessly between cycling and walking and light rail—signature multimodal moves of the cycling global as they circulate between upscale neighborhoods and inner-city amenities without being slowed by the car. Or you might see aspirational cycling globals plying traffic in the gig economy with Foodora or Uber Eats bags strapped to their backs. Those with lower levels of cycling capital (Lee et al. 2016), so long as they carry the connexionist spirit of the new capitalism—much like some of their predecessors who were driven by a Protestant work ethic or keen sense of frugality and discipline (Weber 2002[1934])—can take solace in the fact that cycling globals maintain a competitive marketplace through which, one day, the aspirational, too, might ascend to the lofty lap of luxury.

(Self-)Driving Lessons

Imagine yourself as a Canadian kinetic elite on the West Coast in 2052, disembarking from your off-grid property in the Okanagan Valley. Heading to work at your mining tech company in downtown Vancouver, you ask Pyrrhi to pour you a coffee with a little something extra in it (feels like Friday). You rub your eyes and relish the French impressionist blur of a landscape shooting by outside the window as you speed along. You still remember the days when the 400-kilometer (250-mile) route took you over four hours, a grinding commute. Your kids cannot even fathom it. Then Pyrrhi came along, the self-driving car that whisks you from your private wilderness to your global boardroom in under an hour. Pyrrhi is that much faster than previous cars but also safer and more environmentally friendly, requiring less fuel and room on the road while rarely running into other cars and animals—reducing the violence and stress that put you off driving automobiles in the first place. Moving in a car with greater efficiency allows you to spend more time with your family. And in the "office" of Pyrrhi, you might help move a mining tech play through a major equity funding round before you even reach the boardroom.

As a millennial you managed to avoid the terrifying ritual of securing a driver's license. At first you were content with high-speed rail, private plane travel, public bike shares, and (to indulge your guilty aesthetic pleasure) high-end racing bicycles decorated with the wings of butterflies. But Pyrrhi was so user-friendly and luxurious that you took the plunge. Your only complaint is how everything unexpectedly changed when everyone bought a self-driving car. It is not simply that other people have them, too; as a prominent business executive, you take great pride in generating wealth and jobs for your community and raising its standard of living to new heights. Rather, the problem is, after so many people started dwelling in self-driving cars and buying property farther and farther away from the city, sometimes it feels like all of Cascadia has been carpeted by new smart roads and parking farms. True, you can afford the private skyways and skyparks that skip the cues. But it wasn't supposed to be like this. Faster, smarter, greener self-driving cars supposedly optimize time and space—so why is everyone, you wonder with genuine concern, spending nearly all of their time in them? Why is Pyrrhi warning you every other day about some software glitch or cyberattack that left the occupants of a self-driving car lost, hacked, or locked in and nearly cooked alive in the sun? You let go of such thoughts as Pyrrhi glides into your skypark. Time to bank the big bucks.

The post-Fordist marketization of the car in North America, growing through divergent neoliberal urbanisms and the seductive allure of self-driving technology for solving sociologically complicated "car troubles" (Conley and Tigar McLaren 2009), points at two market lessons for twenty-first-century cycling. The first lesson is to mobilize what markets do best, which is to engender monetary profit, creative innovation, and product development through competitive exchanges without undermining the conditions of competition that connect markets to the common good. In practice markets should avoid pushing "market fixes" for complex socio-technical imbroglios that undermine competition by worsening the monopolies and inequalities that prevent people with low market worth from gaining chances to move into states of higher worth, and that ensure the wealthy only grow wealthier. Such fixes often focus on the future, not in an industrial sense of long-term planning but on selling high-tech solutions that optimize short-term profits. The modern bicycle, which still closely resembles the safety bicycle that replaced the dangerous penny-farthing in the 1880s, might seem immune to profitable high-tech fixes. However, such a framing fails to account for an emerging movement toward "smart cities" that harvest big data from new tools like bike counters, machines along bike routes that count the number of cyclists that go by, and ever-more sophisticated bike share systems. These tools come with a lot of market potential. But cycling ought to question the thinking flowing so freely up and down North America's West Coast that high-tech market interventions can make mobility systems everywhere more efficient, particularly as incessant new cycles of disruptive digital technologies suddenly render previous vehicles and systems obsolete. Domestic and industrial assemblages of mobility, in particular, tremble and fray where emerging markets ignore history and long-term planning.

The second market lesson for cycling is to make markets fairer before it is too late. Under well-regulated conditions markets can drive trade and maintain competition that can advance widespread prosperity as a common good. However, deregulated, neoliberal markets that end up marketizing ever-more spheres of collective social life run the risk of undermining the very conditions that sustain competition and the market common good by fueling monopolies, exacerbating inequalities, and degrading nonhuman environments. Worse, neoliberal markets eat up the "moral shares" held by other good mobilities, destabilizing the fundamental plurality of political morality that nourishes the common good (any common good) in the first place. A dangerously sharp edge of moral friction arises here between neoliberal market worth and civic worth, where neoliberal urban growth and development justify extraordinary inequalities of income and capital (Piketty 2014) while "hollowing out" a welfare state that could promote cycling justice (Aldred 2012). This sharp edge suggests that positive market-civic associations may prove particularly important for reducing the moral friction surrounding cycling expansion. However, it is not simply this moral friction that matters. All non-market worths are in trouble if the global kinetic elite become "responsible only to themselves and their like, and no longer interested in societal projects" (Amin 2006; 1010). Abandoning that metaphysical connection made by Adam Smith to the market's common humanity, the neoliberal market fix begets atomizing moral myopia.

To examine how these lessons can guide the assembly of market cycling, I offer three case studies: a multicity comparative analysis of bike share systems, an atypical case study of Vancouver's high-rolling cycling capital, and a day in the life of Mobi, Vancouver's new bike share vehicle. These cases feature unique forms and a diversity of practices and infrastructures by which neoliberal urbanism reconfigures city cycling as a coveted commodity and mode of consumption. Moving between Motor City and "Vancity" helps clarify both the moral weight and multiplicity of market worth.

Commodifying Cycling through Bike Share

After local businesses and business improvement area associations angrily criticized dedicated bike lanes for taking away car parking (see chapter 3), cities and cycling advocates in Canada became savvier about marketing new cycling infrastructure. Up against a sizeable pro-car, pro-business (and pro-parking) population living in postwar suburbs who tend to vote conservative and lead car-dependent lifestyles outside the gentrifying inner city with its cosmopolitan, condo-dwelling elites—defining what Walks (2007) aptly calls the "boundaries of suburban discontent"—Ottawa, Toronto, Vancouver, and other major cities started pushing the "cycling business case" to justify new cycling lanes. At its core the business case for cycling holds that cyclists of all types stop at local businesses with more ease and frequency than motorists, and on average spend more money when they are there (Sztabinski 2009). If arguments about social justice or the environmental and health benefits of cycling fall flat for businesses and suburbanites who simply associate new cycling infrastructure with a reduction in access, reconceiving the cyclist as the model consumer might help change their minds about bike lanes. Stephen, the Windsor Tweed Ride organizer and Motor City cycling businessman (and bike renter) from chapter 3, clarifies how cycling increases consumption:

> It is proven there is a direct, positive economic impact from installing bicycle infrastructure where there are urban businesses. If you have a bike lane in front of your business, you can actually gauge the increase in traffic, an increase in coins in your till. If you're the hair salon that's on a bike lane, you'll get more cyclists than the hair salon that's not on a bike lane. While cycling you see someone

setting up the oranges outside a grocery store that you never saw before. (Interview 2014)

This justification for cycling infrastructure as market infrastructure is traveling far and wide via city governments, universities, the philanthropic sector, and multinational corporations in both high- and low-cycling urban contexts.

One especially profitable avenue thus far for advancing city cycling's business case—with international corporations, market experimentation, city branding, and corporate sponsorships—is public bike share (where "public" and "share" seamlessly morph into "private" and "profit"). A typical bike share scheme describes a mobility service in which users access a bicycle from a station or dock then take it for a short trip (usually under 30 minutes) before later depositing the bicycle at the same or more likely a different dock within a dock network usually limited to inner cities (Gauthier et al. 2013). The idea has its origins in 1960s Amsterdam, evolving from low-tech versions where bikes were left unsecured in public to coin-operated systems, like supermarket carts, to more recent generations featuring credit card readers, mobile phone interfaces, pricing policies that incentivize turnover, and radio frequency identification and GPS tracking of the user/bicycle (De Maio 2003). While *promoters* who initiate such public bike schemes tend to be public sector bodies, *providers* of bike and dock technologies and their *operators* vary between public and private. According to international bike share consultants Beroud Benoît and Esther Anaya (2012, 286–89), while many combinations exist, the most common have private providers and private operators, usually with some sort of joint advertising contract and corporate sponsorship. In organizational practice bike shares are slippery with respect to whether they are a public service or a business, offering a dynamic site for the private-public blurring that characterizes neoliberal urbanism. Where private provision and private operation is prioritized, as in most North American cases, public bike shares are assembling cycling into large international high-tech, data-driven industries investing in city bike shares across the globe. For example, in Seattle three private companies are competing to provide and operate the best public bikes without any docks at all, disrupting the industry through a new leaner model.

Another compelling case of public bike share is Detroit. Like Seattle, Detroit's bike share combines actors, objectives, and financing that cut across private and public lines—but in a very different socioeconomic context, with the city of Detroit just emerging from a historical bankruptcy. Bike share in Detroit originated in Wayne State University's Office of Economic Development, which launched a feasibility study for the idea in 2013. The study featured a sophisticated business case assembled by Lisa, then a project manager at Wayne State, who imagines Detroit bike share not simply as a way to foster mobility in the inner city and better access to shopping and transit but also as a "catalyst of growth. We think bike share will be great not only as a transportation option but also as an economic development tool" (Interview 2014). To employ bike share as a tool for economic growth, she elaborates, requires "a lot of great partnerships with public, private, non-profit, philanthropic sector agencies" and a multifaceted plan for raising money:

> Our fundraising strategy is to apply for federal funding for some of the start-up capital; get some philanthropic money, to fill the match requirement [for the public money], and create a bit of an operating reserve; and then go to the private sector for corporate sponsorships to pay for the balance of operations and maintenance that wouldn't be covered by user fees. (Interview 2014)

While matching public and private monies and corralling state and local transport and public works agencies that slowly came on board (with the help of a government delegation to Copenhagen on which she acted as the nonprofit-sector representative), Lisa slowly crafted a convincing rationale of bike share for elected officials: "This investment will produce a return."

In contrast to Seattle and most other North American systems, the private-public partnership for bike share in America's Motor City projects the expansion of a fairer marketplace. For Lisa Detroit bike share is not simply about ramping up consumption and gentrification. She is well aware of the fact that as public bike share schemes sweep the world, they notoriously fail to incorporate visible minority and low-income populations. Bike share schemes aim to optimize ridership by targeting dense inner cities and adjacent districts with high activity nodes, often to the exclusion of low-income and non-gentrified neighborhoods (Hannig 2015)—or new markets waiting in the wings. Detroit's population fell from a high of almost two million in 1950 to around 700,000 today, which is 85 percent African American and economically struggling: the city can neither afford nor publicly justify a socially inaccessible public bike share system. Thus Lisa's business case challenges the inequitable market trend by, *inter alia*: partnering with local nonprofits to promote bike share sign-up among underserved populations; developing "neighborhood ambassadors" from low-cycling communities to offer hands-on demos and logistical support (MoGo 2018); lowering the bar for sign-ups by not requiring a credit card and splitting annual membership fees over twelve months as opposed to one upfront fee; and departing from the original feasibility study to advocate for a station in the North End neighborhood of Detroit even though it would be socioeconomically challenging.

Detroit's relatively equitable bike share design, inspired by a similar progressive model in Philadelphia, employs public bike share as an economic tool of development for diverse users of varying capabilities. Called "MoGo," Detroit bike share rolled out in 2017 with 430 bikes and 43 stations throughout 10 neighborhoods. It constitutes an affiliate of the Downtown Detroit Partnership (DDP) in collaboration with the City of Detroit, sponsored by the Henry Ford Health System (HFHS) and Health Alliance Plan (HAP). The sensible and clever branding of nonprofit health-care entities as corporate sponsors for public cycling stands in contrast with other pioneering bike share systems, such as Bixi in Montréal, which in 2009 boasted Rio Tinto as a major sponsor (an international mining group with a dubious environmental and human rights record). At the same time, MoGo does not shy away from Detroit's own industrial heritage. Playing off "Motor City," MoGo, says Lisa, now its new executive director, "continues the city's mobility evolution, providing Detroiters and visitors alike with more accessible options to move around the city" (HAP 2017). And even as MoGo expands a more equitable market for bike share, it also sheds light onto the challenges facing other public-private bike share partnerships and the financial gains to be won through privatization and global expansion.

MoGo's equipment provider and operator, PBSC Urban Solutions of Longueuil, Québec, is a global player. PBSC is what the international arm of Bixi Montréal turned into after Bixi, a global trailblazer in "smart bike share" systems created in 2008, fell into dire financial straits. Facing bankruptcy in 2014 Bixi, as a kind of "para-municipal firm of the City of Montréal," faced "$50 million in debt, little liquidity, late deliveries, software bugs and several lawsuits" (CBC News 2016). After Montréal switched from owner to client (like most cities with private providers and operators), Bixi-Montréal—with five thousand bikes—quickly headed toward a budget surplus. Now PBSC is competing with several other large companies to provide new or additional bike share systems to cities across the globe and collect software fees, in what is estimated to be by 2020 an $8-billion industry (CBC News 2016). With forty-five thousand bikes in sixteen different cities around the world, PBSC CEO Luc Sabbatini says, "The product is fantastic. We have over 100 patents in 45 different countries, so there is a lot of intellectual property because of the investment made by Montreal" (Madger 2017). Capturing Montréal's public investment, PBSC is betting big on new technology to improve the product by investing heavily in research and development and capitalizing on a global growth industry. Sabbatini adds: "A city doesn't feel cool if it doesn't have a bike service. This makes our job easier, since we don't have to solicit those markets. Those markets solicit us. We're having trouble meeting the demand" (Madger 2017). By investing in Bixi, MoGo has become part of a dynamic worldwide market, with cities and corporations everywhere seeking to brand themselves through healthy, high-tech bike share.

Wealthy cities on North America's West Coast are raising the stakes for smart bike share schemes by assembling public bike share through international high-tech markets and big data. Vancouver's bike share scheme, Mobi (for "more biking"), rolled out in 2016. It now has about 2,000 bikes and 150 stations in and around downtown after a recent eastward expansion. Mobi's online credit card payments charge a $9.75 minimum up front (plus overage fees) for a day pass with unlimited trips under thirty minutes (with pricier longer-term passes). Forgoing the low-cost, pay-with-cash alternatives seen in Detroit that render bike share there more like a public service, Mobi follows the best business practices of its private operator, Santa Monica–based CycleHop, for targeting Vancouver shoppers and commuters. The largest smart bike share operator in North America, CycleHop, and Mobi's equipment provider, France-based Smoove, provide fobs and radio-frequency ID cards for easy scanning at solar-powered stations during pickup and "stopover" locking for shopping. To make things flow even smoother Mobi's flagship sponsor, Shaw Communications Inc., connects bike share stations to its Shaw Go WiFi network so users can, *inter alia*, track bike and dock availability on their Mobi smart phone app.[2] Signaling how Shaw brands bike share differently than sponsors of other schemes, says Vancouver Bike Share Inc. general manager Mia Kohout: "It's the perfect partnership between smart bikes and smart technology" (Mobi Shaw Go 2016). With corporate partners like Amazon, Apple, Fairmont, and Hootsuite Media, Mobi's smart bike share hails a smart bike share user who is engaged with innovative digital technology and fluent with high-end communications products.

Tracking the routes and habits of smart cycling consumers is generating big bike share data, which Mobi and others are mining with regression-based techniques and machine learning to optimize intelligent and profitable investment. Through Mobi, the City of Vancouver, Smoove, and Cycle Hop are producing reams of personal geolocation data following where, when, and with what intensity different kinds of public bike consumers are ebbing and flowing across central urban districts. As smart phones and chips in smart bikes relay these data to company servers, they raise pressing questions. Who really owns it? How freely does it flow between the diverse array of public and private partners assembling and sponsoring bike shares? It was with a sense of promoting user privacy and data security, for example, that two behemoth bike sharing companies based in China, Mobike and ofo, recently shared their big data with a Chinese government organization seeking to encourage and regulate its booming bike share economy (an authoritarian government blurring the distinction between public and private life in its own way). The bike share company ofo—a $2-billion business operating across 21 countries in over 250 cities with 32 million trips every day on 10 million trademark lemon bikes (named for the shape of a person cycling) (Campbell 2018)—is one of three dockless companies disrupting conventional bike share in Seattle. Like Vancouver, a Canadian tech hub where Amazon recently opened three thousand new jobs (Bailey and Bula 2018), Seattle uses bike share to help mobilize knowledge workers and consumers at the forefront of creating and beta-testing the product lines of big tech. Reinforcing the growing relationship between big tech (Alphabet, Amazon, Facebook, Apple, and Microsoft) and bike share and cycling in general, is big tech's recent game-changing shift from building suburban, car-dependent campuses to rebuilding cities. As titans of tech like Amazon (and Alphabet in downtown Toronto) rebuild cities like Seattle through inner-city real estate with biophilic work amenities, the disruptive bike sharing economy will generate even bigger data for more profitable concerns, building ever-smarter cities.

While they may seem far removed from, and less accessible than, bike share developments in Detroit, ofo and Mobi are very much rooted in the same business case as Mogo. Lisa, Mogo's executive director, alludes to the insertion of bike share into wider global cycles of high-tech, market-driven urban disruption (beyond Bixi) as she humorously reiterates the same case that Stephen made above:

> We think putting the amenity [bike share] in close proximity to business is a good thing. People with [public bike] memberships spend much more. . . . Stations are often placed at high activity nodes, places where there are a lot of shops and restaurants. You get off the

bike and you know, you're thirsty from your two mile ride over, I'm going to run in and grab a lemonade. Or you want to go in and shop at a . . . I was going to say record store but those things don't even exist anymore. So we'll say . . . you can't really say bookstore so much anymore either . . . so you know, shop at a store. (Interview 2014)

The loss of old stores and previous paradigms to creative destruction and reinvention (Schumpeter 2008[1942]), like Bixi's bankruptcy and rebirth into the black, is a signal of a connexionist market world in which a network of globalized cycling firms execute transient, creative, and disruptive project-work that transfers wealth from public to private entities. The greater the enrollment of this connexionist cycling market into the orbit of big tech, the greater risk it runs in compromising market worth by failing to maintain fair and open bike share competition.

Not all bike shares are everywhere the same, even if their bikes or docks look alike. They vary significantly, for example, in their capacity to access socially marginalized and low-income markets. However, what they all seem to share, again to varying degrees, is their embrace of high-tech solutions for attracting talented cycling globals looking for a standard public bike with which to ride the urban core. The sheer number of cities creating different sorts of public-private bike share schemes bodes well for healthy market competition in a global growth industry for city cycling. More ominously for cycling's market worth, bike share as a whole is becoming ever more entangled with monopolistic tech titans whose businesses and urban redevelopment threaten to undermine fair and competitive participation in the marketplace.

Divergent Neoliberal Urbanisms in Hot Markets

As lucrative and global as they have become, bike share schemes cannot be removed from the cities and larger dynamics of neoliberal urbanism of which they are but one product and one producer. Many cycling capitalists and entrepreneurs are aware if not concerned about the displacement, for example, caused or exacerbated by their own efforts to make cycling more hip, attractive, and accessible. Public bike share schemes, in particular, have strong potential to support urban redevelopment and condo-driven intensification that raises financial pressure on cities. With or without permanent stations or docks, bike shares physically overlay and economically reinforce dense inner-city areas where cycling excels at mass mobility, suggesting bike share schemes offer a potent economic development tool for areas preparing for, or already in the throes of, gentrification. As bike shares become another arrow in the quiver of cycling globals and kinetic elites, they may reinforce new forms of gentrification by appealing to the mobility needs of the higher-income tenants with whom increasingly "financialized landlords" (August and Walks 2018) seek to replace poorer renters. In other words, bike share stands to embolden "roll out" style neoliberal urbanism with its profitable private-public partnerships, global financial flows, and cosmopolitan condo-dwelling clientele. By the same token this neoliberal market assembling of cycling capital through bike share conflicts with conservative, pro-car populisms cropping up across Canada. Toronto, especially during its administration by Mayor Rob Ford (2010–14), offers an exemplary case study of such divergent neoliberal urbanisms that simultaneously challenge and extend a post-Fordist system of automobility (Walks 2015). As it happens, so does Vancouver, making a Canadian constellation.

Toronto and Vancouver, besides dominating national broadsheets with their red-hot real-estate markets, share another (not unrelated) political conundrum. Inner cities and postwar suburban districts are both fighting for market solutions to social problems that privilege the actions of the kinetic elite—but one wants cycling and the other associates it with privileged "Moonbeam Mayors" (Proctor 2018) and "Communist pinkos" (Grant 2010). Toronto seems destined for such multiplicitous market politics. Its postwar suburbs (and cities near Toronto, like Oshawa and Windsor) house a preponderance of Fordist industrial workers and commuters tied culturally and economically to the automobile sector. Vancouver, by contrast, stands far removed from Ontario and its autoworkers, the Big Three automakers, and the vast public subsidies for the car industry. Thus it was shocking to urbane elites when a 2015 referendum asking voters in Metro Vancouver to approve or reject a new 0.5 percent sales tax to help fund major sustainable mobility projects (e.g., transit and cycling), widely expected to pass, decisively failed (61.7 percent No, 38.4 percent Yes). At stake in the plebiscite was a $7.5-billion regional transportation plan, much of which would fund new rail systems laying the groundwork for transit-oriented development (TOD) in car-based suburbs around Metro Vancouver. Cycling advocates supported the plan, with TOD the best bet for "rolling out" cycling growth to the suburbs. Also in favor was nearly every mayor in the region (save for West Vancouver, the richest city in Canada), as well as business groups and labor and environmental associations. Campaigning against the transportation plan was mainly the Canadian Taxpayers Federation. Its British Columbian director, Jordan Bateman, the de facto voice of the "No campaign," called the result a "tremendous victory for taxpayers"—a victory in which "No" votes heavily tilted toward postwar, car-dominated districts (Johnson and Baluja 2015).

In one fell swoop, antitax, pro-car populism hobbled the outward march of sustainable mobilities from Vancouver's inner city. The referendum may be viewed as a civic judgment by empowering citizens to have a direct say in transport policy, or less charitably as a democratic "taxpayer tyranny of the majority." However, I concur with Kyle Willmott (2017, 258), who instead reads the referendum as a market extension of a "taxpayer governmentality" by which neoliberal political subjects *qua* taxpayers fight what they characterize as financially irresponsible government. The Canadian Taxpayers Federation persuaded many Metro Vancouverites that their hard-earned money cannot be trusted with TransLink, the publicly funded regional transport authority. While TransLink's board of directors was reorganized in 2007 by a right-of-center provincial government, removing locally elected representatives in favor of business professionals, the Canada Taxpayers Federation still demonized TransLink for lavish government spending and over-regulation. Said Bateman during the campaign: "We'd all be better off if TransLink spent as much time and effort looking to save money and cut waste as it did dreaming up new tax grabs" (CBC News 2014). The lopsided campaign pit a blatantly ideological Taxpayers "Federation" that has about five actual members (Lamont 2016) against what seemed like the rest of political and civil society—showing political parallels to the Stephen Harper government's move in 2010, for example, to axe the compulsory Canadian census.[3] Even stronger resonances lie between Vancouver's referendum and the populist campaigns across North America in the 1910s and 1920s by auto clubs and businesses, who lobbied on behalf of motorists' "inalienable rights of owning and driving their cars without the harassing complications" of government regulation (Norton 2008, 183–84)—campaigns that also framed restrictions on the car as a form of tyranny by unaccountable experts who lacked the common sense of businesspeople.

What helps distinguish today's "roll back" pro-car populism from historical precedents, however, is the other pro-cycling "roll out" brand of neoliberal urbanism with which it clashes—even as both brands promulgate market solutions to public policy problems. Cycling acts as an important tool and brand image for "Vancouverism," a highly profitable style of dense urban development emphasizing slim glassy towers on commercial podiums, expansive views of nature, city parks, and sustainable mobility. Inspiring far-flung facsimiles like the Dubai Marina—a near "perfect clone of downtown Vancouver" in a previously barren stretch of the Great Arabian Desert, "right down to the handrails on the seawall" (Kiger 2014)—Vancouverism is a brand associated with elite opinion, the creative class, and high-rolling real-estate investors, media moguls, and mining magnates who work and play downtown. Such urbane elites recoiled at the populist suburban backlash against transit investments with its disregard for evidence-based analysis and kowtowing to the Taxpayer Federation. "There is no Plan B," said Vancouver mayor Gregor Robertson defiantly after the plebiscite (Johnson and Baluja 2015). But how different is Plan A, billions for sustainable mobilities, under the Vancouverism brand, from a market perspective? Vancouverism's inexorable roll out into the suburbs from the inner city along light-rail lines might look as if it utterly contradicts pro-car, antitax populism. However, while it respects a role for urbanity, smart design, and expertise (Doolittle 2011), Vancouverism nevertheless has unfolded as a cosmopolitan form of "third way" neoliberal urbanism that, like its pro-car suburban counterpart, thrives as an expansion of market solutions that privilege the already prolific flows of private capital and cycling globals. Taxpayer governmentality and Vancouverism form two sides of the same coin.

Despite the referendum setback of 2015, it's been big business as usual for the redevelopment of inner-city real estate in Vancouver. For example, in 2016 Robertson announced the city would buy the almost nine kilometer (six-mile) disused Arbutus rail corridor on Vancouver's wealthy west side from Canadian Pacific Railway for $55 million, so it could transform the corridor into a walking, cycling, and streetcar urban "greenway." Beaming before the media, Robertson proclaimed: "This is Vancouver's chance to have a New York–style High Line," referring to the disused elevated rail line in Manhattan that became a park and New York City's most visited destination (Bliss 2017). Vancouver's purchase pleased local homeowners whose community gardens had been disturbed by Canadian Pacific's plan to sell off bits of the corridor for handsome sums. It angered others, notably legacy businesses and social enterprisers like Doris (see chapter 3) in Chinatown, in whose protection and revitalization Vancouver has shown far less financial interest after underinvesting in the neighborhood for more than a century. For the Arbutus, Robertson imagines a High Line–like rejuvenation of an economically fallow corridor into a greenway rich with multiple uses and sustainable mobilities following the urban philosophy of Jane Jacobs (1961). His administration spied an opportunity here to resurrect Vancouver's streetcars (after their untimely death in 1958), which would not only stimulate TOD and prime cycling conditions but also—in much the same way bike share creators promote their product—act as "place-makers" that attract millions of tourists a year (Bula 2017). The fact that Vancouver is directing such large sums of public money to such smart TOD in such a wealthy urban enclave shows one example in which the city's policies privilege the multimodal mobilities of cycling globals and the kinetic elite.

A much bigger market test for cycling capital and Vancouver(ism) is the city's $1.73-billion Northeast False Creek (NEFC) redevelopment plan (City of Vancouver 2018). Covering 143 acres of mainly undeveloped land, the public jewel of the plan is a new $200-million park in the close-packed heart of the city. The new 31-acre waterfront park, long promised to NEFC condo buyers who have been protesting its delay with green lights on their windows, will replace some underused, yet extremely valuable land on the north shore of False Creek once Vancouver's Georgia Street Viaducts come down (see chapter 2). It seeks to integrate adjacent neighborhoods (Chinatown, Downtown Eastside, Yaletown, Strathcona, and Mount Pleasant) with starkly diverging mobility needs and capabilities. Thus it makes much more sense to compare this project rather than Arbutus to New York City's famed High Line. Like the area surrounding High Line, which includes a large visible minority population and public housing projects, the presence of Chinatown and the Downtown Eastside further increases the lucrative potential of False Creek's new park community for triggering wider spread urban revitalization. Even more to the point, James Corner himself, whose company designed and constructed the High Line, was brought in as lead landscape architect to work similar magic at False Creek. Corner envisions big things for his new park project: "We believe this park will become, in a sense, the new central park, the new centrepiece, both symbolically and literally physically for all of the various neighbourhoods that surround it" (Stewart 2017).

On one hand, Vancouver's new central park and billion-dollar public-private redevelopment partnership, of which it is a part, shows strong market potential for growing dense cycling-friendly development and future ranks of cycling globals. An inherent limitation of Vancouver-ism in Vancouver is a lack of floor space, hemmed in as the city is by the very shorelines and mountains that give this style of urbanism its nature motif. By demolishing the viaducts, Vancouver effectively unlocks a blank slate for new growth, a singular opportunity "to create a new vibrant and resilient community" on "the last remaining piece of large undeveloped land in the downtown" (City of Vancouver 2018, 70).

Hardly just a new park ensconced by condo developments, the NEFC "is planned to become home to 10,000–12,000 new residents and will provide work space for 6,000–8,000 new jobs" (City of Vancouver 2018, 150). To help move these new residents and workers and immense flows of tourists, the NEFC plan entails new cycling links, including a greenway with dedicated bike lanes that "will become the spine of the new integrated park" (City of Vancouver 2018, 104). And the future central park community is already surrounded by some of the best and busiest dedicated bike routes in North America (Perkins 2018)—including that iconic seawall that Dubai re-created in the Arabian Desert. A sign that the NEFC redevelopment will entail a fair contest for who gets to live, work, and ride in the area, the plan (City of Vancouver 2018 163) includes 1,800 affordable social housing units, community center–provided child care, and other new public amenities (although the city's definition of affordable is questionable) (Pablo 2018). Moreover the plan is framed in the context of reconciliation with the Musqueam, Squamish, and Tsleil-Waututh Nations, on whose unceded territory the site lies, and emphasizes cultural redress for the historical exclusion of Chinatown and Vancouver's black community—accommodating cultural activities and gathering spaces for these groups (City of Vancouver 2018, 19–24).

On the other hand, Vancouver's future central park community also shows signs of eroding the conditions of competition and social mobility that underlie its market worth. Not unlike its bike share growing into the orbits of monopolistic high-tech companies, Vancouver's inner-city redevelopment in general has become increasingly cornered by the international business of real estate, much of which, in turn, is dominated by a small number of mega developers, like Concord Pacific. Formed in 1987 to develop Concord Pacific Place on the former Expo Lands after purchasing them from the City of Vancouver, Concord Pacific, led by Hong Kong billionaire Li Ka-shing (with a current net worth of USD 34 billion), launched Vancouver into higher-stakes real-estate development (Proctor 2016). The corporation specializes in large-scale master plans for "skyline defining communities" (Concord Pacific n.d.), including CityPlace, a 44-acre (18-hectare) mega development under construction in downtown Toronto. Concord's 10.2-acre (4-hectare) waterfront site at NEFC will vertically dominate NEFC and align with Vancouver's vision of NEFC as an events and entertainment district. Preliminary plans for Concord's piece of NEFC (Meiszner 2017) entail signature floating restaurants, cafés, pubs, and high-end retail businesses lining pedestrian laneways and filling the podiums of the two tallest (41-story) towers in the NEFC plan. That one company owns and will profit from so much valuable vertical city space by tailoring it to luxury market housing and amenities does not by itself prove cycling capital flowing through NEFC will become either unfairly monopolized (and not by the communities with whom the redevelopment plan hopes to reconcile) or out of reach for aspiring cycling globals.

However, consider how the High Line transformed New York City. With nearly 8 million people flocking to the High Line by 2016, only seven years after it opened, lucrative park-oriented development followed, through condos, restaurants, and museums. Laura Bliss describes the High Line effect (2017): "The High Line is set to generate about $1 billion in tax revenues to the city over the next 20 years" as "overwhelmingly white" visitors overtake a racially diverse neighborhood. It is precisely in response to such rapid and extreme levels of urban redevelopment or "real-estate imperialism" (Schjeldahl 2014) that the City of Vancouver hired a chief resiliency officer, Katie McPherson, in 2017 to help it prepare for the trauma, displacement, and havoc wrought by gentrification, comparable to that of a natural disaster (Li 2018). With the high-powered architects of the High Line currently crafting NEFC's public park, McPherson may soon have her hands full. The fact remains: although Concord Pacific and city planners may see Northeast False Creek as an undervalued blank slate for rewriting city life, it is very much part of an already existing community, albeit one long demonized and unjustly racialized as an opium den and needle-infested "zit" (CBC News 2017). Altogether the way urban redevelopment has been unfolding throughout inner-city Vancouver, via High Line–inspired mega projects aligned with old money neighborhoods and high-stakes real-estate deals backed by the city in public-private partnerships with billionaire tycoons, is highly problematic for cycling, from a market perspective. The freedom of non-wealthy people to compete with wealthy people in the race to become part of Vancouver's growing cycling market, due to larger factors related to the city's development, continues to dwindle.

As Vancouver's post-Keynesian "third way" market capitalism, so smartly invested and branded through cycling and urban intensification by Mayor Robertson, grows ever more unequal and monopolistic, it undermines a competitive cycling marketplace in which everyone has an opportunity at moving from states of low worth to states of high worth. Along with high-tech bike share gearing city cycling toward kinetic elites and well-heeled consumers, one might conclude that the neoliberal market of Vancouverism is slowly severing cycling from the common good. That Robertson, a putatively progressive leader elected with a mandate to lessen the city's growing inequities and street homelessness, happens to be the neoliberal architect here rather than someone like Stephen Harper or suburban industrial workers fighting for their right to drive, while ironic, is not uncommon. Robertson emblemizes what Jason Hackworth (2007) calls "soft edge" neoliberalism, wherein left-of-center governments while in power rather than redressing end up reinforcing and even extending the programs of urban austerity and market solutions brought in by their right-leaning predecessors (Fanelli 2016). Rather than individuals "as metaphysical as the collective beings of sociology" (Boltanski and Thévenot 2006[1991], 44), diverging neoliberal urbanisms in Vancouver, particularly its downtown brand, risk reducing the city's cycling humans to mere atoms of consumption.

A Day in the Life of Mobi

The following vignette is a composite of many different people and of stories I've collected by hanging around Mobi stations and talking to Mobi users in downtown Vancouver between May and June of 2018. I call the composite "Noah." Part knowledge economy worker, part tourist, and part consumer, Noah's experience captures a broad range of common and less common bike share practices in one of Canada's global cities.

Noah deplaned at Vancouver International Airport (YVR) excited to hop on a Mobi. Noah enjoys flying to Toronto and Montréal and using bike share there, and before arriving in Vancouver for a working holiday they were in Seattle where they tried ofo with mixed results. Noah loves that Seattle is pushing the envelope with dockless bike share systems, because it was easy to find one that was near their hotel downtown and download the app on their mobiles. However, while snapping a skyline picture across the bay in West Seattle, a young man stole Noah's ofo bike, prompting them to vigorously chase him down. Then their partner, after leaving her ofo on the ferry back downtown, may have triggered a search-and-rescue mission for a missing cyclist by the United States Coast Guard (Lloyd 2018). So Noah is looking forward to Mobi, a conventional system like those in Toronto and Montréal with docks as well as Wi-Fi and access to all the urban amenities of which they are interested in taking advantage.

After YVR, through which Noah—a Canadian American citizen and biometrically Trusted Traveler with a Nexus card—flows with relative ease, they head downtown on the Canada Line, Vancouver's newest transit line that opened before the city hosted the 2010 Olympics. After thirty-four minutes on the train, Noah reaches City Centre Station, climbs up the stairs, and immediately finds a Mobi dock (see photo 28). They had packed light and finished their priority e-mails on the plane, so Noah decides to put off heading to the Pacific Rim Fairmont (a favorite place to stay on international business trips). They quickly register their credit information with Mobi on their mobiles, brush off some pigeons, and slip on a shower cap–like liner underneath the helmet provided at the station. Then, after punching a user code, they are on their way. They first skip around the Financial District, taking in the architecture of some firms with whom they are in business or have heard about, easily finding another Mobi after a half hour transpires. For some light shopping after brunch, they visit Salvatore Ferragamo where they find the perfect thousand-dollar Italian sneakers they were looking for, then a few more things at Louis Vuitton inside the Fairmont Hotel Vancouver and some exclusive concessions at Nordstrom.

28. Mobi bikes in Vancouver's City Centre. Photo by author.

29. Mobi bikes at Stanley Park in Vancouver. Photo by author.

Noah does not usually splurge at places like this and chalks it up to how close it is and easy to reach.

After a post-shopping siesta, Noah hops on another Mobi near their hotel and heads for some nature time in Vancouver's world-class Stanley Park. While switching bikes and picking up a snack at English Bay (see photo 29), Noah needs to wait a few minutes before a Mobi employee, a sociable young man attending the University of British Columbia (UBC) in the fall, makes room at the dock station. The system only has two vans, he tells Noah, for redistributing Mobi bikes that invariably end up clogging stations at popular downhill destinations like Stanley Park. Noah suggests that Mobi should incentivize uphill rides as free trips, like another city's bike share system they used once but whose name they couldn't remember. Wheeling around Stanley Park on the seawall, Noah finds the scenery so enthralling that they put a GoPro camera on their helmet and livestream the view as it unfolds to their colleagues, friends, and families around the world. Noah marvels at the cluster of tankers, bulk carriers, and containerships in the bay waiting for their cargo to arrive before docking at terminals. It reminds Noah of the entire globe. When a beautiful beach full of sunbathers presents itself with no dock station around, Noah wishes they were in Seattle where you can leave your public bike (just about) anywhere (not on ferries) but then remembers Mobi comes with a cable lock for making short stops. A short stopover becomes an unexpectedly longer one when, on the beach wielding their work iPad with a data plan, Noah decides to finish off a side project they were working on, drawing creative inspiration from an oceanic mountain backdrop. Disembarking again, Noah suddenly recalls Mobi's overage fees (five dollars every additional half hour), but it does not cause them too much worry.

Back in the city Noah happens upon Hastings Street and the Downtown Eastside (DTES), crossing the point where urban luxury suddenly turns into street homelessness, a higher police presence, and ambulances that remind Noah that Vancouver is mired in an opioid crisis. They are of different minds about the DTES. At first they feel awkward, fearful, and a little angry or ashamed that the police have not done more to clean up the area. However, as Noah, fortified after a wine bar, spends a little more time in the DTES actually chatting with a few people in the laneways about their lives, their feelings grow both more complicated and more sympathetic. Feeling peckish they flow into Chinatown where Noah finds a suitable cocktail bar with pleasing small plates, whose ambience incorporates traditional Chinese medicine with apothecary mixologists and titillating burlesque. Emerging from the dark bar Noah takes a couple tries at punching in their user code, before looking across the street. They see the Chinatown Memorial Monument beside an empty, fenced-off parking lot. Walking over to read a municipal notice on the fence, they discover the controversial new condo development people in the bar were just taking about. Noah thinks probably anything is better than an empty parking lot and wonders why the developers cannot compromise and make a deal with the city and the neighborhood over what to build.

Riding out of Chinatown through Andy Livingstone Park, Noah watches the bright afternoon sun dance along the top of Yaletown's condo towers as people play soccer, shoot heroin, walk their dogs, and cart their worldly belongings all in the same bewildering space. The recurring rumble of a SkyTrain streaking by draws their attention to the Georgia Street Viaducts (see photo 30), where automobiles stream above the trains into the inner city. Why would Vancouver, thinks Noah, where money sprouts not from hydrocarbons in the ground but from buildings on top of it, have built such a noisy, unsightly highway in the sky for the automobile? The land around it has gone to waste. Imagine how much more money the city, developers, local businesses, and job creators could make and further invest if this wasteland were something else. Such imaginings float away from Noah's mind as they finally make their way back to Pacific Rim Fairmont. They smile with excitement about tomorrow.

Against Neoliberal Urbanism: Market Mobility Futures

This chapter on market mobilities focuses on different kinds of bike share schemes and divergent forms of neoliberal urbanism that show the multiplicity of ways in which cities and developers are commodifying cycling and generating cycling capital. Given the explosive growth of the global bike share industry and heady urban redevelopment of the "inner global city," the market potential for city cycling, in terms of short-term profits, has never looked brighter. In many cities cycling has become a potent symbol for lucrative gentrification, festooning the "planning porn" and promotional images published by cities and developers.

However, the very same urban developments, placed in historical and comparative context, emit signals of an increasingly opaque cycling market. In a sclerotic marketplace, cycling capital is hoarded by kinetically privileged cycling globals (Elliott and Urry 2010) who champion the new connexionist spirit of capitalism (Boltanski and Chiapello 2005[1999]) and can afford to buy space and time (and feel like they belong) in luxury urban environments. In any moral assemblage of mobility predicated on the common good, persons at

30. Georgia Street viaducts, Vancouver. Photo by author.

lower states of worth must have the opportunity to hustle and access higher states of worth, and vice versa—people of high worth cannot be immune from losing it. More than any other moral assemblage of cycling, markets under political and urban conditions of neoliberalism (Peck 2010; Walks 2009; Harvey 2005) show a creeping rigidity and lack of mobility between states of worth. Through growing monopoly and inequality, the cycling marketplace not only grows unmoored from the Fordist organization of industrial capitalism but also increasingly fails to maintain the free competition that encapsulates good markets.

Neoliberal market assemblages of cycling are neither ubiquitous nor inevitable. Their strongest coalescence in Canada occurs within the centers of the nation's global metropolises (Toronto, Vancouver, and Montréal), where the financialization and "high tech-ification" of urban redevelopment and gentrification compound market winnings and losses to stratospheric new peaks and valleys. Given the rapid growth and densification of Canada's largest cities, however, which expect millions of migrants to join them in the coming decades, it is possible these places provide bellwethers of more dramatic changes to come for cycling. Therefore these urban meccas will offer seminal testing grounds for whether market assemblages of cycling can learn and diverge from the car's history of monopolies, bankruptcies, externalization of social and climate costs, and ongoing "market fixes" through digital technology and big data. Another key test: Can cycling's marketization avoid the kind of political and cultural sclerosis created by the car's close relationship with conservative suburbs and exurbs whose values and votes oppose that of central cities, or will it simply exacerbate city-suburb fractures further by feeding new downtown brands of neoliberal urbanism? To save (still very much emerging) cycling markets from themselves, cycling businesses, their public regulators, and transport planners should, *inter alia*, invest in relatively equitable public-private partnerships for bike share (e.g., Detroit's system) that unite rather than divide central cities and suburbs, and regulate hot cycling and housing markets to maintain fair competition and access while protecting smart cities and citizens' proprietary rights to their own data.

Despite political push back from Canada's suburban forces of pro-car populism, cycling's neoliberal market expansion into the inner global city already carries enormous moral weight in defining cycling's worth. This is obviously not just a market problem. As the market world of cycling grows hegemonic, it undercuts Adam Smith's fair marketplace while also eroding other common goods or ways of making cycling worthy through a higher calling for humanity. In the individualizing, hyper-competitive world of neoliberal market assemblages of cycling, there is no such thing as a "cycling society," no time to "commit cycling sociology." Nor is there much time for protecting the larger, more-than-human environment, even as climate change poses an existential crisis for humans and other species of life on earth. If the externalization of costs associated with the degradation of nonhuman environments around the world constitutes the largest failure of markets (Stern 2006), ultimately the health of cycling markets (and every other anthropocentric assemblage of cycling) depends on an ecological reckoning.

31. Mike cycles through Leslie Spit, downtown Toronto, Ontario. Photo by author.

5. Ecological Mobilities

Enacting Nature through Cycling

What makes mobilities ecologically good? What makes a bike lane good for "cycling nature"? What ecological lessons might cycling take from driving? These questions invite no easy answers. Relative to other moral assemblages of mobility, ecological mobilities have only just begun to transform the ways in which human and nonhuman beings live together. Politically, ecological worth takes us beyond the pale of anthropocentric traditions, industrial systems, global markets, and social citizenships. Political ecology rests on the extension of moral worth to nonhuman beings and nonhuman environments, with wide-ranging debate over what sorts of entities deserve ecological worth and how this worth can be "put to the test" (Latour 1998; Lamont and Thévenot 2000). As the limited electoral success of green parties attests, ecology faces tremendous difficulty infiltrating popular politics.[1] Based on complex associations across multiple time-space scales, ecological problems such as climate change and global habitat degradation generally fail to penetrate the realm of personal concern. At the same time, where ecological judgments do gain widespread political traction, it is often in combination with other, more conventional moral evaluations (Lamont and Thévenot 2000; Latour 1998). Indeed from carbon markets and battles over whale hunts to new forms of urban sustainability, a thick cloud of uncertainty surrounds "how actors may credibly test green worth" (Blok 2013, 494).

Compounding the political uncertainty surrounding ecology, on a practical level it is unclear how people bring ecological worth into their everyday, lived mobilities. It appears that many people engage in sustainable practices, including cycling, for reasons other than ecology. To me this came as a surprise early during my research in Vancouver, Canada, where cycle tracks reach into world-renowned urban wilderness parks (Kheraj 2013). Surely in Vancouver, a city known both for wild nature and urban sustainability, many people would be motivated to cycle for the environment! On the contrary: Vancouverites appear to cycle mainly because it is easy to do so. They resemble people elsewhere, including places where mass cycling is successful. As Denmark states on its official website:

> While many guests in the Danish capital seem to think that Copenhageners must be really concerned with the environment since so many use a bike, it's just not the reason why Copenhageners ride. Many Copenhageners are of course focused on environmental issues but, when asked, only 1 per cent of Copenhageners mention it as the main reason. Cycling is the preferred means of transport because it's the quickest and easiest way to get around town. (Danish Government 2017)

That cyclists focus on convenience shows that the intentions behind why people choose to cycle, by themselves, are not likely to yield significant ecological insights. This focus also shows the limits of neoliberal transport policies that help consumers use market signals to make better choices. A much broader lens is needed to understand how in practice cycling can animate an ecological common good.

Enacting Nature

To illuminate ecological mobilities, I explore not why people choose to cycle but how, and with what infrastructures, when they engage in "cycling nature." In the absence of standardized political tests of ecological worth, or "conventional co-ordinating devices" (Thévenot 2002, 14) for making equivalence between disparate ecological entities, ecology rarely prevails over formal political judgments of cycling (although see Chihyung 2016; Canadian Parks and Wilderness Society [CPAWS] 2017). I contend that ecological mobilities emerge, however, through the everyday judgment, social practice, and infrastructuring of nature, wherein tidy divisions between the "social" and "natural" dissolve. Through sensuous urban entanglements of social and natural entities, or "everyday environmentalism" (Loftus 2012), people develop and mobilize a moral sense of nature. My data suggest that many people, even if they do not cycle for ecology or the environment per se, say they cycle to (or with) nature they judge to be good, even in the city, often with assistance from commuter infrastructure. The quantity of this broad sort of cycling nature grows immensely once dominant representations of nature—pristine, undisturbed spaces set apart from human culture and activity—are set aside in favor of ecologically valuable models of practice and infrastructure that cultivate attention to nonhuman beings. My analysis will not judge which specific nonhuman beings and environs are the most deserving of ecological worth.[2] Rather than rush to define the one right way of judging ecology, I provisionally attribute ecological worth to a mundane yet nimble, multi-sensorial mode of enacting and infrastructuring nature on the move with, rather than at the expense of, some rather ordinary nonhuman beings (e.g., rivers, trees, fish, and birds).

Following nature as an ongoing enactment brings ecological mobilities slowly into focus through many piecemeal associations between humans and nonhumans in the weeds of everyday life. As Anders Blok warns (2013, 506), apprehensions of "the novel ecological order of worth" (Latour 1998; Thévenot 2002) are premature: contemporary environmental controversies show that "there are not one but several common ecological worlds." A slower approach to the politics of ecology grounded in the day-to-day experience of enacting nature is needed to follow the emergence of ecological plurality. This approach destabilizes, however, what is often seen as "nature." Neither a set of fixed traits nor simply a sociocultural construct, nature as enactment relies on performative and cultural effort (Cronon 1996) but also the transformative agency of nonhuman actors and infrastructures (Mol 2002; Lund 2013). Focusing on the enactment and by material extension the infrastructuring of nature in the city builds on everyday environmentalism (Loftus 2012). It also reveals a slower approach to enacting nature grounded in the experience of cycling—inspired, in part, by that of driving—which emboldens ecology under the guise of an urban Gaia (Latour 2017). In places such as Canada ecological judgments of mobilities too often ignore the city and quickly cast new cycling infrastructure in a negative light.[3] More generally, cosmopolitan urban ecology is underexplored and latent with possibility (Gandy 2013). All this boils down to a simple practical question: Positively speaking, how does a good bike lane for nature in the city come about? More provocatively, what happens if we raise the bar for "nature" all the way to "wilderness"?

Cycling nature confirms that even the wildest nature, wilderness, is assembled and transformed by human practice and intervention, and can usually be found wherever people say they find it (Vannini and Vannini 2016). Both the city and the production of urban space (Lefebvre 1991) offer a powerful "critical case study" (Flyvbjerg 2006) of wilderness: as a place where people least expect to find it, the city acts as a black swan for wilderness. For example, even Phillip and April Vannini, who cast a wide "ecumenical" net, argue wilderness "can potentially unfold in any number of different wild places, from protected areas to the bush just outside of town" (2016, 24). Taking wilderness *into* town, I flesh out the idea of "wilderness mobilities" in the next section as a conceptual tool for analyzing cycling nature in a habitat assembled for cycling. A unique ecological assemblage of mobilities that ushers wild nature into everyday life, wilderness mobilities confront persistent and widely held notions of urbanity as that which is not wild (Haupt 2013). Drawing on ecologically qualified infrastructures (public passageways constructed to bring people to nature), wilderness mobilities trace ways of cycling that connect everyday ecology to dreams, adventure, play, and the historical technique of "driving nature." Ultimately what makes mobilities good, ecologically speaking, is the cultivation of wilder natures wherein people pay closer attention to nonhuman beings as worthy ends unto themselves.

Wilderness Mobilities

When a child left to their own devices enters the woods, sometimes the woods make off with their entire imagination. For example, one summer during early 1990s suburbia in Nova Scotia, when I was ten, three friends and I were climbing trees on the edge of the woods. That's when we spotted a rope, unfathomably large, lying half coiled inside an industrial yard at the bottom of a long, steep hill like some dinosaur snake. By our estimation it could tow and lift an entire city. Over a few days we devised a plan, and throughout that July we executed "Rope City." Every day we rose before dawn, biked to the woods, scrambled down a rocky hill, and hopped a fence into the snake pit. Yard by painstaking yard, we dragged that rope. Under the chain-link fence, we dragged. Up the rocky hill, in plain view, we dragged. Deeper into the woods, we dragged. And at long last, gazing hungrily up into a deciduous canopy, we lifted, exploiting counterweights, spikes, and younger siblings. After absconding uphill into the woods with an impossibly large rope using eight hands and eight feet, we threaded the dinosaur snake over thicker branches near the tops of large trees, creating what we imagined to be a new kind of city in a forest. Rope City came about tenuously through adventure and play with enchanted objects in a wild "wasteland" (Gandy 2013), an "edge space" shot through with traces of human waste and multiple ways of (de)valuing things. Looking back at it now I see a grainy synecdoche for an ecological city wherein nature comes alive as a wild, unfamiliar world that is both like a city and not like a city at all.

You might have a childhood memory like this, too, if you went unfettered into the woods, or some other wild at the edge of your world; if you do, now it may seem like a dream. Dreams tamper with relations between objects, time, and space. As a result they fall away in ordinary life pretty abruptly. As Georg Simmel once abruptly put it, "Everyone knows how quickly we forget dreams because they are placed outside the meaningful context of life-as-a-whole" (1998[1895], 222). At the same time, dreams dabble in reality making. They may begin with the most familiar, banal things—brushing your teeth, driving your car, eating

Corn Flakes or Cheerios—before turning unfamiliar and strange—
teeth fall out on the floor, cars defy physics, and the next grocery aisle
over is a fjord where you sense the presence of ancient whales. In this
world-bending activity, dreams share an important quality with adventure. Both challenge the physical realities from which they derive and
depart. Simmel described adventure in the wild alpine, for example,
as a momentary "dropping out of the continuity of life" that inevitably
"takes on the quality of a dream" (Simmel 1998[1895], 222). To be sure,
dreams of adventure, when co-opted by elite mobilities (Birchnell
and Caletrio 2013) and wrapped up in escapist fantasies of the wild
(Sheller 2007), undermine, reify, and socially stratify the very nonhuman environments to which they aspire. At the same time, dreams and
adventures carry the potential to feed and inspire novel, artful ways
of moving with nature, not as an adventure "getaway" bent on leaving
urban coexistence behind, but as a way of embracing city wilderness.

Think of wilderness mobilities less as epic vehicular voyaging to
virginal nature aided by all manner of adventure travel and ecotourism
agencies (Braun 2002), and more as banal, temporary tripping into
more-than-human time-space askew from life-as-a-whole. Less a place
of escape than a playful mode of attention or banal utopianism (Gardiner 2004), wilderness mobilities stretch human kinaesthetic engagements beyond anthropocentric life into wider webs with nonhumans,
such as trees and coyotes (Fusselman 2015), that creep deep into cities.
Donna Haraway (2016, 23–24) nods to the ecological importance of
play: "Perhaps it is precisely in the realm of play, outside the dictates
of . . . settled categories, and function, that serious worldliness and
recuperation become possible." For a non-transport example, compare a typically sterile, injury-proof playground in North America to
Savage Park in the middle of Tokyo (Fusselman 2015). At Savage Park,
like Rope City, children play with fire, jump out of trees, and mangle
strange, out-of-place objects into temporary habitats using enchanted
tools they personify. Watching her kids play at Savage Park, Amy Fusselman marvels at "how hungry my boys always seem in their play
for moments when their actions could take on real gravity" (2015, 18).

Central to wilderness mobilities, "workful-play" combines instrumental elements of planned action (build a treehouse) with playful movements that neither make money nor optimize infrastructure (leap out of it!) so much as expose and map a person's practice onto more-than-human habitat (urban wild). Rewilding the city, however, will take more than injecting a little loosely supervised chaos into parks.

Driving Lessons

Imagine yourself in the summer of 1909 at the wheel of a Ford Model T, careening down a tree-lined parkway at fifteen miles per hour in early twentieth-century Buffalo. Parkways, introduced here in North America during the 1890s by Frederick Law Olmsted, convey you to water, trees, and wildlife. Unlike the linear freeway or circular cul-de-sac, the parkway allows you to engage in curvilinear car driving along winding waterways (a largely forgotten kind of automobile habitat). These "park roads" (Scott 2012) cultivate a particular mode of attention and embodied technique of mobility (Mauss 1973). With minimal signage and few trucks and traffic stops, while driving you can contemplate, and take pleasure in, the beauty of nature along landscaped vistas. Park roads develop your car driving skills—eyes on road ahead, hands touching wheel, feet traversing pedals. But on the park road, you drive slowly around the bend, soak in biodiverse surroundings, and become attuned and connected with water—if only for a fleeting moment.

The park road, preconceived and planned, is critical to the active infrastructuring (Star 1999) of nature through "pleasure driving." Its unusual curves, vistas, and waterfront access facilitate a workful-playful mode of automobility.

In postwar practice, parkways for driving fell victim over time to utilitarian modifications and faster, more violent automobility, showing the limits (and expiry date) of the best-laid city plans and park road ideals (Scott 2012). However, the idea and early execution of park roads, I propose, augur compelling possibilities for wilderness mobilities, even mass cycling habitats wherein ecological mobilities thrive outside the functionalist walls erected by mid-twentieth-century transport engineering and modernist infrastructure (see chapter 2).[4] What makes the early twentieth-century parkway more inspiring for assembling such habitat in the twenty-first century than, say, the Trans-Canada Highway or even the new Trans-Canada "Great Trail," a 24,000-kilometer (15,000-mile) multiuse trail system that spans the country—even though both were (and continue to be) designed to afford mobilities through wilderness—is simple: parkways explicitly reassembled cities. With one of the highest urban concentrations of people among advanced economies—82 percent of Canadians live in large or middle-sized cities (Statistics Canada 2017a)—the majority of people in Canada currently reside in spatial conditions ripe for transformation into cycling habitat.

In what follows I analyze the assembling of ecological mobilities by everyday cycling over three crescendoing acts. In each act I shadow people cycling as they make their way into robust cycling habitat on ecologically qualified infrastructure.[5] Together the three acts show, with the aid of stills from video data, how cycling enacts nature through playful techniques of mobility, banal adventure, and ecological infrastructure that animate wilderness mobilities. They also reveal salient points of moral friction between ecological and other moral assemblages of mobility, especially civic mobilities. Act I follows Marilyn cycling nature in Ottawa, whose National Capital Pathways materialize wilderness mobilities as a prominent and visible part of capital urban culture. Act II dips into Toronto's underworld, wherein Mike enacts a less visible nature across a vibrant postindustrial "wasteland." And Act III moves far stage left into Finnish cycling territory, following Ansa and Inari, to show what happens when ecology's moral equipment fortifies the bones of the city and cultivates its growth as a whole. By curtain fall these three acts illustrate how cycling nature, more forcefully than driving it, assembles an ecologically good means of living together.

Enacting Nature through Cycling

Act I. Capital Pathways: Perfect Chaos

After stuffing a blanket, beer, and a book into her backpack, Marilyn signals toward the Ottawa River. Tying together English, French, and

Algonquian nations, the Ottawa River tugs her toward wild nature. Some objects for this voyage differ from those she takes with her while cycling to work, but the basic equipment remains the same: helmet, packed lunch, sunglasses, and her ten-year-old hybrid bicycle. Unlike cycling to her workplace, to which she always prefers the most efficient route, for the river she's quick to say, "There are different ways to get there." The intimate knowledge of the way her old bike handles the ground immediately shows. Act I begins in a standstill, then Marilyn starts rolling slowly around her house up a slant, like a tightrope walker, weaving around piles of gravel and furniture in the driveway of someone who obviously does not own a car. Marilyn cycles out of her driveway appearing relaxed, as if she were enjoying island time, or time that moves slower than usual.

Island time shatters at the end of the block, as Marilyn approaches what she calls "Scary Scott Street," a four-lane arterial road notorious for speeding motorists, near Ottawa's urban core. She says later, "I would probably do this [turn left on Scott] on a weekend. It's Friday, so it's a little different. It's not that hard to cross Scott Street on a weekend. Cars think they own this street." After a school bus blazes by, without hesitation Marilyn floats into the street, head looking right, bike moving left, exploiting a small gap in traffic in the forelane before shooting forward again through a gap emerging in the far lane. She "talks" to speechless motor vehicles with her body. Scott Street talks to her in a way, too, with its painted bike lane and procession of miniature plastic kids on lawns meant to ward off dangerous drivers. The bike lane does little to soothe cyclists when motorists blow by at seventy kilometers (forty-five miles) per hour, even stoic cyclists like Marilyn. She says, "It's the most direct route to work, so I usually take it to work instead of the river [pathway]. But I'm going to see how many more minutes it is along the river. . . . I'm very brave to be on Scott Street. Many people are avoiding it, and maybe I should too."

Scott Street exemplifies modern car-driving habitat, where self-conscious, safe cyclists feel compelled to plan and execute their movements carefully, with a keen sense of situational awareness, intentional

32. Marilyn traverses "Scary Scott Street" in Ottawa. Photo by author.

agency, visual conspicuity, and individual responsibility. The material objects Marilyn relies on to safely negotiate car habitat—the painted bike lane, her helmet, the bicycle itself—are stripped to their core functions as linear instruments for getting from point A to point B. Painted bike lanes also hint at the presence of cycling habitat, although a thin one Marilyn is happy to quickly traverse (see photo 32). This part of the voyage shows how cycling nature, as a whole trip, unfolds in part through geometric channels used primarily as a means to an end, where humans and nonhumans (e.g., raccoons) know well not to linger.

After darting along Scott Street, Marilyn turns north onto familiar side streets, where traffic slows and functional rules of the street relax. Her biking body's intimate knowledge of the side streets is on display as she playfully skirts potholes and cracks. Not yet removed from an ocean of motor noise, but slipping deeper into cycling territory, familiar streets embed Marilyn's person—her body, her memories, and mental maps—deeper into the diversity of her surroundings, which now, she later describes, begin to open up and expand through sounds, smells, and emotions. Marilyn rounds a corner by a playground and hears some kids playing. I hear the shrill cries of children debating. Marilyn listens and says she recalls a place she knows well, a place that ushers her on toward the river.

Moments later Marilyn reaches the end of a cul-de-sac and takes off. She sails through a narrow chain-link channel and enters a protected cycling habitat called the National Capital Pathway system. Capital Pathways are planned landscapes of mobilities that afford access to relatively spontaneous forms of nature along waterways. Technically they are multiuse pathways separated from car traffic and built along rivers, canals, and other natural areas across Ottawa in the 1970s. Today, after much expansion, they span more than 600 kilometers (373 miles) across the region.⁶ Originally these shared multiuse pathways were designed for recreation and connecting people with nature in the city. Many run parallel to parkways that were built for this purpose with car driving in mind. However, some residents began using Capital Pathways to try utility cycling and commuting, as these routes can be efficient, and today Capital Pathways support eclectic mixtures of playful-purposeful-nature biking. As if on the verge of something exciting, Marilyn's pace quickens when she spots the river through the trees up ahead.

After riding seamlessly under a line of cars driving overhead along a parkway overpass, Marilyn turns a corner onto the Ottawa River Pathway, joining a loose parade of, *inter alia*, pedestrians, cyclists, inline skaters, dogs, birds, insects, and fuzzy pollen grains finding their way along the river. Later Marilyn elaborates why she's thinking of switching from Scott Street to the Pathway for commuting, even though it might add five to ten minutes to her journey (not insignificant for someone who typically runs late and prefers to bike as the crow flies). When I ask why, she says, "Nature. It's very therapeutic to see the water and the trees and beautiful views of Ottawa." Though Marilyn is loath to give up her pace, her biking here soon changes. Carving a neat curvilinear path around bird-watchers, baby strollers, and some incorrigible geese, Marilyn says she's listening for people, wind, trees, birds, and water. When she meets and briefly acknowledges the non-humans, they become more like companions rather than instruments for her cycling. The river wilderness pathway helps Marilyn become acquainted with and concerned for the life in her vicinity.

Some will no doubt question the depth of nature Marilyn enacts so quickly on an orderly path in a major metropolis designed to invite a diversity of differently abled persons-without-cars to move along with the river. For example, while Simmel (1998[1895], 219) acknowledged the civic worth of railways built into the Alps that led to a "wholesale opening-up of and enjoyment of nature"—because "countless people who previously were barred because of their strength and means are now able to enjoy nature"—he also lamented that the "lure of the ease of an open road, and the concentration and convergence of the masses" lead to "an average sensibility" of nature, one that may be more "egoistic" than "educative." This begs the question: What creates a "heightened" sense of the wild? Even Simmel (1998[1895], 222) admits he "disagrees with that foolish romanticism which saw difficult routes, prehistoric food and hard beds as an irremovable part of the stimulus of the good old days of alpine travel." Marilyn's not scaling the Alps, but her cycling can be interpreted as a sophisticated enactment of wilderness. Her cycling shows how play mobilized as serious action temporarily pulls her away from the banal flow of life-as-a-whole into making associations with nonhumans. The embedding of her ecological, slightly reckless way of cycling within the materials of Ottawa's Capital Pathways makes it more significant, mobilizing its repeated practice through hard infrastructure.

At last Marilyn finds what she was cycling for. Act I comes to a close as she veers off the pathway down a hill, dismounting elegantly while still riding, waiting to step off the pedal until the last second before she strolls across a sandy beach. From the second Marilyn sailed through a chain-link channel into the urban wild, time and space were reassembled into an ecological endeavor. That she broke off into a different, wilder nature was confirmed by the sound of it. Turning off the car grid cut the incessant motorized noise and asphalt-rubber friction that blankets automobile habitat like a vast sonic glacier. Sitting and listening expansively by the river, Marilyn casts her attention to a broad, biodiverse cast of living beings.

As we talk later, higher above the Ottawa River in Major's Hill Park, Marilyn tells me cycling is not the only way for her to experience nature in the city. Sometimes, she says, cycling "feels too fast" and she prefers walking with nature. This prompts me to ask her if there is a nature connection between her cycling and walking. Does walking nature help Marilyn cycle nature, and vice versa? She says,

> I'm a pretty good pedestrian and cyclist. . . . Yeah, I think it does. Especially, around a lot of that, kind of, chaos, but perfect chaos or something? Like in Barcelona? With all the cyclists, runners, regular pedestrians, skateboarders, and cars I guess . . . that's kind of like here along the pathway.

Marilyn calibrates her cycling with slower ways of enacting nature. So what at first seems like unruly entanglements between wilderness and built infrastructure, multiuse pathways and incorrigible Canadian geese, upon closer inspection turns into a "perfect chaos," a marvelous mess on the brink of order and disorder. Down by the river the risk of violence is much lower than that of "Scary Scott Street," but not low enough to discourage cycling that, like children playing at Savage Park, takes on real gravity.

Act II. River Valley Trails: You Have No Idea What the Ravines Are until You're in Them

Meanwhile 450 car-driving kilometers (280 miles) southwest of Canada's capital in the middle of the nation's largest city, Toronto, Mike reassembles bicycle parts into a vehicle made for handling nature. He owns more than three bikes, but less than four, and takes them apart and puts them back together again according to the type of voyage he imagines. As I mentioned in the book's introduction, for nature Mike prefers a fixed gear. It might take a little more work to ride, because he can never stop pedaling. But in wild environments like Toronto's Don Valley, Mike places a premium on the "extra feel" or more intimate, embodied technique he attributes to riding a fixed-gear bicycle, and his tinkering shows a dynamic process of attunement. He carefully recalibrates his bike to create a way of feeling out his wider environment. In turn the change in bicycle recalibrates Mike; how he moves when he cycles, how he pays attention and to whom.

Mike cycles nature in a starkly different context than Marilyn. Ottawa's Capital Pathways—parkways for cycling—enjoy iconic status in "the nation's city." They play a visible and celebrated role in a political production of space (Lefebvre 1991) carefully planned to extol wilderness as a Canadian value alongside Ottawa's parks, greenbelt, parkways, and north-gesturing neo-Gothic parliamentary architecture (Di Leo Browne 2016). By contrast much of Toronto's wilderness, including its River Valley Trails, lies underground, obscured underneath the city's flat concrete crust. These still-evolving trails show "infrastructures as dynamic relational forms" (Harvey and Knox 2015) that vertically challenge planar notions of the city (Graham 2016) through easy-to-miss subterranean networks (Starosielski 2015). As Mike puts it, "Most people don't really know its river ravine systems are there." Act II begins behind Mike's apartment in Regent Park, a 1940s mixed-income social housing project and gentrifying neighborhood in downtown Toronto. Act II ends in murky river water at the bottom of a ravine in a valley that was nearly destroyed by industry, sprawl, and a superhighway called the Don Valley Parkway (a parkway in name only). In spite of these different contexts, Act II picks up and carries important threads from Act I. Like Marilyn, Mike rides with a sense of adventure from the concrete heart of the city into the urban wild, activating planned infrastructures that embed workful-play in a passage that temporarily trains his attention to nonhuman beings.

After Googling detours in a city always under reconstruction, Mike takes his saddle and gets rolling. A slow sense of Saturday ease he enjoyed in his backyard shatters as fast as Marilyn's island time. After leaving his driveway Mike pours into a heavy intersection at Parliament and Dundas Streets, slowing down using backward pressure with his legs rather than a hand break. His fixie generates speed and slowness differently than Marilyn's free-wheeler. He is quick to slow and loath to stop, even in the thick of modern car habitat. Putting toes down on the ground, for Mike, means rupturing a continuous, pleasurable process of flow, a flow for which he constantly alters his pace (making my shadowing complicated). He shoots ahead then slinks along. He cranks his handlebars to increase his angle with streetcar tracks before safely sliding across their crevice. Without much room to maneuver, Mike swerves like a sidewinder to negotiate the bustling street and take his space (see photo 33). Like Marilyn, in car habitat Mike enters spaces that always seem to be already unfolded around his bicycle-body. He dodges buses, streetcars, spontaneous jaywalkers, swarms of cabs, diesel-belching trucks, and predictable pedestrians walking many lines. The entire time riding up Parliament, Mike's toes stay inside their pedal cages. Improbably, given the sea of floating objects and crosscurrents, he holds on to his own flow.

The enactment of nature through cycling, like that of motorcar driving on a parkway, entails a particular embodied technique. Marcel Mauss (1973) observed that techniques of the body, while ingrained, can change completely across generations. Take swimming, he says: "The habit of swallowing water and spitting it out again has gone. In my day swimmers thought of themselves as a kind of steam-boat" (1973, 71). Despite generational shifts, techniques enter "every attitude of the body" and resist personal change. Of swimming like a steamboat, Mauss observes, "It was stupid, but in fact I still do this: I cannot get rid of my technique" (1973, 71). This interplay of change and stability in habits impacts the growth of ecological mobilities. Cycling expansion depends both on new generations rejecting the car and people transitioning their own lives from driving to cycling. Additionally ecological cycling depends on people who already cycle learning to ride with the nonhuman environment rather than against it.

33. Mike cycles up Parliament Street, Toronto. Photo by author.

At first Mike's cycling technique emphasizes work over play. Like dance performers he defers to dominant rules and rhythms that time and space his flow; he alters his speed before reaching stop lines, drifting behind idle cars instead of always squeezing by them. A little more subversively, when traffic freezes at intersections he floats glacially into forbidden space, smoothing the edges around stops and starts just as the lights turn, as if to gently question their delegated authority. Like Mauss's swimming, Mike's cycling is sewn into his muscle memory. He says, laughing, "What's my technique like? It's masterful. Nah, I don't think a lot about my technique." And yet Mike's technique has changed over three decades. He once prioritized high speed, fighting to keep it, burning red lights and running stop signs. He says, "My usual way of biking used to be go 100% all the time, and exhaust yourself." But after getting doored on Parliament Street, ticketed for running a red light, and encountering aggressive motorists in Toronto "who hate cyclists," Mike took pains to adjust his technique. Now, "I go steady and pretty conservative. I'm just trying to make it a bit slower and actually enjoy it, then I'm much more likely to do it. It's not just a work-out." Still Mike's old habits creep up on him. Eyeing an opening in traffic, he suddenly rips into the middle of Parliament Street, carving a fast arc into a familiar neighborhood called Cabbagetown. He cannot get rid of his technique.

On a slow, familiar side street leading to the river, Mike's cycling opens up to his surroundings. Feeling easy he swings around manhole covers then swerves again, right off the car grid into a park. Unlike Marilyn's seamless tunnel, at the liminal gates of nature Mike negotiates a cricket match, shifting constellations of dog-human companions, and finally stairs. These stairs create a notable point of moral friction between ecological and civic mobilities. They question the social design of ecological cycling infrastructures, asking who and what kinds of bodies gain access. Furthermore these stairs raise a political trouble directly for ecology: Into exactly what sort of nature is Mike descending? While portaging Mike surveys a tight bundle of modern mobility channels, whose leakage undermines the health of the river and the ravine around it (from right to left in photo 34). Mike spies an arterial road; a rail corridor; the River Valley Trail (newest right-of-way); a perfectly linear stretch of the Don River; and the Don Valley Parkway. The river was twisted and channeled into a linear instrument by engineers in the 1880s to expand and rationalize its flow for markets, industry, and high-speed rights-of-way. Bombarded by waves of "technological progress" and haunted by diluted industrial contamination, this riparian stretch of edge space, like Rope City, traces a prolific urban wasteland (Gandy 2013).

Flirting with high speed, Mike starts along the River Valley Trail and just as he turns a corner runs into a cluster of oncoming cyclists (see photo 35). An oncoming speeding racer suddenly disturbs the pack, a rude weekend warrior at whom a woman riding a rental from Bike Share Toronto scowls. As trails become more accessible, mixing different styles and skills, work and play, they help ameliorate some ecological-civic frictions, like social exclusion, while exacerbating others, such as

34. Mike portages down to the river. Photo by author.

incivility (Elias 2000). Ecological cycling, to an extent, hangs on this civic complexity. As ever more people engage in cycling nature, they may share space for cultivating non-instrumental associations with nonhuman beings, or just co-opt nature for themselves.

A thin moral edge between ecological and civic mobilities presses into Mike's cycling again, moments later up the River Valley Trail under a large bridge. A mural-in-the-making catches his attention. Mike pulls over and the artist beckons, explaining how the city government turned the River Valley Trail into a larger "Pan Am Path," a civic legacy project for the 2015 Pan American Games held in Toronto. The Pan Am Path is billed as "an 85-kilometre effort to unearth and enliven Toronto's ravine underworld" (Merringer 2015). It makes nature more accessible by inviting persons without cars to use and reimagine biodiverse places like the Don River Valley. It simultaneously enrolls the river's "improvement"—wherein something "more could be made of the ravines that snake through Toronto" (Merringer 2015)—into a

35. Mike negotiates other cyclists. Photo by author.

civic world in which equitable rights of passage and solidarities generally exclude nonhuman beings.

The mural on the trail raises more ecological trouble: What makes nature beautiful, adventurous, and artful anyway? The wasteland offers a clue. For Mike it is has something to do with the sumac trees. I watch as they call his attention. Saying good-bye to the civic artist, he heads uphill and pauses by the bellowing, leaky superhighway for a sumac weaving itself around a fence. Spontaneously sumacs pop up around the valley through seeds but also rhizomatic new shoots, or suckers, which over time create a complex individual. Sumac trees constitute but one prolific organism that thrives in this river ravine. Part of the art and beauty of this dynamic habitat relates to how it entwines, mimics, erodes, and is eroded by the industrial human infrastructures that were thought to have destroyed it. Once viewed as empty and devoid of life, some urban wastelands or "unreal estate" (Herscher 2012) are increasingly seen by scientists, artists, and citizens as prolific "eco-

36. Mike takes a dip in the Don River. Photo by author.

ducts," "ecological refugia," and bastions of biodiversity in the emerging "cosmopolitan ecology of cities" (Gandy 2013, 1305). For Mike, who is drawn to the eroding shorelines and ever-shifting riverbanks where traces of industrial objects shape the ravine, some wastelands in Toronto offer a compelling urban wild that challenges conventional notions of wilderness as far away, intact, and unspoiled. Here, while Mike winds carefully down into the river valley, his cycling shows how ecologically worthy wastelands can help recompose multifarious more-than-human environments.

At this moment "a workable aesthetic theory of urban nature that moves beyond neo-romanticist antinomies and the ontological strictures of the bounded human subject" (Gandy 2013, 1303) is not on Mike's mind, although he is highly aware of his self as being interconnected with nonhuman life. At the bottom of the ravine his dusty wheels want to take a dip in the river (see photo 36). Like Marilyn, Mike says something about water and how its surrounding life pulls him into the wild. Sometimes he detours through the River Valley Trail on his way to work, combining work with play and nature through cycling.

Act III: Pyörätie: You Don't Have to Think Where to Do That

Meanwhile 6,314 kilometers (3,923 miles), as the crow flies, northeast of Toronto in downtown Oulu, Finland, Ansa laughs at me and dances away dramatically on her bike when I say, "Just bike naturally!" The whole question of "cycling nature"—or cycling at all, as something to be treated separately for analysis—strikes her as odd. The reason is, no one in Oulu hangs their identity on cycling:

> Everyone here uses bikes, so it's not like somewhere else where riding a bike is more like a hobby. Here it's just normal, like walking, everyone has one. You get a bike when you're three, four . . . five or six. So people are not wearing tights, and they don't have the fancy bikes. They actually use the bike to get from point A to point B. Like today, I've been going to work, and back home, and then to dance practice, and then out here . . . so, I'm using it to get around. (Interview 2015)

Similarly, Inari, another young woman from Oulu, stares at me blankly after I ask her to describe how she chooses when and where to cycle, and how she bikes to nature. It's not like Helsinki, she says, where cars, limited infrastructure, and a lack of familiarity ("am I allowed to bike here?") compel her to seriously contemplate her cycling ahead of time. "In Oulu you don't have to think where to do that. It's so normal, I don't really think about it." Four times closer to the Arctic Circle than Helsinki in the land of the midnight sun, the city of Oulu faces its own physical challenges in expanding cycling. Yet Oulu, whose rates of cycling, summer and winter, dwarf those of cities in Canada, offers a good glimpse of ecological cycling futures.

Act III pushes cycling nature sideways, physically across the Atlantic Ocean but also politically into a different urban universe, to show how cycling might reassemble Canadian ecology. It begins in Oulu's urban core, not far from the mouth of Oulujoki (River Oulu), an ancient river crossroads like Ottawa and Toronto. It ends in Oulujoki's delta on the Hupisaaret Islands in a public city park older than Canada (Inari), and chasing the ocean sunset (Ansa). Ansa and Inari's cycling breaks off from Marilyn and Mike's in a way already illuminated: ubiquity and normalcy. In the banal, unthought-of nature of Oulu's cycling, wherein bikes stick out as much as cars in Canada, Oulu is no different than other thriving cycling cities like Copenhagen and Amsterdam. However, Oulu stands apart from larger European cycling cities as a renowned global capital of winter cycling (Babin 2014). Assisted by diligent maintenance, Oulu's high levels of cycling survive interminable subarctic nights. But winter is not the part Oulu plays here. Nor is it the only, or even principal, way in which Oulu's cycling might reimagine Canada's.

On the surface the pyörätie (cycle path) in Oulu looks similar to Toronto's River Valley Trails and Ottawa's Capital Pathways. Drawing persons-without-cars, mingling work and play, the pyörätie weaves the non-car city with more-than-human nature. Indeed Ansa and Inari, apart from taking cycling for granted, enact cycling nature in much the same way as Marilyn and Mike (albeit without the head armor). For example, Inari starts her journey downtown, spending more time navigating among differently mobile humans than nonhuman beings, with help from the odd "cycle-only" path. Looking relaxed from the get-go, Inari cycles slower than my other research participants. Yet like all the others, she never really stops. Gliding through parks, pausing at intersections, wending her way around people walking and talking, sliding through parking lots and construction sites, Inari holds on to her flow as tight as Mike did on Parliament Street in downtown Toronto. Ansa, for her part, cycles as fast as Marilyn; describing her style, she says, "in a hurry, that's my signature." Before long both Finnish women flow easily from Oulu's urban core to the waterways that define the city's wilderness.

The wind picks up off the north Baltic Sea as Ansa takes a pyörätie from the city library onto Pikisaari, or Pitch Island. Pitch takes its name from the heavy industry that dominated this shipbuilding base since the 1600s until the latest wave of artisans moved in after the 1970s. When

37. Ansa passes the owl watchers. Photo by author.

explaining the natural appeal of Pitch, with a gloaming ocean looming just over the toothy horizon, Ansa touches on the traditional value of the place and the educational worth of its new art institutions. She also reflects on her ability to notice things more generally. Ansa describes how her cycling not only transforms the way she pays attention to the things around her but also to the ways in which her surroundings themselves change. Cycling the pyörätie, she says,

> you see a lot more. You can't see nature in the same way if you're sitting in a car. On a bike you can pause, and also you get the smells, and you feel in the wind. Especially now that it's getting . . . well it should be getting warmer, but the summer *is* coming. Trees are getting greener. You notice better, when you're riding a bike. If you ride the same paths, you notice the change. Like just a few weeks back, there wasn't any green things, and then one day I'm coming home, and it's slowly getting green. I notice it. (Interview 2015, italics in the original)

While the ability of people cycling to "stop and smell the roses" is touted loudly in arguments over cycling's economic benefits (see chapter 4), given the scale of climate change and habitat degradation triggered by the Anthropocene, perhaps it is time to reemphasize those proverbial roses as ends unto themselves. One thing Ansa "notices better" while cycling to the ocean is other people cycling to watch and record owls who inhabit Oulujoki's delta on the top edge of Europe (see photo 37). The ornithological sighting points to a larger balance in Finland between civic equality and ecological integrity: an expansive "everyman's right," or public right of access to wilderness, extending to foreigners living in the country. This balance depends on limiting ecological-civic moral friction by enacting legal responsibilities *for* nature, which is: 1) usually expressed negatively as restrictions (no fishing in rapids and currents; no picking or gathering of berries and mushrooms on the endangered list); or 2) expressed more positively, cultivating what Haraway (2016) calls active human "response-ability" *to* other species. Response-ability entails facing up to profound wilderness troubles and becoming less impervious to multispecies' suffering inflicted by the Anthropocene. In a small but systematic way, Ansa's cycling helps advance human response-ability to other species. Attuning affective, vulnerable, and multi-sensorial cycling (Larsen 2014; Aldred 2013; Furness 2010; Spinney 2006) to Pitch Island increases her care and attention for a fragile nonhuman environment.

Where Ansa darted through Pitch Island due west for the ocean, Inari, cycling her own way, skirts Pitch and heads north, seamlessly switching like a train from one pyörätie to another. She hops across islands that are very slowly moving themselves, periodically crackling and popping back up into shape ever since the glaciers that once smothered them melted away. When Inari lands on Oulujoki's north shore she slows and starts quietly riding in a straight line. It almost seems like she zones out. By her description:

> If there is light wind and the sun is shining, and the speed is kind of light because [much of Oulu is] so flat, you can just do the best

you can or as hard as you can. With the velocity and the wind in your hair you can . . . think. You can think. You don't have to think too much about the biking, you can just be in your own thoughts.

Inari often thinks of nature during these quiet moments of contemplation. Because so many pyörätie, she says, create "quite peaceful" routes, "some in the middle of the forest," they equip her cycling movement with a mindfulness, a multi-sensorial sense of presence that forms another "sensory strategy" (Jungnickel and Aldred 2014) cyclists use to notice the world. Analogous to people cycling in traffic listening to music from earbuds, not to disengage from the city (as many assume) but rather to stay engaged using sonic strategies, Inari lets the more-than-human environment itself, assembled with the pyörätie, remove her ears and her mind from regular distractions. If wilderness mobilities entail a high level of noticing, their practical accomplishment also demands some level of "not noticing." Far from zoning out, Inari's meditative capacity to momentarily remove the noise of everyday life helps her attune with a nonhuman world larger than her immediate vicinity.

The ecological promise of Oulu's pyörätie lies in the spread of this prolific Finnish cycling path (an idea originally adapted from Sweden, says Oulu's cycling coordinator, Timo) into the structure or "bones" of the city. This is what distinguishes the pyörätie from the wilderness pathways explored in Acts I and II. While they all share the same basic form and came about through prescient planning, only the pyörätie became a widespread policy that transformed the city's growth. According to Timo and Jorma, Oulu's chief cycling planner, in the 1970s pyörätie were implemented at the beginning of urban development as the most direct way to travel between neighborhoods and the city center. As a result the pyörätie continues to afford the most effective way to get somewhere. The pyörätie neither qualifies as a special piece of infrastructure nor fades away in landscapes of automobility, like in Canada. By using the pyörätie to plan the city, Timo explains, Oulu was able to reach the point where not only cycling but cycling nature has always been part of routine life. You go somewhere, you take your bike. Many people have said to me, they have this moment in the day when they feel like, out of the loop, a moment for themselves to breathe and enjoy and relax for a while. And especially in Oulu, where you have cycling routes going inside the city structure using the green areas and all the parks, it can be really relaxing. (Interview 2015)

Despite having physical and policy roots in the city structure, the pyörätie still faces challenges. Timo observes "a change in generations," toward increased reliance by young people on parents for car rides as "the city sprawls." Recent weather fluctuations have wrought havoc with Oulu's formidable winter maintenance. Still, as a basic planning principle the pyörätie remains politically intact, keeping a window open into what wilderness mobilities might look like in other cities were they to cultivate and distribute their young pathways and river trails.

As Inari crosses back over the Oulujoki she nears the wild she was aiming for, which illuminates further infrastructures for ecological mobilities. Passing a line of small children standing on their toes to peer over the bridge rail—some enraptured by the river coursing through a hydroelectric power plant, others gesturing to a nearby ladder giving salmon and other fish safe passage from the sea—Inari wriggles through a stream of cyclists, tricyclists, trailers, and strollers off the bridge before rolling nonchalantly into Hupisaaret Islands City Park. The park represents what Inari first imagined when I asked if I could shadow her "cycling nature." I can see why. The 150-year-old city park covers an archipelago teeming with a multiplicity of island lives plunked down in a busy river delta. Crisscrossed by waterways and wooden bridges (and some of the city's busiest cycling routes), the park draws a biodiverse cast of humans and nonhumans into greenhouses, botanical gardens, outdoor play spaces, and wilder areas. Despite its ecological complexity Hupisaaret Islands is not a separate cloth cut from Oulu. The entire journey here, Inari never left the pyörätie, and here again lies the promise of this ecologically qualified cycling path, with its citywide activation of workful-play and regular tripping into more-than-human time-space. The pyörätie weaves together urban wilderness mobilities.

Meanwhile, as Ansa chases the ocean sunset, I watch as a smile gradually floods her face. Maybe it was the twilight hour, but of all the scenes from this foray to Finland, Ansa's emotional connection with her environment, during a rare moment of slowness akin to Inari's meditative cycling, punctuates the pleasure of becoming aware of a wider, wilder world and one's small presence within it. The rolling motion of cycling, the pyörätie, the river's delta, the ocean, and the forest, even the owls and fish, all play a role in associating Ansa expansively with her surroundings. As she nears the edge of the illuminated world, she becomes giddy. In her words, cycling consists of a lot of things, and these things are

> more exciting in nature. Like it's nice to walk there, but it[']s also cool to ride a bike there, it's a bit more dangerous [laughs] . . . it's not really dangerous, but . . . I feel like a little kid when I'm riding a bike in the forest, you know? (Interview 2015)

After the Curtain Falls: Ecological Mobility Futures

This chapter on ecological mobilities focuses on whole voyages to foreground the urban experience of cycling nature. I trace moral assemblages of ecology that follow people cycling in places they themselves judge to be ecologically good, and show how quotidian cycling practices enact nature in the city. Crucial to this urban enactment is the infrastructuring of nature, which unfolds as an ongoing contested and everyday process across ecologically qualified pathways and wilderness trails. These pathways and trails offer policymakers and transport planners a pragmatic tool for instantiating an amorphous common good in more-than-human urban environments. They include nascent networks in urban Canada—one deeply embedded in the political production of the nation's city (Ottawa), the other lurking below the city in postindustrial edge space (Toronto)—and a more consolidated network of such infrastructure in Finland (Oulu). Together these cases illuminate a plural, cosmopolitan urban ecology (Gandy 2013) and everyday environmentalism (Loftus 2012) that hint at novel ways of living and moving together with other species. Ecological mobilities are a work in progress. For example, when you hear the phrase "cycling justice," do you imagine many nonhuman beings beyond dogs and cats or is it "cycling social justice" that really comes to mind? Still, as ever more people engage in cycling nature, ecology shows political potential for becoming a powerful way in practice to attribute and deny mobilities' moral worth. The enactment of nature by cycling is an opportunity to refine ecology into a common good people can work with.

In short, mobilities become ecologically good when they contribute to the mutual flourishing of human and nonhuman beings. Such flourishing slowly begins as people notice, follow, and engage nonhumans, not as tools for adventure travel or ecotourism but as morally worthy entities in their own right. This outline for an "ecological mobilities test" may be thin, but it challenges anthropocentric imaginaries of the common good. A political minefield lies ahead of ecology as it transforms from a scientific, religious, or aesthetic endeavor into a common good. Consequently I propose a slow approach to following ecological mobilities grounded in experience, tracing how ecology enters mobility practice via the weeds and edges of day-to-day life as a playful mode of expanding human attention, building on a brief but decisive historical lesson of parkway driving. Cycling animates ecology, in particular, where hard infrastructures and city planning make cycling nature widespread. I refer to this way of cycling as wilderness mobilities when it becomes an adventurous, dreamlike re-noticing of the familiar city as something larger, stranger, and full of nonhuman agencies. Wilderness mobilities grow when human noticing, along with some strategic forms of "not noticing," progresses to acknowledging nonhuman beings as ends and not instruments. I leave to further analysis the task of exploring exactly how it can lead toward more fulsome kinds of care for nonhuman beings. On the basis of my analysis I offer two provisional conclusions.

First, I conclude that however ecological mobilities play out, they will contest for what, and for whom, the "city" and "nature" are, because the enactment of wilderness does not suddenly stop at the urban growth boundary. The interwoven problems of designing an urban planet, animating nature, transitioning to post-carbon mobilities, and redefining the common good suggest ecology's moral-political project may be as fragile as the fleeting human-nonhuman associations on which it is built. Given this deep-seated uncertainty, ecological mobilities can benefit through further empirical modeling of their growth along diverse enactments of nature. Hopefully North American cities will continue to experiment with wilderness infrastructure; exemplary models like Oulu will, with any luck, inspire transoceanic imitation.

Second, I conclude that ecology strongly justifies an expansion of cycling nature at the expense of driving it. Flowing outward from civic mobilities wherein people cycling use more of their senses and less violence than people driving to engage fellow citizens in public space, ecological worth expands as people make room in the old anthropocentric polis for civil engagement with nonhuman beings. This ecological transformation can be viewed less as an attack on the car, although it offers a forceful criticism, than as a positive extension of early forms of parkway driving. As such, cycling nature offers a morally game-changing "pilot project" aimed at opening up hearts and minds as much as decrying ecologically devastating aspects of automobility.

Cycling is, of course, not in every situation good for nonhuman environments. True, cycling may produce minuscule carbon emissions, habitat degradation, and roadkill compared to driving. But cycling also requires energy for its production and practice, sometimes in unsavory political situations. In 2012 South Korea, for example, wrapped up new pathways for cycling wilderness in a massive river-damming project whose ecological devastation seemingly dwarfs the cycling pathways' ecological value (Chihyung 2016). While cases like South Korea's call for multilevel research, in which ecological practices and objects are weighed and compared across multiple scales, cycling's ecological advantage over driving nature remains clear given the ecological devastation of automobility. A much bigger political problem for ecology than cycling is finding widespread practical and infrastructural expression.

Another question lingers: Does noticing nature and becoming familiar with living nonhumans through cycling actually translate into the kind of ecological concern and care that would lead to their flourishing? My analysis suggests it might. I set out shadowing people cycling nature so I could observe fine-grained, fleeting details of their connection to their surroundings, like body language, and the interview statements made by them elaborate a connection with nonhumans. While my research participants' actions and words suggest cycling does foster such concern, some of my observations were more ambiguous than others. For instance, all of my participants said they enjoy walking as much as cycling with nature. In other words, cycling clearly may not be the only (or best) mobility to foster ecological associations. Feet on the ground play a critical role (Ingold 2004). However, there are still good reasons to recommend cycling for ecological care. Putting aside for a moment its collaborative potential with walking, cycling, with its middle speed between driving and walking, affords a strong way of connecting the animation of nature to everyday mobility needs for work, school, socializing, and shopping, using minimal urban infrastructure. The political transformation of city life by ecological cycling, where it currently revolves around the car, could be world repairing. The powerful collaborative tendency of cycling and walking to extend and enrich each other (Pooley et al. 2013) only adds to the potential for cycling to help nourish nonhuman life.

Another, even thornier, question is, if cycling nature suffers from all the same civic problems that limit access to cycling in general, should people just focus on civic actions like voting, protesting, lawmaking, reporting, and regulating rather than following the playful practices and fleeting objects tied up with a worth as ill-defined and politically fluid as ecology? This represents a fair and challenging limitation, a question that cannot be addressed by critical case study design (Flyvbjerg 2006), cross-national comparison (Lamont and Thévenot 2002), and Finnish ingenuity (Babin 2014) alone. At issue is whether ecology stands up and holds together as a discrete common good with its own forms of enactment, or whether ecology should more properly be viewed, for example, as a shadow of the civic world and the extension of human rights and human laws to other species. Herein lies yet another wrinkle: Even *if* ecology stands up as its own, bona-fide moral worth, should we not cultivate it anyway using tested civic practices, objects, and institutions?

To such thorny moral questions I conclude that ecology stands up and that civic tools, under contemporary moral conditions, can lift it further. People cycling are not only their community, rights, or citizenship but always also their environments. As cycling nature shows, ecology dances around provocatively with civic mobilities, generating frictions between divergent moral assemblages, not all of which need be negative. Civic-ecological relations carry the potential to help counter the moral world's political colonization by neoliberal capitalism. Yet the civic tools of human equality, democratic rights, and social justice do not easily translate to multispecies injustice, animal personhood, or justifying the similarities and differences, for example, between mycelia, rivers, forests, salmon, bonobos, and *sapiens*. Putting aside their powers of cross-pollination for a moment, if civic tools ultimately fail as good ecological tools, then the kit needs more tools. If rights fail to fit on rivers and forests, ecology needs its own political vehicles. If "social" solidarity fails to cover oceans and atmospheres before yet more human-driven extinctions roll around, then ecology stands up as its own worth, along with the political question of its enactment.

To what futures do ecological mobilities beckon? How can ecological mobilities reassemble the good city in concert and friction with other moral assemblages of mobility? On the one hand, the whole political ecological project could fail. The Anthropocene might go on minimizing nonhuman agencies (Hathaway 2015) or devolve into a Misanthropocene (Clover and Spahr 2014). Gaia might remain an ineffectual god (Latour 2017) while wilderness sells out to highway-dependent franchises of "neo-pastoral urban spectacles" (Gandy 2013). On the other hand, ecology might politically thrive in the future and become a conventional way of equating disparate ecological entities and attributing moral worth. Apparently simply becoming available as a moral vocabulary does not guarantee ecology's political use, or that of any other common good, in any particular conflict or urban planning controversy. This again begs the question lying at the foundation of this book: Why have a plurality of good mobilities at all? One good reason for examining a plurality of common goods, and their intersecting moral assemblages, is because particular worths can colonize large moral territories and stifle the "good city" altogether. Keeping this moral territorializing activity in mind, the political failure or success of ecology may ultimately lie in ecology's capacity to manage moral friction and create momentum with other common goods. I take up the need for a coalition of moral assemblages of mobility including political ecology in the book's conclusion.

38. A bike leans on a tree in Sunset Park, Vancouver. Photo by author.

Conclusion

Good Cycling Futures

A bounded yet fundamental plurality of morally worthy infrastructures, practices, and judgments about human and nonhuman flourishing assemble the good cycling city. I hope this book, by bringing canonical political philosophies of the common good to bear on the sociology of mobilities, elucidates a moral blind spot within the mobilities paradigm. I also hope it advances the theoretical provocation that more multiplicity exists in each unique world of morality than is commonly assumed (Blok 2013), particularly as dramatic, territorializing relations between five different moral assemblages unfold across urban nations such as Canada. In spite of, and almost certainly because of, this plurality and multiplicity of political morality, humans are left without any hard and homogeneous sense of shared commonality in their collective life. Humans instead face a profound indetermination of the good life, the good city, and indeed, good mobilities. Moral worth remains tenuous at best.

If there is one overarching "driving lesson" to draw from family car adventures, superhighway worlds, national hitchhiking tours, self-driving boosterism, and driving with nature on how to go about making cycling good, it is undoubtedly the fragility and fluidity with which mobilities become assembled through domestic, industrial, civic, market, and ecological worth. These canonical moral worths can be identified readily enough in planning debates and political conflicts at multiple scales across Canada. They arrive on scene whenever politicians, bureaucrats, scientists, local community members, citizens, parents, commuters, and businesses, instead of more narrowly defined interests, appeal to the common good in order to solve a problem, a higher common principle that says even the losers in a given battle win because humanity (or more-than-humanity) itself gains. But such appeals to bolster mobilities' moral worth are by no means guaranteed. Canada, like many other affluent secular societies, struggles to hold on to a sense of overarching commonality in a world riven with hyper-partisanship, deepening inequality, and indeed, *immoral mobilities*, wherein vast differences of wealth and privilege are justified by rejecting the dignity of some humans. Compounding this uncertainty, even when moral worth is mobilized it depends on the situation, where its character is often contested and states of high and low worth are not permanently ascribed to persons or objects but are also challenged and redistributed through political tests and public controversies. This fluidity of moral worth is necessary in liberal democracies, and it opens the door to clashes among differently worthy practices and infrastructures. Some moral mobilities assemble vast territories, while others wither.

And yet for all their multiplicity, fragility, and territorial conflict, moral assemblages lift mobilities up into the hallowed halls of the common good, where whole humanities and more-than-just-humanities flourish. A key contribution of this book lies in this idea of moral assemblages of mobility. Moral worth may most obviously announce itself where people make public appeals to social equity, the efficiency of systems, the gross domestic product (GDP), etc. But it takes a bewildering array of objects, nonhuman beings, and everyday practices to support the actual, ever ongoing assembly of moral mobilities. Qualified objects such as bollards, dollars, and ancient riverways may not be as easy to identify as agents of larger moral infrastructures, but without them moral worths cannot leave the minds of philosophers or polemics of politicians to become part of physical environments. Recognizing the worth embedded in particular configurations of objects and practices—say, the domestic worth of bikeways, the civic worth of cycle tracks, or the ecological worth of wilderness pathways—offers transport planners and policymakers a valuable grammar for making moral mobilities in the first place but also for challenging dominant assemblages.

I also hope this book says something empirically important about the ways in which cycling can help people put down roots, plan urban mobilities, expand mobility justice, compete fairly with money, and notice nonhuman beings. The five moral assemblages I trace constitute unique meetings of political philosophy and sociology, but they also together compose a history and a politics of urban mobility. Historically they follow the development of car capitalism and post-Fordist neoliberalism in tension with tradition, democracy, and, eventually, the environment. Power relations between moral assemblages in Canada have shifted, in particular, through the coalescence of industrial and market worth against other forms of worth, the postwar conquest of market worth through neoliberalism, and the fiery emergence of political ecology. The car played a decisive role in each of these tectonic moral shifts. If cycling simply repeats the car's mistakes and emboldens neoliberal urbanism, it risks trading a plurality of worlds in which people pursue a better humanity for a hollower homogenous world in which the "good life" becomes an amoral measure of money and luxury without any responsibility to those who do not have either. In this hollower world no such grand and lofty projects as society or sociology thrive. Therefore the best way moral mobilities can be put into action, as an idea but also as a history and a politics, entails the contestation and forceful rejection of immoral but also *amoral mobilities* that lack any connection whatsoever to the flourishing of a higher common humanity. Given the obviously capitalistic forces at play behind contemporary moral disconnection, the strongest way for cycling to apply the lessons of driving, I conclude, is to advance a liberal democratic politics of mobility centered on civic, domestic, and ecological mobilities.

Before fleshing out an aspirational and progressive politics of cycling at the end, I trace four "moral vectors" of mobility across the book as a whole. These multi-moral (inter-assemblage) vectors are obscured by each chapter's deep dive into the multiplicity of unique assemblages, from which the whole is always filtered differently through the lens of each part. Vectors flow across different parts. While the book's metanarrative periodically surfaces through "moral frictions" with a more global perspective, this narrative divides and combines moral assemblages across one especially great rift in history and politics that does not exhaust the inter-assemblage possibilities of cycling. Other intriguing moral vectors both reinforce and contravene this rift. They help distill the complex fissures and chasms developing across a pluralistic "moralityscape." In so doing they put the entire moral idea of mobilities into finer perspective as a single tumultuous whole.

Moral Vectors of Mobility

Imagine moral vectors as arrows moving through each piece of a moral assemblage of mobility—judgments, practices, and infrastructures—and the moral frictions arising from all the assemblages.

(Planning) Judgments

The process of planning city cycling creates a moral vector of judgments that crosses the "great rift" between capitalist and noncapitalist moral worths. City planning shows moral interdisciplinarity. While a positivistic technical science of urban planning and engineering animates industrial worth, the social and political process of planning cycling cannot be reduced to industrial logics alone. The planning process also features community participation and private urban developments that afford its travel into other moral worlds. Thus it makes sense to talk of cycling's "civic plans" and "business plans" that combine industrial judgments with meanings and materials from civic and market assemblages. City planning even reaches into domestic and ecological assemblages, for example, through not-in-my-backyard style reactions against change (or NIMBYism), heritage policies, and the rewilding movement. In a certain sense city planning, as a formal yet indispensable way of judging and reassembling the worth of cycling, simply amounts to a narrative process of telling contemporary stories about urban socio-technical change. The most compelling stories arguably make space for voices of unfamiliar strangers (Eckstein 2003), and the quality of cycling planning narratives should be judged by their capacity to include authors and voices that resonate across moral fault lines.

I characterize this vector of judgments as a set of "waves" of cycling planning in Canada that roughly divide the first two decades of the twenty-first century. First-wave cycling planning (2001–10) champions cycling's industrial worth, wherein cycling is engineered uniformly across the city via standard painted bike lanes that ignore differences of place, history, and the body. Some cities in Canada, anachronistically, tread water here still. Most cities, however, are now riding a second wave of cycling planning (2010–20), exemplified by narratives about the need for dedicated bike lanes that invite more kinds of people to cycle. Second-wave cycling planning pivots toward civic judgment, aiming for cycling inclusion. Yet as dedicated lanes in turn feed cycling development and gentrification that deepen racialized and neighborhood-level exclusion, a third-wave cycling planning appears imminent. Such a third wave can push planning stories further yet toward cycling justice by using an intersectionality lens to evaluate complex cycling inequalities. Complicating the civic direction of this planning vector, however, cities increasingly create space with large developers and global investors in public-private partnerships. Ushering market worth further into the process of planning cycling, such partnerships challenge, and further inspire, the coalescence of its third wave.

This succession of cycling planning waves does not emanate everywhere in a straightforward, irreversible way—for example, Toronto during the Rob Ford years showed a second wave crashing and a city rewinding to the first wave (CBC News 2011). City planning, furthermore, whether technocratic and top-down or grassroots and community-driven, is not the only way to justify and critique cycling. Parents, voters, consumers, corporations, community associations, social movements, and ordinary humans searching for nature judge and evaluate cycling's moral worth beyond planning. Yet city planning, rippling especially from industrial out through civic and market assemblages, forms a powerful vector of formal judgments of cycling that include actors from multiple worlds in the process of authoring and plotting its expansion.

(Sociotemporal) Practices

The active doing of city cycling opens up two salient paths, or vectors, of practice. Cycling in every moral assemblage shows a multi-sensorial, embodied, and affective practice that more intimately situates people into the world than the motor vehicle. People in the city when they cycle become more prolific shoppers, more connected to local places, safer and more engaged citizens on the move, more efficient road users, and slower, deeper observers of nature and wilderness. However, further illuminating the complexity of cycling assemblages as a whole, one moral vector of practices contravenes the great capitalist-noncapitalist rift, while the other reinforces it.

The first moral vector of practice pits civic and market mobilities, strange bedfellows on the whole, against domestic, industrial, and ecological mobilities on the matter and depth of time. While a more intimate world connection characterizes all moral assemblages of cycling, this multi-sensorial performance takes on a noticeably deeper sense of duration through industrial futures, domestic pasts, and ecological cycles, rhythms, and orbits. For a sense of industrial duration, try cycling outdoors near the mass, velocity, and noise of a superhighway built for uninterrupted, high-speed car travel; it will intimately expose you to historical and contemporary futures of automobility. Dedicated bike lanes may not yet exude the same sense of permanence, but industrial pilot projects often turn into taken-for-granted infrastructures that might signal a long future. With equal depth but in the opposite direction, a sense of domestic duration pervades home and family. Riding with your parents or children and sewing into place your kins' memories and traumas, and those of your local community, move and unfold home into time immemorial. With varying depths and curvilinear directions, riding along rivers, forests, and oceans with a biodiversity of plants, animals, and fungi introduces and exposes people to the manifold life spans and temporalities of nonhuman beings. With nonhuman beings and their temporalities spontaneously distributed throughout, and often obscured by, the built urban environment, they often playfully creep up on people cycling (and ambling) as humans re-notice the city as a stranger place full of nonhuman agencies. Between industrial futures, domestic pasts, and such ecological clockworks lies an extraordinary set of practices for coming into closer contact with time. In contrast to these longitudinal moralities, civic and market worth take cross-sectional snapshots of equitable societies and prof-itable economies.

Another prominent moral vector of practices travels across assem-blages by the active doing of cycling as "a together," one that expresses human and nonhuman beings as social, convivial animals. Unlike the durational course of cycling practice, this conviviality vector reinforces the great rift. Industrial and market mobilities tend to motivate indi-vidualistic styles of cycling where people cycling are conceived as (and conceive of themselves as) singular units, system users and consum-ers moving instrumentally and rationally from point A to point B. In contrast domestic, civic, and ecological mobilities afford more sociable styles of cycling as a more-than-one. Family co-cycling, impromptu and organized "bike gangs," and riding with sociable nonhuman beings (e.g., crows) allow more conviviality than biking either directly to and from work as efficiently as possible or biking for competitive consumption. Thus, unlike the way cycling interacts with time, a different vector of practices based on co-cycling as a together pulls the analytical story back to capitalist versus noncapitalist moralities.

(Infrastructuring) Multiplicity

The physical embedding of cycling into the built urban environment generates vectors of infrastructure that also both contravene and rein-force the great rift. One intriguing vector of infrastructures based on modal integration isolates civic mobilities, and their materialization as dedicated bike lanes, from the rest. Only dedicated bike lanes fully isolate cyclists. Across domestic bikeways, industrial systems, ecological pathways, and corridors of consumption, infrastructures show a range of ways of integrating cycling with pedestrians and other self-propelled vehicles (ecological pathways), plus slower-moving motor vehicles (domestic bikeways) and faster-moving motor vehicles (industrial and market infrastructures). This infrastructural multiplicity suggests that achieving cycling justice and building the good cycling city may not be as straightforward as building dedicated bike lanes. Slow and safe encounters with "vehicular others" may even play an important role in inculcating some of the very habits and virtues (e.g., civility, empathy) necessary to build widespread social and political support for cycling equity among different kinds of road users. To be sure, dedicated bike lanes, particularly in high traffic areas, contain substantial power to expand the city cycling franchise by actively inviting people cycling into streets to which they can actually feel they safely belong. Yet dedicated lanes do not offer a civic panacea, especially when we account for their positive association with gentrification. Thus a compelling puzzle, particularly for third-wave cycling planners, revolves around infrastructuring complex urban spaces that maximize cycling access and growing demand through different combinations of cycle tracks and passageways that cyclists share with others. In the experimental spirit of the cycling engineer-bricoleur, previously settled infrastructural forms may need to be undone, as has already happened in some Canadian cities where dedicated bike lanes, for example, have been formally revised to accommodate other self-propelled and electronically assisted vehicles, like e-bikes, inline skates, skateboards, and wheelchairs.

Delimiting the "good bike lane" as any passageway that removes cyclists from fast-moving motor vehicles opens up another vector of infrastructures, one that reinforces the great (non)capitalist moral rift. While on one hand the strong association of dedicated bike lanes with cycling justice and civic mobilities runs the risk of "design determinism" (Golub et al. 2016), on the other hand, it also offers a powerful point of material leverage for advocates, planners, and engineer-bricoleurs seeking to expand civic cycling. Similarly, strong associations with particular infrastructural formations exist for domestic mobilities in local neighborhood bikeways and ecological mobilities in shared pathways and wilderness trails. Together these civic, domestic, and ecological formations create a vector of infrastructures where bike lanes themselves travel as "immutable mobiles" of stable configuration across different urban contexts. By contrast industrial and market infrastructures show markedly less configurational stability. Industrial cycling systems combine infrastructures that optimize efficiency, while market-driven bike lanes mobilize whatever passages maximize consumption and profit—which all vary widely across different contexts. The impact of this path of infrastructures for cycling expansion is uncertain. The ability of bike lanes outside the orbit of neoliberal capitalism to "travel" across different contexts bodes well for pouring a material foundation for more progressive city cycling. At the same time, the infrastructural plasticity of capitalist assemblages of mobility may, in some cases, help market and industrial mobilities co-opt cycle tracks, bikeways, and multiuse trails into the circuits of cycling-oriented development and consumption—particularly where these civic, domestic, and ecological infrastructures are not reinforced by strong public judgments and practices.

Moral Frictions

Moral frictions between the five unique moral assemblages generate the largest moral vectors across the book as a whole. By way of summary these moral frictions tell a story of centripetal forces converging the assemblages together, and equally strong centrifugal forces threatening to explode them apart. At the start domestic mobilities form a thin, yet long-standing arc of stable tension all the way to ecological mobilities in the end, as people animate traditional knowledge and become familiar with their nonhuman surroundings. Off in the middle distance looms a storm brewing between civic and market mobilities, gaining fuel from the city's unaffordable housing. Turning to the moral core of industrial capitalism, fissures grow between industrial and market mobilities and threaten to tear capitalism apart, with the former trying to restrain the latter from privatizing infrastructure and reducing engineering to profit. Pivoting from there into the storm glimpsed at the start, civic mobilities rage as inequities grow more complex. Civic inequities become caught up in the fissures of capitalism and magnified around the fulcrum of urban intensification and gentrifying redevelopment. Friction grows even fiercer when market mobilities overtake industrial mobilities in the overflowing currents of neoliberal capitalism. Under the storm's eye, domestic, civic, and industrial mobilities start to swirl like a hurricane around market mobilities. A plurality of unique moral assemblages begins to collapse into a single neoliberal market, one whose returns grow increasingly large, uneven, and divorced from the flourishing of a common humanity, even one based on markets. Before a plurality of good mobilities disassembles, nonhuman beings intervene. Ecological mobilities arbitrate in the end against the moral closure of neoliberal capitalism, mounting an equal force of moral opening by destabilizing the very notion of a common humanity upon which market mobilities, and every other moral assemblage, depends. To characterize what this ecological push back might look like, I return to the fable from the book's introduction, retelling it from the perspective of coyotes.

To Burn or To Not Burn Down the World?

The City Council meeting did not go as planned. Coyotes, of course, did not want to attend. Meetings with other animals give them anxiety.

"Are coyotes competent enough to join the City?" needles their inner voice. *"Are coyotes smart enough? Are they sufficiently* social?"

But tensions between bees, crows, raccoons, beavers, and foxes had grown so hot as of late that coyotes feared the City would soon combust into violence. So they made a plan. Coyotes would swallow their fear of meetings and simply tell the old Council what coyotes could see plainly from the shadows: not foxes, but their money and everyone's avarice were threatening to rend the City into pieces. The coyotes' plan might have worked. But instead of taking coyotes seriously, Council escalated the political crisis further by debating the deportation of foxes as enemy aliens.

With their heads spinning, coyotes take leave of the Council and retreat to their hovel. There they deliberate whether they ought to intervene and help the other animals should the City descend into chaos. Some coyotes wonder, why should they? After all, the other animals have wantonly abused the City's water, land, and atmosphere while otherwise refusing to respect the great neighborhood of coyotes. At the same time, most coyotes, while studiously avoiding the other animals, have gotten to know the foxes. In a strange, interspecific way, they even relate with them—despite their despicable treatment of the world.

Not long thereafter, while surreptitiously noting the nocturnal comings and goings of City Hall, coyotes by chance overhear a most disturbing conversation. Some high crows and bees are quietly plotting to cull corrupt foxes. In an instant, time for deliberation closed, chaos had come and coyotes would not sit idly by and watch the City implode. With utmost haste coyotes warn the moderate bees and crows with connections to the suburbs who might prevent their radical colleagues from lighting the first match of war. But it was too late. Before the moderates could reach the radicals, innards were spilling. [As it happened the radicals, though well positioned, completely missed their targets at first from a lack of nerve and poor execution. It was only after targeted foxes misguidedly returned to the scene of their own botched assassination that the radicals could finish the job.]

With even greater haste coyotes pivot and seek out moderate foxes, beavers, and raccoons with inner-city ties to try and temper their response, for the good of the City. Tragically, just as coyotes begin to bend some amenable ears, angry bees and crows elsewhere, eyeing a chance to capitalize on the cull, press into the suburbs, rounding up foxes and ransacking their enterprises. Convening an emergency deliberation on a ravine overlooking foxes as they prepare a counter-attack, coyotes see the writing on the wall. Not long after weighing the pros and cons of running away, and lamenting their lack of agency over animal affairs, coyotes resolve to defend the City. They know it means meeting in lethal conflict with powerful foxes, whose territorial expansion coyotes have closely followed from the start. When the brutal counterattack ends, foxes only barely prevail in fending off coyotes and usurping a City divided.

In the years that follow, oppressive heat and fox rule compel coyotes to lay low. After coyotes almost derailed the countercoup, increasingly fascist foxes brand coyotes as outsiders stealing scarce resources and sapping a strong, prosperous homeland (the irony of which alone makes coyotes cringe). Democratic demagogues arise, claiming they can transcend the coyote-fox divide through new "sunny ways" that throw away old left-right politics. But they offer thin foil for strongmen, autocratic foxes who muzzle the media and demolish dissent. Coyotes must now track the other animals with utmost situational awareness. In the suburbs coyotes avoid a hostile population dominated by beavers and raccoons in a friendlier, flatter environment with room to run. In the tighter inner city coyotes use the friendlier faces they find in crows and bees to a negotiate a more hostile, vertical environment with stricter surveillance and fewer ways out. Relying on their physical and social dexterity, coyotes creep deeply into each of these worlds. They slowly piece together the political machinations of foxes, who move with dangerous ease throughout the City.

Around the suburbs coyotes watch as mega-housing tracts, new highways, and patriotic fervor engulf the countryside. Fox-financed development sprawls so fast that raccoons and beavers scarcely notice the new inequalities it creates. After scrapping the City's road tolls and development levies, foxes replace greenbelts with sweeping stadiums and plazas for police parades, rewarding loyal beavers and raccoons with cheap beer and lavish rallies against entitled, out-of-touch elites who would raise their taxes, threaten their jobs, and choke off economic growth. Beneath the bombast, slipping out bedroom windows in hushed tones, coyotes pick up signs of a subtle, even more corrosive shift. Beavers and raccoons, trapped in a silo of fox news, slowly lose their capacity to empathize or even talk with the crows and bees whom they once lived beside and respected as neighbors. Instead they view the world, and identify themselves, through their differences with downtown dilettantes and cosmopolitan fools.

Crossing from the suburbs to the inner city, once a leisurely trek, now takes coyotes weeks of careful planning and tunneling. Upon resurfacing, the sky no longer shows, hiding behind shiny thickets of perpetually rising luxury sky dwellings. With fire and sanitation services lost to severe cuts, coyotes find cover under a smoky haze, from which they barely discern downtown. The same inequality spreading across the suburbs takes on more acute proximity in the city core, where growing masses of beggar bees and crows eke out a living beside their superrich brethren, separated by but a window, police sting, or cold, blank stare. Coyotes watch as the wealthiest bees and crows cocoon and pleasure themselves into blissful ignorance, while forgetting the way luck made their success and chalking the failure of the poor up to personal irresponsibility. With foxes tightening a noose around the inner city, coyotes listen to bees and crows caught in their own silo of college radio propaganda mainly complaining about redneck raccoons and bumpkin beavers.

Coyotes confirm from painstaking cross-world reconnaissance that fox money and everyone's avarice were dividing and vanquishing the City. That coyotes had a hunch this might happen when they first spied foxes cunningly co-opting forgotten spaces between the City and the countryside brings them no solace. The latest field reports show increasingly militaristic rallies in the suburbs and fox forces amassing by conduits into the City's core. Coyotes once more despair about their lack of power over animal affairs. Just then, by random chance, they intercept a deeply disturbing fox communiqué: "*cheap beer exhausted; so, too, fresh water; exterminate downtown.*"

At their makeshift hovel in uncharted territory, coyotes arbitrate over what to do next. One coyote who had just returned from the field says foxes have lit fires across the suburbs to rile up beavers and raccoons. Another coyote just returning from a deep dive with crows and bees notes the same distraction downtown. Then, rather than running away, coyotes resolve to reassemble the affairs of animals who clearly no longer know how to live together. Channeling their inner trickster, coyotes start whipping up the flames so they might destroy private property in the territory of foxes—so, the City. They hope a cataclysmic natural disaster, short of annihilation, will cure modernity's malaise and reunite the animals by mobilizing the City against a threat to its very existence. . . .

Not long after the great forest fire burned the old City to the ground, taking down many noble (and even more shoddy) structures with it, a new City begins to bud. Delicious and rare mushrooms abound. The first deliberation of coyotes, after the great forest fire, takes place solemnly in a fallow field where some important coyotes and crows have perished. Coyotes agree to grow a better City by first rehabilitating the neighborhoods of crows and bees before shifting precious resources to the designs of beavers, raccoons, and foxes.

Toward a Plurality of Good Cycling Futures

This book's metanarrative and moral fables conceal an Anglo-Canadian bias. How relations among "moral animals" or assemblages of mobility unfold over time might look very different from the standpoint of, say, Belarus, compared to Canada and the United States. Belarus might have entire other moral assemblages and frictions that I have here not even considered (e.g., where the lingering impacts of Soviet communism have worked to suppress markets). And even between Canada and the United States salient differences emerge, given the awesome power of market mobilities in America, where, for example, corporate titans like the Koch brothers can kill public transit projects across the country (Tabuchi 2018). Canada, too, has a powerful, pro–fossil fuel politics of automobility—for example, note Ontario's 2018 election of Doug Ford (brother of the late Toronto mayor Rob Ford) as provincial premier, whose campaign promised scarcely more than to roll back carbon pricing and bring back buck-a-beer and cheap gasoline. But the market machinations of the Koch brothers are on another scale. Of course such a geopolitical, international comparison of moral mobilities lies beyond the scope of this book. I highlight it here as a fruitful area for future sociological research that extends insight into the significance of geographical and historical context for moral mobilities.

Cross-contextual comparison is critical for imagining a plurality of good cycling futures. I articulate this simple insight in chapter 3 as a foundation for an expansive conception of cycling justice, and it flows in my book through a cross-city sampling of case studies. Cycling judgments, practices, and infrastructures vary between and within urban contexts. After all, the city is where cycling stands the greatest chance of becoming a form of mass mobility that rivals or even surpasses the car—and thus where cycling faces formidable and diverse political challenges. Canada, one of the most highly urbanized, yet car-dependent countries in the world, offers good case studies (Flyvbjerg 2006) for this urban sociological puzzle, including: "most likely" cases of cycling expansion (Ottawa) with paradigmatic cases of infrastructure (Ottawa's Laurier Avenue); "least likely" cases of cycling expansion (Motor City); and "extreme cases" of cycling gentrification (Vancouver). Comparing these kinds of cases, and the tensions and counterintuitive movements within them, creates a broad basis for thinking about where and how city cycling will grow. As with countries, which particular moral assemblages and frictions are most relevant for any particular city, as they develop their own blends of cycling infrastructures, cultures, and technologies, will vary. By the same token, which political strategies might best advance a progressive moral politics of cycling will look different from the standpoints of Vancouver, Winnipeg, Motor City, Toronto, Ottawa, and Dartmouth. However, from the cases as a whole, "stretched" further through comparative insights from Detroit, Seattle, and Oulu, we can glean some shared starting points.

A Pan-Canadian, progressive cycling politics should adopt a liberal democratic focus on expanding civic, domestic, and ecological cycling. Under industrial capitalism, market and industrial worth threatened to crowd out the others, while in these neoliberal times market worth threatens to become the sole arbiter of the common good and altogether corrode political morality. So in the liberal democratic interests of cultivating a plurality of moral assemblages of mobility—which ultimately means people can, to an extent, decide for themselves what sort of good life they want to lead—civic, domestic, and ecological cycling ought to take priority for a progressive cycling politics. Such a politics might take any number of forms across a variety of scales. I imagine it proceeding through two particular, mutually reinforcing aspirations: a national city cycling plan and a liberal democratic cycling education.

Canada needs a national city cycling plan that coordinates and bankrolls new local neighborhood bikeways, multiuser nature trails, and dedicated cycle tracks in cities from coast to coast to coast. More important than the specific content of its industrial assembly—recall that these infrastructures offer relatively "immutable mobiles"—is that it offers a "civic plan," one ideally in line with third-wave cycling planning. By its national nature such a civic plan should focus on making city cycling equally accessible for all urban Canadians and ameliorating complex, intersectional cycling inequalities within and between cities and their neighborhoods.

Equally important, a national city cycling plan should reassemble and re-narrate a Canadian identity and "Canadian good life" that for too long has been associated through popular culture and politics with the car, the suburbs, and a romanticized northern wilderness. In other words, without knocking the worth of Justin Trudeau's "highway bike lanes for the middle class" ("Trudeau Announces Bike-Only Lanes for Trans-Canada Highway" 2015), a national cycling plan has to be an all-class *city* plan. Ideally a national city cycling plan would proceed as both a product and generator of urban empowerment. Like its outdated cultural stereotypes that elide cities in which most of its people live together, Canada's institutions have not caught up to urban reality. Its constitution, first written in 1867, did not empower cities because they did not yet exist, instead defining municipalities as mere "creatures" of the provinces (Fanelli 2016). Consequently cities now suffer from a fundamental lack of decision-making and revenue-generating power, even as they face added social responsibilities downloaded by higher levels of government. This is partly why they sprawl so greatly. Political sparks since the early 2000s of a "New Deal for Cities" have yet to ignite meaningful change. But demographic trends ensure these sparks will continue to fly in the fastest growing country in the G7. Canada's rural population is aging far faster than those in cities, while growth, concentrated in large cities, continues to tilt away from the once-booming car-friendly suburbs toward cycling-friendly urban centers, "with young professionals and aging baby boomers alike opting for the downtown-condominium life" (Press 2017). A New Deal for Cities is a New Deal for Cycling—and vice versa.

A national city cycling plan would not only qualify cycling for federal resources as a "strategically" important mode of transport but also link cycling to an evolving cosmopolitan sense of Canadian nationhood. For example, Canada's multicultural sense of nationhood has been most recently rattled by an acknowledgment and deep examination of the country's cruel efforts throughout its history to "cause Aboriginal peoples to cease to exist as distinct legal, social, cultural, religious, and racial entities in Canada" (Truth and Reconciliation Commission of Canada 2015, 1). A national city cycling plan that addresses the deep injustices suffered by First Nations, Métis, and Inuit at the hands of Euro-Christian settler colonialism will be better than one that does not. The increase in the urban population of Indigenous peoples unfolding for decades in Canada (Statistics Canada 2017a) points to the civic-domestic potential for cycling to enhance urban Indigenous mobilities. Including Indigenous voices and perspectives in local and national city cycling planning should be a priority.

Another potentially significant linkage between a national city cycling plan and Canada's evolving sense of itself connects cycling justice with the more-than-human environment. Like the Trudeau government's lackluster movement on urban empowerment, its environmental policy has been less than inspiring. Trudeau touts a "third way" beyond economic growth versus environmental protection that includes strongly supporting Canada's fastest-expanding source of greenhouse gas emissions, Alberta's oil sands operations, by expanding pipeline capacity to the Pacific Ocean. However, an ecological correction in Canadian politics seems inevitable, when the mutually reinforcing forces of climate change, biodiversity loss, and habitat degradation eventually become an arbiter that compels Canada to embrace and identify with environmental protection as an existential source of social solidarity. Coyotes are a-comin'. Like a New Deal for Cities, a New Deal for Sustaining Human and Nonhuman Life on Earth will find a notably strong steward in cycling.

Besides a national city cycling plan, a Pan-Canadian progressive cycling politics requires a democratic education (Gutmann 1987). Specifically, Canada needs a stalwartly public and liberal democratic education in cycling, wherein humans actively learn how to care about their local communities, practice good citizenship, and execute environmental stewardship in their everyday self-propelled lives. Civic virtues like empathy with other road users and public reasonableness—the capacity of people to frame their demands of government and society within the common good—is in short supply as of late, just when humans need it most. Besides intergenerational trauma in Indigenous communities, climate change, creeping authoritarian populism, and hyper-partisan politics molding separate cultural worlds and realities reinforced through social media silos, Canada, as elsewhere, suffers from growing socioeconomic inequalities that further corrode people's commitment to liberal democracy and the common good. Extreme market wealth, for example, renders kinetic elites disconnected from societal projects, forgetful of the external supports that have helped create their wealth and prone to withdraw into their own, gated worlds. Canadians do not usually live in ghettoes surrounded by the same sorts of people. Yet Canada's top one percent of income earners comprise:

> A community of people who overwhelmingly tend to live in segregated neighbourhoods; who often withdraw their children from the public school system to educate them in their own schools; who have a high likelihood to hire and work for only people from their closed circle; who tend to marry their own kind and whose children are far more likely than members of other communities to live and work strictly within their group. (Saunders 2017)

Growing inequality and the ghettoization of the wealthy present a critical threat to cycling justice by preventing different kinds of people from learning to live and travel together. A democratic cycling education desperately needs wealthy people to participate, pay their taxes, and contribute to the common good. A democratic cycling education requires people of all social classes, ethnocultural identities, creeds, and capabilities to become good citizens together.

Public school shows the strongest potential for housing a democratic cycling education, where people can practice their deliberation and public reasonableness with unfamiliar voices in strange environments from an early age. Cycling to and from school and play on bikeways, nature trails, and cycle tracks, instead of getting passively chauffeured by their parents, can teach children and young adults to propel their own discovery of human differences and diverse urban spaces and urban durations. Cycling should become an important, convivial part of the public school curriculum, not necessarily as a sport or competitive endeavor, but rather as a lifelong democratic tool for engaging local communities, practicing civility and empathy in public space all while noticing and appreciating the nonhuman world. The precise nature of a public democratic cycling education will of course vary by urban context. Windsor, Dartmouth, Winnipeg, and other cities without extensive cycling networks around public schools should focus on putting more cycle tracks and traffic-calmed bikeways on the road to expand their existing multiuse trails. Vancouver's cycling education should broach gentrification across the lines of social class, race, and gender. So should Toronto's. Ottawa should continue to educate the nation by exchanging ideas and research with other advanced cycling countries in Northern Europe and elsewhere, and by showcasing advanced city cycling practices and infrastructures. Tying Canada's cities together, a national city cycling plan should accelerate knowledge transfer across provinces and school systems. Top-down national plans, however necessary, are also insufficient (and education is under provincial jurisdiction in Canada). Bottom-up grassroots community engagement is critical for expanding cycling justice (Golub et al. 2016). Decentralized public schools in cities across the country that invite everyone to learn together are the best place to start.

While trying to imagine an expansive liberal democratic cycling justice back in chapter 3, I said I would return to "one of the great unresolved questions of political philosophy" (Kymlicka 2001, 257), which this book, in a roundabout way, encircles. Here we find ourselves at the focal point. How do people become excited to live with one another in social and political solidarity? How do citizens unite around justice and the common good in the first place, besides through world war (and great forest fires)? It is probably neither excitement about justice and equality alone, nor one conception of the common good. One's too thin, the other too heavy handed to account for solidarity and unity in, or between, the nation-states in which we currently live. Rather:

> Social unity requires something in between these two approaches: it requires that citizens share more than simply liberal principles, but less than a shared conception of the good life. What could this be? (Kymlicka 2001, 261)

I think "this" could be a bounded plurality of fundamentally different conceptions of the good life. I nominate domestic, industrial, civic, market, and ecological assemblages of the common good. I do not suggest they should ever necessarily share equal standing, but rather more like an equilibrium in which they balance each other out as moral forces. If any one of these moral worths tries to snuff out another, conflict ensues. Market tyranny is not inevitable in Canada. Neither is driving a car. If cycling can apply the moral lessons of driving, it will cultivate as it grows an urban cornucopia.

Notes

Introduction

1. The NCC is a federal crown corporation that plays three roles: "long-term planner of federal lands, principal steward of nationally significant public places, and creative partner committed to excellence in development and conservation" (http://ncc-ccn.gc.ca/).
2. For more on the beginnings of this concept of moral assemblages, in the context of the Russian Orthodox Church's approach to drug use and HIV, see Zigon (2010). For more on "assemblage theory" see DeLanda (2006). To see the concept of assemblage applied persuasively in the context of wilderness, see Vannini and Vannini (2016).
3. For example, Rivera purposefully enlarged the engine block–piercing spindles to mimic the Toltec sculptures of pre-industrial Mexico, which were seen as guardians or protectors of civilization. For a guided virtual tour, see http://www.dia.org/.

1. Domestic Mobilities

1. When you were a kid your father, driving around the Ontario countryside in goggles on hand-graded roads full of craters without a windshield, had to bring his own gasoline, fix his own car, and be prepared to build his own roads and bridges out of rocks and wood planks. Sure, he had to find a team of horses to haul him out of a slough or two, but even today "there still is a sense of adventure in donning one's goggles, leather gauntlets, and long cotton duster and setting off for a Sunday drive" (Francis 2006, 43).
2. Notably, fathers in my research in many ways cycled with children very similarly to mothers. However, fathers tended to incorporate carrier cycling (including tandems and tag-alongs) with their children into pre-existing cycling routes and routines, whereas mothers more frequently adapted their cycling routines to accommodate more complex trip-

chaining, where new, emergent routes and routines served multiple activities and destinations.

3. Atypical or "extreme cases," methodologically, can "reveal more information because they activate more actors and more basic mechanisms in the situation studied" (Flyvbjerg 2006, 229).

4. Hastings Street is a major artery near, and running parallel to, Adanac. While she rides along Adanac, memorable points along Hastings periodically emerge and pick off Celestina's attention perpendicularly, creating new folds in her mental map.

2. Industrial Mobilities

1. A note on usage: by Motor City, I mean both Windsor and Detroit.

2. Cycling advocacy in Motor City during the late twentieth century gained strength as Michigan's off-road biking community began lobbying for city cycling infrastructure and the conversion of rails to trails. It also took a step forward on the Canadian side through the construction of recreational off-road facilities around Windsor guided by the city's 1991 Bicycle Use Development Study (BUDS).

3. These pathways are owned and managed by the National Capital Commission, a crown corporation responsible for long-term planning of federal lands (http://ncc-ccn.gc.ca/places-to-visit/parks-paths-and-parkways/multi-use-pathways-in-the-capital).

4. Neatly illustrated on a graph entitled "Ottawa Hull and Environs Forecast of Population Trends" (Gréber 1950, 51), half a million people were projected to inhabit greater Ottawa by the end of the twentieth century, or by 2020 at the latest. The postwar baby boom, supported by the rise of Canada's welfare state, meant that greater Ottawa reached 500,000 inhabitants not by 2000 or 2020, but in 1966. This was the same year that the city completed land acquisition for the greenbelt (spending $40 million, in 1966 dollars), and two years after private developers began circulating proposals to systematically "leapfrog" the nascent urban growth boundary (Gordon and Scott 2008, 137). Gréber's plan was part of a "dismal" record of postwar projections under challenging demographic conditions (George 2001, 113).

5. Advances in forecasting methodology have facilitated specialized "derived projections" (George 2001) that examine a diversity of variables related to land use.

6. Specifically the 2013 *Ottawa Cycling Plan* begins to distinguish cycling needs for women and men and older cyclists and children. This more

advanced industrial thinking is a hallmark, I propose, of second-wave cycling planning, which I explore in chapter 3.

7. Dartmouth merged with Halifax in 1996 as part of the sprawling Halifax Regional Municipality. The name "IKEA Halifax" irks some Dartmouth residents and confuses some consumers.

8. www.dartmouthcrossing.com.

9. https://thegreattrail.ca/about-us/faq/.

4. Market Mobilities

1. There was a brief glimmer of hope in the early 2000s, when then–prime minister Paul Martin (the architect of Canada's 1995 slash-and-burn neo-liberal budget) introduced the idea of a "New Deal" for cities. It quickly fizzled into a minor sharing of gas tax revenue to support public transit.

2. Shaw, intriguingly, leads us back to this chapter's driving lessons and self-driving cars. In May 2018 the company completed its first 5G technical trials, taking a significant step toward next-generation wireless technology. Whether Canadian companies will be able to turn their 5G inventions into market gold through self-driving cars, smart cities, and bike share systems, or whether China has already "outmaneuvered everyone" by building an extensive pipeline of intellectual 5G property through Canadian universities (Silcoff 2018), is a touchy issue in Canada—a country known more for its scientific and industrial breakthroughs than for converting their inventions through entrepreneurialism into market wealth.

3. Stephen Harper's cabinet similarly used arguments about protecting everyday working people from burdensome, even tyrannical regulatory intervention by the state to effect a seemingly self-destructive government policy to undermine good data that united a wide range of businesses, urban elites, social service providers, and scientific experts in opposition.

5. Ecological Mobilities

1. In a recent British Columbian election, for example, hailed by national media as a historic election for the Green Party, the Greens won three of eighty-seven seats in the legislature and became "kingmaker" by ousting the reigning right-of-center party by supporting the left-of-center party.

2. My cautious approach acknowledges the inherent difficulty of morally ranking nonhuman beings and environments that frequently contravene anthropocentric notions of the individual and the human life span (Bouchard 2013). Additionally it avoids dwelling on the celebrity species

(e.g., whales and polar bears) that garner outsized attention in popular ecological debates.

3. For example, the Icefields Trail, a proposed paved multiuse pathway in Jasper National Park in Alberta, enraged environmentalists in 2017 by threatening to destroy a small but important amount of critical habitat for at-risk species (Canadian Parks and Wilderness Society [CPAWS] 2017).

4. Cycling habitat refers to the "natural environment" of cyclists (Scott 2016). While the material cultures, meanings, and performance of city cycling vary widely, the basic ingredients of good cycling habitat are internationally generalizable: safe (separated from cars), connected, legible, and desirable routes that take people cycling where they want to go, preferably without body armor. I would add to this rather aspirational standard of good cycling habitat in the city by including access to wild nature.

5. In the summer of 2015 I asked cyclists in cities across Canada and Oulu, Finland, if they could bike to nature they judged to be good and visited it on a regular basis (including on the way to work), and if I could shadow them with a helmet-mounted GoPro camera and later interview them about it with use of the footage. These ride-alongs and video-elicitation interviews generally took three to four hours. I define ecologically qualified infrastructure for cycling as public multiuse pathways and trails separated from car driving whose design, construction, and public justification lay, at least in part, in the access and enjoyment of nature. The three acts represent a purposive, theoretically driven sample of such infrastructure.

6. Of these pathways 236 kilometers (147 miles) are owned and maintained by a federal urban planning agency unique to Canada, the National Capital Commission.

References

Aldred, Rachel. 2013. "Incompetent or Too Competent? Negotiating Every-day Cycling Identities in a Motor Dominated Society." *Mobilities* 8, no. 2: 252–71.

———. 2012. "Governing Transport from Welfare State to Hollow State: The Case of Cycling in the UK." *Transport Policy* 23:95–102.

———. 2010. "'On the Outside': Constructing Cycling Citizenship." *Social & Cultural Geography* 11, no. 1: 35–52.

Aldred, Rachel, Bridget Elliott, James Woodcock, and Anna Goodman. 2017. "Cycling Provision Separated from Motor Traffic: A Systematic Review Exploring Whether Stated Preferences Vary by Gender and Age." *Transport Reviews* 37, no. 1: 29–55.

Amin, Ash. 2006. "The Good City." *Urban Studies* 43:1009–23.

Anderson, Gillian, Joseph G. Moore, and Laura Suski, eds. 2016. *Sociology of Home: Belonging, Community, and Place in the Canadian Context.* Toronto: Canadian Scholars.

Aronczyk, Melissa. 2005. "'Taking the suv to a Place It's Never Been Before': suv Ads and the Consumption of Nature." *Invisible Culture: An Electronic Journal for Visual Culture* 9.

Associated Press. 2011. "Report: Ambassador Bridge Owners Reap Profits from Tax-Free Gas Sales." April 25, 2011. https://www.mlive.com/news /detroit/index.ssf/ 2011/04/report_ambassador_bridge_owner.html.

August, Martine, and Alan Walks. 2018. "Gentrification, Suburban Decline, and the Financialization of Multi-Family Rental Housing: The Case of Toronto." *Geoforum* 89:124–36.

"Automobiles More than Summer Toy." *Globe*, January 16, 1920, ProQuest Historical Newspapers, 15.

Babin, Tom. 2014. *Frostbike: The Joy, Pain and Numbness of Winter Cycling.* Victoria bc: Rocky Mountain.

Bachelard, Gaston. 1994[1958]. *The Poetics of Space*. Boston: Beacon.

Bailey, Ian, and France Bula. 2018. "Amazon to Open New Vancouver Office, Create 3,000 jobs." *Globe and Mail*, April 30, 2008. https://www .theglobeandmail.com/canada/british-columbia/article-amazon-to-open -new-vancouver-office-create-3000-jobs/.

Bauman, Zygmunt. 2003. "Utopia with No Topos." *History of the Human Sciences* 16, no. 1: 11–24.

Benoît, Beroud, and Esther Anaya. 2012. "Private Interventions in a Public Service: An analysis of Public Schemes." In *Cycling and Sustainability*, edited by John Parkin, 269–302. London: Emerald.

Berg, Maggie, and Barbara Seeber. 2016. *Slow professor: Challenging the culture of speed in the academy*. Toronto: University of Toronto Press.

Bijker, Wiebe E. 1997. *Of Bicycles, Bakelites and Bulbs*. Cambridge MA: MIT Press.

Binnema, Ted, and Melanie Niemi. 2006. "'Let the Line Be Drawn Now': Wilderness, Conservation, and the Exclusion of Aboriginal People from Banff National Park in Canada." *Environmental History* 11:724–50.

Birtchnell, Thomas, and Javier Caletrio, eds. 2013. *Elite Mobilities*. London: Routledge.

Bliss, Laura. 2017. "The High Line's next balancing act." *City Lab*, February 7, 2017.

Blok, Anders. 2013. "Pragmatic Sociology as Political Ecology: On the Many Worths of Nature(s)." *European Journal of Social Theory* 14, no. 3: 251–61.

Blok, Anders, and Marie Leth Meilvang. 2015. "Picturing Urban Green Attachments: Civic Activists Moving between Familiar and Public Engagements in the City." *Sociology* 49, no. 1: 19–37.

Blokker, Paul. 2011. "Pragmatic Sociology: Theoretical Evolvement and Empirical Application." *European Journal of Social Theory* 14, no. 3: 251–61.

Boltanski, Luc, and Eve Chiapello. 2005[1999]. *The new spirit of new capitalism*. London: Verso.

Boltanski, Luc, and Laurent Thévenot. 2006[1991]. *On Justification: Economies of Worth*. Princeton NJ: Princeton University Press.

Bonham, Jennifer. 2011. "Bicycle Politics: Review Essay." *Transfers* 1, no. 1: 137–46.

Bouchard, Frédéric. 2013. *From Groups to Individuals: Evolution and Emerging Individuality*. Cambridge MA: MIT Press.

Braun, Bruce. 2002. *The Intemperate Rainforest: Nature, Culture, and Power on Canada's West Coast*. Vancouver: UBC Press.

Brenner, Neil, and Nik Theodore. 2002. "Cities and the Geographies of 'Actually Existing Neoliberalism.'" *Antipode* 34, no. 3: 349–79.

Brodie, Janine. 2002. "Citizenship and Solidarity: Reflections on the Canadian Way." *Citizenship Studies* 6, no. 4: 377–94.

Brown, Jeffery. 2006. "From Traffic Regulation to Limited Ways: The Effort to Build a Science of Transportation Planning." *Journal of Planning History* 5, no. 1: 3–34.

Brown, Lindsay. 2015. "When Hipsters Dream of the 1890s: Heritage Aesthetics and Gentrification." *Briarpatch Magazine*, May 7, 2015.

Bula, Frances. 2017. "Vancouver Mulling Streetcar Network Despite Problems in Some Other Cities." *Globe and Mail*, December 3, 2017. https://www.theglobeandmail.com/news/british-columbia/vancouver -mulling-streetcar-network-despite-problems-in-some-other-cities /article37175706/.

Bullard, Robert, Glenn Johnson, and Angel Torres. 2004. *Highway Robbery: Transportation Racism and New Routes to Equity*. Cambridge: South End.

Burgess, Ernest. 1925 [1970]. "The Growth of the City: An Introduction to a Research Project." In *City*, edited by Robert Park, Ernest Burgess, and Roderick McKenzie. Chicago: University of Chicago Press.

CAA. n.d. "CAA—More than 100 Years of History." Canadian Automobile Association South Central Ontario. Accessed October 1, 2010. https:// www.caasco.com/in.

Campbell, Charlie. 2018. "The Trouble with Sharing: China's Bike Fever Has Reached Saturation Point." *Time*, April 2, 2018. http://time.com/5218323 /china-bicycles-sharing-economy.

Canada's Ecofiscal Commission. 2014. "Smart, Practical, Possible: Canadian Options for Greater Economic and Environmental Prosperity." Accessed November 12, 2017. https://ecofiscal.ca/reports/smart-practical-possible -canadian-options-for-greater-economic-and-environmental-prosperity/.

Canadian Charter of Rights and Freedoms. 1982. Part I of the Constitution Act, 1982, being Schedule B to the Canada Act 1982 (UK), c 11.

Canadian Parks and Wilderness Society. 2017. "CPAWS Responds to Parks Canada's Announcement of Public Consultation on the Proposed Icefields Trail." Accessed January 6, 2017. http://cpaws.org.

Castells, Manuel. 1997. *The Power of Identity: The Information Age*. New York: Wiley-Blackwell.

CBC News. 2018. "Portage Bridge Work to Close Lanes This Summer." April 19, 2008. https://www.cbc.ca/news/canada/ottawa/portage-bridge-ottawa -gatineau-close-1.4626273.

———. 2017. "'This Is a Zit': Neighbours Decry Needles, Other Trash in Andy Livingstone Park." June 14, 2017. https://www.cbc.ca/news/canada /british-columbia/andy-livingstone-park-1.4161504.

———. 2016. "Montreal's Bixi Continues to Pursue Global Domination: With 15 Cities Offering Its Bike-Sharing Systems, Company Can't Keep Up with New Demand." April 16, 2016. https://www.cbc.ca/news/canada/montreal /bixi-bike-sharing-cities-1.3539443.

———. 2014. "PST Hike of 0.5% Proposed for Metro Vancouver Transit Referendum." December 11, 2014. https://www.cbc.ca/news/canada /british-columbia/pst-hike-of-0-5-proposed-for-metro-vancouver-transit -referendum-1.2870043.

———. 2011. "Jarvis Bike Lanes to Be Removed." July 13, 2011. https://www .cbc.ca/news/canada/toronto/jarvis-bike-lanes-to-be-removed-1.980377.

CBC News Radio. 2017. "It's Dangerous to Call the Trans Canada Trail Complete, Says Cyclist." *The 180 with Jim Brown*, April 23, 2017.

Chihyung, Jeon. 2016. "Dams and Bikes: How to Destroy Rivers and Enjoy Cycling along Them in South Korea." Paper presented at Cycling and Society Conference, Lancaster, UK, September 2016.

Chittley, Jordan. 2015. "Ontario Drivers to Face Higher Set Fines for Distracted Offences, Dooring Cyclists." *Globe and Mail,* August 27, 2015. https://www.theglobeandmail.com/globe-drive/news/trans-canada -highway/ontario-drivers-to-face-higher-set-fines-for-distracted-offences -dooring-cyclists/article26127042/.

Chrysler. 2012. TV advertisement. Aired: February 2012.

City of Detroit. 2005. *Nonmotorized Urban Transportation Master Plan.* Prepared by Giffels-Webster Engineers, Carter-Burgess, ArchiveDs, Brogan & Partners for the City of Detroit, Traffic Engineering Division and Department of Public Works.

City of Ottawa 2013. *Ottawa Cycling Plan.* Accessed June 13, 2013. http:// ottawa.ca/en/ residents/ transportation-and-parking/cycling/ ottawa-cycling-plan.

———. 2008. *Ottawa Cycling Plan.* Accessed September 12, 2009. http://www .ottawa.ca/residents/onthemove/cycling/ottawa_cycling_plan_en.html.

City of Vancouver. 2018. *Northeast False Creek Plan.* Accessed June 5, 2018. http://vancouver.ca/files/cov/northeast-false-creek-plan.pdf.

———. 2017. *Greenest City: 2020 Action Plan: 2016–2017 Implementation Update.* Accessed May 15, 2017. http://vancouver.ca/files/cov/greenest-city -action-plan-implementation-update-2017.pdf.

———. 2016. *Walking + Cycling in Vancouver: 2016 Report Card.* Accessed May 15, 2017. http://vancouver.ca/files/cov/walking-cycling-in-vancouver -2016-report-card.pdf.

City of Windsor. 2001. *Bicycle Use Master Plan: Final Report.* Accessed November 2017. https://www.citywindsor.ca/residents/traffic-and -parking/transportation-planning/documents/bump%20-%20executive %20summary.pdf.

Clarke, P. 2012. "No Bike Lane Say Laurier Businesses and Residents." *Centretown News*, March 23, 2012.

Clover, Joshua, and Juliana Spahr. 2014. *#Misanthropocene 24 Theses.* Accessed June 2, 2017. http://communeeditions.com/misanthropocene/.

Colville-Andersen, Mikael. 2012. *Cycle Chic.* London: Thames and Hudson.

Concord Pacific. n.d. "About." Accessed June 2, 2018. https://www .concordpacific.com/about.

Conley, Jim. 2009. "Automobile Advertisements: The Magical and the Mundane." In *Car Troubles: Critical Studies of Automobility and Auto-Mobility*, edited by Jim Conley, J., and Arlene Tigar McLaren, 37–57. Aldershot: Ashgate.

Conley, Jim, and Arlene Tigar McLaren, eds. 2009. *Car Troubles: Critical Studies of Automobility and Auto-Mobility.* Aldershot: Ashgate.

Corfu, Nina. 2017. "Cyclist Hopes Halifax's Plan Will Mean No More Bike Lanes to Nowhere." *CBC News*, December 20, 2017. https://www.cbc.ca /news/canada/nova-scotia/devonshire-barrington-bike-lane-to-nowhere -halifax-cycling-coalition-halifax-1.4450605.

Cox, Rosie. 2006. *The Servant Problem: Domestic Employment in a Global Economy.* London: I. B. Tauris.

Crawford, Blair, and Beatrice Britneff. 2015. "Ghost Bike Debate: Permanent Memorial for Cyclists Proposed." *Ottawa Citizen*, October 31, 2015. https://ottawacitizen.com/news/local-news/national-memorial-for-cyclist -proposed.

Cresswell, Tim. 2014. "Mobilities III: Moving on." *Progress in Human Geography* 38, no. 5: 712–21.

———. 2010. "Politics of Mobility." *Environment and Planning D* 28, no. 1: 17–31.

———. 2006. *On the Move: Mobility in the Modern Western World.* New York: Routledge.

Cronon, William. 1996. "The Trouble with Wilderness: Or Getting Back to the Wrong Nature." *Environmental History* 1, no. 1: 7–28.

Cupples, Julie, and Elisabeth Ridley. 2008. "Towards a Heterogeneous Environmental Responsibility: Sustainability and Cycling Fundamentalism." *Area* 40, no. 2: 254–64.

Cycling in Cities, University of British Columbia (UBC). 2017. "Safety and Travel Mode." Accessed March 22, 2018. http://cyclingincities.spph.ubc.ca /injuries/.

Danish Government. 2017. "A Nation of Cyclists." Ministry of Foreign Affairs of Denmark

website, August 1, 2017. https://denmark.dk.

de Certeau, Michel. 1988. *The Practice of Everyday Life*. Vol. 1. Berkley: University of California Press.

DeLanda, Manuel. 2006. *A New Philosophy of Society: Assemblage Theory and Social Complexity*. New York: Continuum.

De Maio Paul. 2003. "Smart Bikes: Public Transportation for the 21st Century?" *Transportation Quarterly* 57, no. 1: 9–11.

Dennis, Kinglsey, and Kohn Urry. 2009. *After the Car*. Cambridge: Polity.

Detroit Slow Roll. 2014. "Mission Statement." Accessed July 4, 2014. http:// www.slowroll.bike/.

Dickinson, Janet, and Les Lumsdon. 2010. *Slow Travel and Tourism*. London: Earthscan.

Di Leo Browne, Timothy. 2016. "National Style in the Architecture of Parliament: Whose Nation, Whose Style?" *Canadian Journal of Urban Research* 25, no. 1: 49–62.

Dobbin, Murray. 2003. "December 2003: Liberal or Neoliberal?" *Canadian Centre for Policy Alternatives*, December 1, 2003. https://www.policyalternatives .ca/publications/ monitor/december-2003-liberal-or-neoliberal.

Doolittle, Robyn. 2011. "Toronto Needs a Third Way, Leaders Say." *Toronto Star*, July 28, 2011.

Durkheim, Emile. 1965 [1912]. *Elementary Forms of Religious Life*. Translated by Joseph Ward Swain. New York: Free Press.

Eckstein, Barbara. 2003. "Stories in the Practice of Planning." In *Story and Sustainability: Planning, Practice, and Possibility for American Cities*, edited by Barbara Eckstein and James A. Throgmorton, 13–38. Cambridge: MIT Press.

Elias, Norbert. 2000. *The Civilizing Process: Sociogenetic and Psychogenetic Investigations*. Oxford: Blackwell.

Ellingsen, Winfried G., and Knut Hidle. 2013. "Performing Home in Mobility: Second Homes in Norway." *Tourism Geographies* 15, no. 2: 250–67.

Elliot, Anthony, and John Urry. 2010. *Mobile Lives*. London: Routledge.

Fainstein, Susan. 2010. *The Just City*. Ithaca NY: Cornell University Press.

Fanelli, Carl. 2016. *Megacity Malaise: Neoliberalism, Public Services and Labour in Toronto*. Winnipeg, Manitoba: Fernwood.

Fassin, Didier. 2008. "Beyond good and evil?: Questioning the Anthropological Discomfort with Morals." *Anthropological Theory* 8, no. 4: 333–44.

Featherstone, Mike. 2004. "Automobilities: An introduction." *Theory, Culture, and Society* 21, nos. 4–5: 1–24.

Flyvbjerg, Bent. 2006. "Five Misunderstandings about Case-Study Research." *Qualitative Inquiry* 12, no. 2: 219–45.

Forks North Portage Corporation. 2018. "The Forks." Accessed March 1, 2018. https:// www.theforks.com/about/the-forks.

Francis, Daniel. 2006. *A Road for Canada: The Illustrated Story of the Trans-Canada Highway*. Vancouver: Stanton Atkins & Dosil.

Freudendal-Pedersen, Malene. 2015. "Whose Commons Are Mobilities Spaces?—The Case of Copenhagen's Cyclists." *ACME: An International E-Journal for Critical Geographies* 14, no. 2: 598–621.

———. 2009. *Mobility in Daily Life: Between Freedom and Unfreedom*. Farnham: Ashgate.

Freudendal-Pedersen, Malene, and Ole B. Jensen. 2012. "Utopias of Mobilities." In *Utopia: Social Theory and the Future*, edited by Michael Jacobsen and Keith Tester, 197–218. Farnham: Ashgate.

Furness, Zack. 2010. *One Less Car: Bicycling and the Politics of Automobility*. Philadelphia: Temple University Press.

Fusselman, Amy. 2015. *Savage Park: A Meditation on Play, Space, and Risk for Americans Who Are Nervous, Distracted, and Afraid to Die*. New York: Mariner.

Gandy, Matthew. 2013. "Marginalia: Aesthetics, Ecology, and Urban Wastelands." *Annals of the Association of American Geographers* 103, no. 6: 1301–16.

Gardiner, Michael. 2004. "Everyday Utopianism: Lefebvre and His Critics." *Cultural Studies* 18, nos. 2–3: 228–54.

Garrard, Jan, Susan Handy, and Jennifer Dill. 2012. "Women and Cycling." In *City Cycling*, edited by John Pucher and Ralph Buehler, 211–34. Cambridge MA: MIT Press.

Gauthier, Amy, Colin Hughes, Christopher Kost, Shanshan Li, Clarisse Linke, Stephanie Lotshaw, Jacob Mason, Carlosfelipe Pardo, Clara Rasore, Bradley Schroeder, and Xavier Treviño. 2013. *The Bike-Share Planning Guide*. New York: Institute for Transportation and Development Policy.

General Motors. 2009. TV advertisement. Aired June 2009.

George, M. V. 2001. "Population Forecasting in Canada: Conceptual and Methodological developments." *Canadian Studies in Population* 28, no. 1: 111–54.

Gollom, Mark. 2017. "Has Ambassador Bridge Owner Matty Moroun 'Outmanoeuvred Everybody'? Liberals Say No." *CBC News*, September 25, 2017. https://www.cbc.ca/news/business/bridge-gordie-howe-ambassador -moroun-windsor-detroit-1.4294977.

Golub, Aaron, Melody L. Hoffman, Adonia E. Lugo, and Gerardo F. Sandoval. 2016. *Bicycle Iustice and Urban Transformation: Biking for All?* London: Routledge.

———. 2016. "Introduction: Creating an Inclusionary Bicycle Justice Movement." In *Bicycle Justice and Urban Transformation: Biking for All?*, edited by Aaron Golub, Melody L. Hoffman, Adonia E. Lugo, and Gerardo F. Sandoval, 1–19. London: Routledge.

Gordon, David L. A. 2001. "Weaving a Modern Plan for Canada's Capital: Jacques Gréber and the 1950 Plan for the National Capital Region." *Urban History Review* 29:43–61.

Gordon, David L. A., and Richard Scott. 2008. "Ottawa's Greenbelt Evolves from Urban Separator to Key Ecological Planning Component." In *Urban Green Belts in the Twenty-First Century*, edited by Marco Amati, 129–48. Aldershot: Ashgate.

Graham, Stephen. 2016: *Vertical: The City from Satellites to Bunkers*. London: Verso.

Graham, Stephen, ed. 2009. *Disrupted Cities: When Infrastructure Fails*. New York: Routledge.

Grant, Kelly. 2010. "Don Cherry Slams 'Pinkos' in the 'Left-Wing Media' during Ford Inauguration." *Globe and Mail*, December 7, 2010. https:// www.theglobeandmail.com/news/toronto/don-cherry-slams-pinkos-in -the-left-wing-media-during-ford-inauguration/article1318666/.

Gréber, Jacques. 1950. *Plan for the National Capital: General Report Submitted to the National Capital Planning Committee*. Ottawa: National Capital Planning Service.

Green, Judith, Rebecca Steinbach, and Jessica Datta. 2012. "The Travelling Citizen: Emergent Discourses of Moral Mobility in a Study of Cycling in London." *Sociology* 46, no. 2: 272–89.

Gutmann, Amy. 1987. *Democratic Education*. Princeton NJ: Princeton University Press.

Guy, Simon, and Elizabeth Shove. 2000. *A Sociology of Energy, Buildings and the Environment: Constructing Knowledge, Designing Practice*. London: Routledge.

Hackworth, Jason. 2007. *The Neoliberal City: Governance, Ideology, and Development in American Urbanism*. Ithaca NY: Cornell University Press.

Hall, Peter. 2015. "The social life of truck routes." In *Transport, Mobility, and the Production of Urban Space*, edited by Julie Cidell and David Prytherch, 117–33. Abingdon: Routledge.

———. 2002. *Cities of Tomorrow: An Intellectual History of Urban Planning and Design in the Twentieth Century*, 3rd ed. Oxford, UK: Blackwell.

Hannam, Kevin, Mimi Sheller, and John Urry. 2006. "Editorial: Mobilities, Immobilities and Moorings." *Mobilities* 1, no. 1: 1–22.

Hannig, James. 2015. "Perceptions of Bike Sharing in Underserved Communities within Milwaukee and the Twin Cities." Master's thesis, University of Wisconsin–Milwaukee.

HAP. 2017. "Detroit Bike Share to Introduce City's Newest Transit System, MoGo, Detroit Bike Share." Accessed April 26, 2018. https://www.hap.org/news/2017/04/detroit-bike-share.

Haraway, Donna J. 2016. *Staying with the Trouble: Making Kin in the Chthulucene*. Durham NC: Duke University Press.

———. 1991. *Simians, Cyborgs and Women: The Reinvention of Nature*. London: Free Association.

Harvey, David. 2005. *A Brief History of Neoliberalism*. Oxford: Oxford University Press.

Harvey, Penny, and Hannah Knox. 2015. *Roads: An Anthropology of Infrastructure and Expertise*. Ithaca NY: Cornell University Press.

Hathaway, Michael. 2015. "Wild Elephants as Actors in the Anthropocene." In *Animals in the Anthropocene: Critical Perspectives on Non-Human Futures*, edited by the Human Animal Research Network Editorial Collective, 221–42. Sydney: Sydney University Press.

Haupt, Lyanda L. 2013. *The Urban Bestiary*. New York: Little, Brown.

Heidegger, Martin. 2002 [1954]. "Building, Dwelling, Thinking." In *Basic Writings: Martin Heidegger*, edited by D. Farrell Krell, 347–63. London: Routledge.

Henderson, Jason. 2006. "Secessionist Automobility: Racism, Anti-Urbanism, and the Politics of Automobility in Atlanta, Georgia." *International Journal of Urban & Regional Research* 30, no. 2: 293–307.

Herscher, Andrew. 2012. *The Unreal Estate Guide to Detroit*. Ann Arbor: University of Michigan Press.

Hilderman, Thomas, Frank, and Cram Planning and Design. 2015. "Oodena Celebration Circle." Accessed December 15, 2017. https://www.theforks.com/uploads/public/ files/attractions/oodena_info.pdf.

Hoffman, Melody L. 2016. *Bike Lanes Are White Lanes: Bicycle Advocacy and Urban Planning*. Lincoln: University of Nebraska Press.

Holden, Meg. 2017. *Pragmatic Justifications for the Sustainable City: Acting in the Common Place*. London: Routledge.

Holden, Meg, and Andy Scerri. 2015. "Justification, Compromise and Test: Developing a Pragmatic Sociology of Critique to Understand the Outcomes of Urban Redevelopment." *Planning Theory* 14, no 4: 360–83.

Hommels, Anique. 2008. *Unbuilding Cities: Obduracy in Urban Sociotechnical Change*. Cambridge MA: MIT Press.

Horton, Dave. 2007. "Fear of Cycling." In *Cycling and Society*, edited by Dave Horton, Paul Rosen, and Peter Cox, 133–52. Aldershot: Ashgate.

Horton, Dave, Paul Rosen, and Peter Cox, eds. 2007. *Cycling and society*. Aldershot: Ashgate.

HUB. 2018. "Bike the Night presented by MEC." Accessed April 25, 2018. https://bikehub.ca/bike-events/bike-the-night-presented-by-mec.

Hughes, Thomas P. 1983. *Networks of Power: Electrification in Western Society, 1880–1930*. Baltimore MD: Johns Hopkins University Press.

Ingold, Tim. 2008. "Bindings against Boundaries: Entanglements of Life in an Open World." *Environment and Planning A* 40:1796–1810.

———. 2004. "Culture on the Ground: The World Perceived through the Feet." *Journal of Material Culture* 9, no. 3: 315–40.

Jacobs, Jane. 1961. *The Death and Life of Great American Cities*. New York: Random House.

Jarvis, Anne. 2016. "Detroit Gets It." *Windsor Star*, May 31, 2016.

Jensen, Ole B. 2012. "If Only It Could Speak: Narrative Explorations of Mobility and Place in Seattle." In *Technologies of Mobility in the Americas*, edited by Phillip Vannini, Lucy Budd, Ole B. Jensen, Christian Fisker, and Paola Jiron, 59–77. New York: Peter Lang.

———. 2009. "Flows of Meaning, Cultures of Movement: Urban Mobility as Meaningful Everyday Life Practice." *Mobilities* 4, no. 1: 139–58.

Johansson, Pernilla, and Stacy Liou. 2017. "Public Spheres on the Move: The Embodied Deliberation of Cycling in Los Angeles." *Space and Polity* 21, no. 1: 59–74.

Johnson, Lisa, and Tamara Baluja. 2015. "Transit Referendum: Voters Say No to New Metro Vancouver Tax, Transit Improvements." *CBC News*, July 2, 2015. https://www.cbc.ca/news/canada/british-columbia/transit

-referendum-voters-say-no-to-new-metro-vancouver-tax-transit
-improvements-1.3134857.

Jones, Phil. 2005. "Performing the City: A Body and a Bicycle Take on Birmingham, UK." *Social and Cultural Geography* 6:813–30.

Jungnickel, Katrina, and Rachel Aldred. 2014. "Cycling's Sensory Strategies: How Cyclists Mediate Their Exposure to the Urban Environment." *Mobilities* 2:238–55.

Kaye, Julie, and Daniel Béland. 2014. "Stephen Harper's Dangerous Refusal to 'Commit Sociology.'" *Toronto Star*, August 22, 2014.

Keenan, Greg. 2015. "Made in Mexico: An Emerging Auto Giant Powers Past Canada." *Globe and Mail*, February 13, 2015.

Kheraj, Sean. 2013. *Inventing Stanley Park: An Environmental History*. Vancouver: UBC Press.

Kiger, Peter J. 2014. "How Vancouver Invented Itself." *Urban Land Magazine*, February 14, 2014.

Kymlicka, Will. 2001. *Contemporary Political Philosophy*. Oxford: Oxford University Press.

Lamont, Dougald. 2016. "Canadian Taxpayers Federation Has 5 Members—Why Should We Care What They Think?" *CBC News*, October 16, 2016. https://www.cbc.ca/news/canada/manitoba/canadian-taxpayer-federation-opinion-lamont-1.3802441.

Lamont, Michèle, and Laurent Thévenot, eds. 2000. *Rethinking Comparative Cultural Sociology: Repertoires of Evaluation in France and the United States*. Cambridge: Cambridge University Press.

Larsen, Jonas. 2014. "(Auto)Ethnography and Cycling." *International Journal of Social Research Methodology* 17:59–71.

Latour, Bruno. 2017. *Facing Gaia: Eight Lectures on the New Climatic Regime*. Cambridge: Polity.

———. 2007. *Reassembling the Social: An Introduction to Actor-Network Theory*. New York: Oxford University Press.

———. 1998. "To Modernize or to Ecologize? That's the Question." In *Remaking Reality: Nature at the Millenium*, edited by Noel Castree and Bruce Willems-Braun, 220–41. London: Routledge.

Laurier, Eric, Hayden Lorimer, Barry Brown, Owain Jones, Oskar Juhlin, Allyson Noble, Mark Perry, Daniele Pica, Philippe Sormani, Ignaz Strebel, Laurel Swan, Alex S. Taylor, Laura Watts, and Alexandra Weilenman.

2008. "Driving and 'Passengering': Notes on the Ordinary Organization of Car Travel." *Mobilities* 3:1–23.

Ledsham, Trudy, George Liu, Emily Watt, and Katie Wittmann. 2012. "Mapping Cycling Behaviour in Toronto." Report for the Toronto Cycling Think and Do Tank. School of the Environment, University of Toronto.

Lee, Do Helen Ho, Melyssa Banks, Mario Giampieri, Xiaodeng Chen, and Dorothy Le. 2016. "Delivering (In)Justice: Food Delivery Cyclists in New York City." In *Bicycle Justice and Urban Transformation: Biking for All*, edited by Aaron Golub, Melody L. Hoffman, Adonia E. Lugo, and Gerardo F. Sandoval, 114–29. London: Routledge.

Lefebvre, Henri. 1991. *The Production of Space*. Oxford: Blackwell.

Li, Wanyee. 2018. "Experts Say Vancouver Must Prepare for a New Kind of Emergency—Gentrification." *Toronto Star,* May 7, 2018.

Lloyd, Sarah A. 2018. "Leaving a Shared Bike on the Ferry Will Trigger a Coast Guard Search and Rescue." *Curbed Seattle,* April 10, 2018. https://seattle.curbed.com/2018/4/10/17219888/bike-share-ferry-coast-guard.

Loftus, Alex. 2012. *Everyday Environmentalism: Creating an Urban Political Ecology*. Minneapolis: University of Minnesota Press.

Longhurst, James. 2015. *Bike Battles: A History of Sharing the American Road*. Seattle: University of Washington Press.

Lubitow, Amy. 2016. "Mediating the 'White Lanes of Gentrification' in Humboldt Park: Community-Led Economic Development and the Struggle over Public Space." In *Bicycle Justice and Urban Transformation: Biking for All?*, edited by Aaron Golub, Melody L. Hoffman, Adonia E. Lugo, and Gerardo F. Sandoval, 249–59. London: Routledge.

Lugo, Adonia E. 2013. "CicLAvia and Human Infrastructure in Los Angeles: Ethnographic Experiments in Equitable Bike Planning." *Journal of Transport Geography* 30:202–7.

Lund, Katrín. 2013. "Experiencing Nature in Nature-Based Tourism." *Tourist Studies* 13, no. 2: 156–71.

Madger, Jason. 2017. "*Bixi:* PBSC *Urban Solutions Brings Bike-Sharing to the World (Part 3)*." *Montreal Gazette,* January 20, 2017.

Mahood, Linda. 2018. *Thumbing a Ride: Hitchhikers, Hostels, and Counterculture in Canada*. Vancouver: UBC Press.

Mapes, Jeff. 2009. *Pedaling Revolution: How Cyclists Are Changing American Cities*. Corvallis: Oregon State University Press.

Markan, Zak. 2016. "Dartmouth Crossing Brook Boasts Surprising Trout Life." *CBC News*, April 19, 2016. https://www.cbc.ca/news/canada/nova -scotia/dartmouth-crossing-fish-life-1.3541356.

Martens, Karel, Daniel Piatkowski, Kevin J. Krizek, and Kara Luckey. 2016. "Advancing Discussions of Cycling Interventions Based on Social Justice." In *Bicycle Justice and Urban Transformation: Biking for All?*, edited by Aaron Golub, Melody L. Hoffman, Adonia E. Lugo, and Gerardo F. Sandoval, 86–99. London: Routledge.

Massey, Doreen, B. 1993. "Power-Geometry and a Progressive Sense of Place." In *Mapping the Futures: Local Cultures, Global Change*, edited by John Bird, Barry Curtis, Tim Putnam, George Robertson, and Lisa Tickner, 60–70. London: Routledge.

Mauss, Marcel. 1973. "Techniques of the Body." *Economy and Society* 2, no. 1: 70–88.

McDowell, Linda. 2007. "Spaces of the Home: Absence, Presence, New Connections and New Anxieties." *Home Cultures* 4, no. 2: 129–46.

McIlvenny, Paul. 2015. "The Joy of Biking Together: Sharing Everyday Experiences of Vélomobility." *Mobilities* 10, no. 1: 55–82.

McIntosh, Jeff. 2017. "Big Canadian Cities See Faster Suburban Growth Despite Bid to Boost Density." *Globe and Mail*, April 14, 2017.

McLaughlin Motor Car Co. 1922. *Reference Book*. Oshawa: General Motors of Canada.

Meiszner, Peter. 2017. "Massive Northeast False Creek Area Plan to Transform Waterfront." *Urban YVR*, November 18, 2017. https://urbanyvr.com /northeast-false-creek-plan-nefc-2017.

Merringer, Ian 2015. "Pan Am Path Knits an Underworld within Toronto." *Globe and Mail*, June 19, 2015.

Miguelez, Alan. 2015. *Transforming Ottawa: Canada's Capital in the Eyes of Jacques Gréber*. Ottawa: Old Ottawa.

Mobi Shaw Go. 2016. "Vancouver Bike Share Picks Up Speed with Shaw Sponsorship." Press Release, accessed May 13, 2018, http://newsroom.shaw .ca/materialDetail.aspx?MaterialID=6442451915.

MoGo. 2018. "MoGo Neighborhood Ambassadors." Accessed June 15, 2018. https://mogodetroit.org/mogo-neighborhood-ambassadors/.

Mol, Annemarie. 2002. *Body Multiple: Ontology in Medical Practice*. Durham NC: Duke University Press.

Moore, Joseph. 2016. "Car Free Day! Urban Homemaking, Projects and the Neighbourhood Politics of Home." In *Sociology of Home: Belonging, Community, and Place in the Canadian Context*, edited by Gillian Anderson, Joseph Moore and Laura Suski, 187–202. Toronto: Canadian Scholars Press.

Morissette, Claire. 2009 [1994]. *Deux Roues, un Avenir: Le vélo enVville*. Montréal: Ecosociété.

Norton, Peter D. 2008. *Fighting Traffic: The Dawn of the Motor Age in the American City*. Cambridge MA: MIT Press.

Office of the Chief Coroner for Ontario. 2012. "Cycling Death Review: A Review of All Accidental Cycling Deaths in Ontario from January 1st, 2006 to December 31st, 2010." Accessed September 1, 2013. http://www .mcscs.jus.gov.on.ca/sites/default/files/content/mcscs/docs/ec159773.pdf.

Pablo, Carlito. 2018. "Questions Raised about 1,800 Social Housing Units Pledged in Vancouver's Northeast False Creek Plan." *Georgia Straight*, February 8, 2018.

Parusel, Sylvia, and McLaren, Arlene Tigar. 2010. "Cars before Kids: Automobility and the Illusion of School Traffic Safety." *Canadian Review of Sociology* 47:129–47.

Paterson, Matthew. 2007. *Automobile Politics: Ecology and Cultural Political Economy*. Cambridge: Cambridge University Press.

Peck, Jamie. 2011. "Neoliberal Suburbanism: Frontier Space." *Urban Geography* 32, no. 6: 884–919.

———. 2010. *Constructions of Neoliberal Reason*. Oxford: Oxford University Press.

Peck, Jamie, and Adam Tickell. 2002. "Neoliberalizing Space." *Antipode* 34, no. 3: 380–404.

Perkins, Martha. 2018. "Burrard Bridge Named Busiest Cycling Route in North America. Eco-Counter Puts Vancouver at the Top of Its List for Canada and the U.S." *Vancouver Courier*, January 24, 2018.

Piketty, Thomas. 2014. *Capital in the Twenty-First Century*. Cambridge MA: Harvard University Press.

Pink, Sarah, and Kerstin Mackley. 2016. "Moving, Making and Atmosphere: Routines of Home as Sites for Mundane Improvisation." *Mobilities* 11, no. 2: 171–87.

Pirie, Gordon. 2016. "Modalities in Transport History." *Journal of Transport History* 37, no. 1: 3–4.

Pooley, Colin, Tim Jones, Miles Tight, Dave Horton, Griet Scheldeman, Caroline Mullen, Ann Jopson, and Emanuele Strano. 2013. *Promoting Walking and Cycling*. Bristol: Bristol University Press.

Popan, Cosmin. 2018. "Utopias of Slow Cycling: Imagining a Bicycle System." PhD Dissertation, Lancaster University.

Press, Jordan. 2017. "Census 2016: Big Cities Home to Big Share of 35 Million Canadians." *CBC News*, February 8, 2017. https://www.cbc.ca/news/politics /cities-population-census-2016-1.3972062.

Price, Matt. 2004. "Economics, Ecology, and the Value of Nature." In *The Moral Authority of Nature*, edited by Lorraine Daston and Fernando Vidal, 183–204. Chicago: University of Chicago Press.

Proctor, Jason. 2018. "Bike Lane Barometer: Judging Vancouver Mayor Gregor Robertson's Legacy: After 10 Years in Office, Mayor's Many Accomplishments Likely Eclipsed by Expansion of Bike Routes." *CBC News*, January 10, 2018. https://www.cbc.ca/news/canada/british-columbia /gregor-robertson-bike-lanes-mayor-vancouver-1.4481920.

———. 2016. "Deal of the Century: Expo 86 Land Purchase Changed Vancouver." *CBC News*, May 4, 2016. https://www.cbc.ca/news/canada/british -columbia/expo-86-china-business-vancouver-1.3560255.

Pucher, John, Ralph Buehler, and Mark Seinen. 2011. "Bicycling Renaissance in North America? An Update and Re-Appraisal of Cycling Trends and Policies." *Transportation Research Part A* 45, no. 6: 451–75.

———. 2006. "Why Canadians Cycle More Than Americans: A Comparative Analysis of Bicycling Trends and Policies." *Transport Policy* 13, no. 3: 265–79.

Putnam, Robert. 2000. *Bowling Alone*. New York: Simon and Schuster.

Quinn, Stephen. 2017. "Vancouver Cyclists Are Reaching Peak Entitlement." *Globe and Mail*, October 20, 2017.

Ramage-Morin, Pamela. 2017. *Cycling in Canada*. Ottawa: Statistics Canada.

Rawls, John. 1971. *A Theory of Justice*. Cambridge: Harvard University Press.

Reevely, David. 2013. "Segregated Bike Lanes Downtown Not as Sure a Thing, Though Laurier's Looks Like a Keeper." *Ottawa Citizen*, March 5, 2013.

Relph, Edward. 1976. *Place and placelessness*. London: Pion.

Robinson, William I., and Mario Barrera. 2012. "Global Capitalism and Twenty-First-Century Fascism: A US Case Study." *Race & Class* 53, no. 3: 4–29.

Rose, Nikolas. 1999. *Powers of Freedom: Reframing Political Thought*. Cambridge: Cambridge University Press.

Rosenbaum, Lee. 2014. "After Detroit's Close Call." *Wall Street Journal*, November 19, 2014.

Sadik-Khan, Janette, and Seth Solomonow. 2016. *Street Fight: Handbook for an Urban Revolution*. New York: Penguin.

Saunders, Doug. 2017. "What Do Working German Women Have that Canadians Don't? Lots of Help from Above." *Globe and Mail*, March 12, 2017.

———. 2017. "Can We Ever Knock Down the Walls of the Wealthy Ghetto?" *Globe and Mail*, July 17, 2017.

Savan, Beth, Emma Cohlmeyer, and Trudy Ledsham. 2017. "Integrated Strategies to Accelerate the Adoption of Cycling for Transportation." *Transportation Research Part F: Traffic Psychology and Behaviour* 46(A): 236–49.

Schjeldahl, Peter. 2014. "High Line Rhapsody." *New Yorker*, October 7, 2014.

Schumpeter, Joseph. 2008[1942]. *Capitalism, Socialism, and Democracy*, 3rd ed. New York: Harper Perennial Modern Classics.

Scott, James. 1998. *Seeing Like a State: How Certain Schemes to Improve the Human Condition Have Failed*. New Haven CT: Yale University Press.

Scott, Nicholas. 2016. "Cycling, Performance and the CommonGgood: Copenhagenizing Canada's Capital." *Canadian Journal of Urban Research* 25, no. 1: 22–37.

———. 2013. "Like a Fish Needs a Bicycle: Henri Lefebvre and the Liberation of Transportation." *Space & Culture* 16, no. 3: 397–410.

———. 2012. "How Car Drivers Took the Streets: Critical Planning Moments of Automobility." In *Technologies of Mobility in the Americas*, edited by Phillip Vannini, Lucy Budd, Ole B. Jensen, Christian Fisker and Paola Jiron, 79–98. New York: Peter Lang.

Scott, Nicholas, and Janet Siltanen. 2016. "Intersectionality and Quantitative Methods: Assessing Regression from a Feminist Perspective." *International Journal of Social Research Methodology* 20, no. 4: 373–85.

Sheller, Mimi. 2018. *Mobility Justice*. London: Verso.

———.2007. "Retouching the "Untouched Island": Post-Military Tourism in Vieques, Puerto Rico." *Téoros-Journal of Tourism Research* 26, no. 1.

———. 2016. "Uneven Mobility Futures: A Foucauldian Approach." *Mobilities* 11, no. 1: 15–31.

Sheller, Mimi, and John Urry. 2006. "The NewMmobilities Paradigm." *Environment and Planning A* 38:207–26.

———. 2000. "The City and the Car." *International Journal of Urban and Regional Research* 24:737–57.

Shove, Elizabeth, and Nicola Spurling, eds. 2013. *Sustainable Practice: Social Theory and Climate Change*. London: Routledge.

Siemiatycki, Matti, Matt Smith, and Alan Walks. 2016. "The Politics of Bicycle Lane Implementation: The Case of Vancouver's Burrard Street Bridge." *International Journal of Sustainable Transportation* 10, no. 3: 225–35.

Silcoff, Sean. 2018. "How Canadian Money and Research Are Helping China Become a Global Telecom Superpower." *Globe and Mail*, May 26, 2018. https://www.theglobeandmail.com/canada/article-how-canadian-money -and-research-are-helping-china-become-a-global/.

Simmel, Georg. 1998[1895]. "The Alpine Journey." In *Simmel on Culture: Selected Writings*, edited by David Frisby and Mike Featherstone, 219–32. London: Sage.

Smith, Adam. 2011[1759]. *Theory of Moral Sentiments*. Gutenberg.

Spinney, Justin. 2016. "Fixing Mobility in the Neoliberal City: Cycling Policy and Practice in London (UK) as a Mode of Political-Economic and Bio-Political Governance." *Annals of the Association of American Geographers* 106, no. 2: 450–58.

———. 2015. "Close Encounters? Mobile Methods, (Post)Phenomenology and Affect." *Cultural Geographies* 22, no. 2: 231–46.

———. 2006. "A Place of Sense: A Kinaesthetic Ethnography of Cyclists on Mont Ventoux." *Environment and Planning D: Society and Space* 24, no. 5: 709–32.

Spotswood, Fiona, Tim Chatterton, Alan Tapp, and David Williams. 2015. "Analysing Cycling as a Social Practice: An Empirical Grounding for Behaviour Change." *Transportation Research Part F* 29:22–23.

Star, Susan L. 1999. "The Ethnography of Infrastructure." *American Behavioral Scientist* 43, no. 3: 377–91.

Starosielski, Nicole. 2015. *The Undersea Network*. Durham NC: Duke University Press.

Statistics Canada. 2017a. Data tables, 2016 Census, accessed December 15, 2017, www12.statcan.gc.ca/.

———. 2017b. "Commuters Using Sustainable Transportation in Census Metropolitan Areas." Government of Canada: Minister of Industry.

———. 2011. 2011 National Household Survey Public Use Microdata File (accessed via Simon Fraser University).

Stehlin, John. 2014. "Regulating Inclusion: Spatial Form, Social Process, and the Normalization of Cycling Practice in the USA." *Mobilities* 9, no. 2: 21–41.

Stern, Nicholas. 2006. *The economics of climate change: The Stern review*. Commissioned by the Government of the United Kingdom.

Stewart, Megan. 2017. "Is Vancouver Ready for the High Line Effect?" *Vancouver Magazine*, June 29, 2017.

Stoczkowski, Wiktor. 2008. "The 'Fourth Aim' of Anthropology: Between Knowledge and Ethics." *Anthropological Theory* 8, no. 4: 345–56.

Sztabinski, Fred. 2009. *Bike Lanes, On-Street Parking and Business: A Study of Bloor Street in Toronto's Annex Neighbourhood*. Clean Air Partnership, Toronto. Accessed May 15, 2012. http://www.bikeleague.org/sites /default/files/bikeleague/bikeleague.org/programs/bicyclefriendlyamerica /bicyclefriendlybusiness/pdfs/toronto_study_bike_lanes_parking.pdf.

Tabb, William K. 2015. "If Detroit Is Dead, Some Things Need to Be Said at the Funeral." *Journal of Urban Affairs* 37, no. 1: 1–12.

Tabuchi, Hiroko. 2018. "How the Koch Brothers Are Killing Public Transit Projects around the Country." *New York Times*, June 19, 2018. https://www .nytimes.com/2018/06/19/climate/koch-brothers-public-transit.html.

Tait, Malcom, and Ole B. Jensen. 2007. "Travelling Ideas, Power and Place: The Cases of Urban Villages and Business Improvement Districts." *International Planning Studies* 12, no. 2: 107–28.

Tarrow, Sidney. 2011. *Power in Movement: Social Movements and Contentious Politics*. Cambridge: Cambridge University Press.

Taylor, Charles. 2004. *Modern Social Imaginaries*. Durham NC: Duke University Press.

Teschke, Kay, Anna Chinn, and Michael Brauer. 2017. "Proximity to Four Bikeway Types and Neighborhood-Level Cycling." *Journal of Transport and Land Use* 10, no. 1: 695–713.

Teschke, Kay, Conor Reynolds, Francis J. Ries, Brian Gouge, and Meghan Winters. 2012. "Bicycling: Health Risk or Benefit?" *UBC Medical Journal* 3, no. 2.

Thévenot, Laurent. 2002. "Which Road to Follow? The Moral Complexity of an 'Equipped' Humanity." In *Complexities: Social Studies of Knowledge Practices*, edited by John Law and Annemarie Mol, 53–87. Durham NC: Duke University Press.

Toronto Public Health. 2012. "Road to Health: Improving Walking and Cycling." Toronto, Ontario: Toronto Public Health.

"Trudeau Announces bike-only lanes for Trans-Canada Highway." 2015. Accessed August 4, 2015. https://thelapine.ca/trudeau-announces-bike -only-lanes-for-trans-canada-highway/.

Truth and Reconciliation Commission of Canada. 2015. "Honouring the Truth, Reconciling for the Future: Summary of the Final Report of the Truth and Reconciliation Commission of Canada." Ottawa: Library and Archives Canada.

Urry, John. 2014. *Offshoring*. Cambridge: Polity.

———. 2006. "Inhabiting the Car." *Sociological Review* 54, no. 1: 17–31.

———. 2004. "The 'System' of Automobility." *Theory, Culture & Society* 21, nos. 4–5: 25–39.

Vannini, Phillip. 2013. "Slowness and Deceleration." In *The Routledge Handbook of Mobilities,* edited by Peter Adey, David Bissell, Kevin Hannam, Peter Merriman, and Mimi Sheller, 116–24. London: Routledge.

———. 2012. *Ferry Yales: Mobility, Place and Time of Canada's West Coast.* New York: Routledge.

Vannini, Phillip, and April Vannini. 2016. *Wilderness.* New York: Routledge.

van Nostrand, John C. 1983. "The Queen Elizabeth Way: Public Utility versus Public Space." *Urban History Review* 12:1–23.

Wagner, Lauren B. 2017. "Viscous Automobilities: Diasporic Practices and Vehicular Assemblages of Visiting 'Home.'" *Mobilities* 12, no. 6: 827–46.

Walks, Alan. 2015. "Stopping the 'War on the Car': Neoliberalism, Fordism, and the Politics of Automobility in Toronto." *Mobilities* 10, no. 3: 402–22.

———. 2009. "The Urban in Fragile, Uncertain, Neoliberal Times: Towards New Geographies of Social Justice?" *Canadian Geographer* 53, no. 3: 345–56.

———. 2007. "The Boundaries of Suburban Discontent? Urban Definitions and Neighbourhood Political Effects." *Canadian Geographer* 51, no. 2: 160–85.

Walks, Alan, ed. 2014. *The Urban Political Economy and Ecology of Automobility: Driving Cities, Driving Inequality, Driving Politics.* Abingdon, UK: Routledge.

Waraniak, Jeff. 2015. "The Rapid Rise of Slow Roll." *Hour Detroit*, March 23, 2015. http://www.hourdetroit.com/Hour-Detroit/April-2015/The-Rapid-Rise-of-Slow-Roll/.

Watson, Matt. 2013. "Building Future Systems of Velomobility." In *Sustainable Practice: Social Theory and Climate Change*, edited by Elizabeth Shove and Nicola Spurling, 117–31. London: Routledge.

Weber, Max. 2002[1934]. *The Protestant Ethic and the Spirit of Capitalism.* London: Penguin Classics.

Williams, Daniel R., and Susan R. Patten. 2006. "Home and Away? Creating Identities and Sustaining Places in a Multi-Centered World." In *Multiple Dwelling and Tourism: Negotiating Place, Home, and Identity*, edited by Norman McIntyre, Daniel Williams, and Kevin McHugh, 32–50. Wallingford MA: CABI.

Willmott, Kyle. 2017. "Taxpayer Governmentality: Governing Government in Metro Vancouver's Transit Tax Debate." *Economy and Society* 46, no. 2: 255–74.

Winters, Meghan, and Kay Teschke. 2010. "Route Preferences among Adults in the Near Market for Bicycling: Findings of the Cycling in Cities Study." *American Journal of Health Promotion* 25, no. 1.

Winters, Meghan, Melissa Friesen, Mieke Koehoorn, and Kay Teschke. 2007. "Utilitarian Bicycling: A Multilevel Analysis of Climate and Personal Influences." *American Journal of Preventive Medicine* 32, no. 1: 52–58.

Winters, Meghan, and Moreno Zanotto. 2017. "2032–Gender Trends in Cycling Over Time: An Observational Study in Vancouver, British Columbia." *Journal of Transport & Health* 5 (Supplement):37–38.

Yang, Lin, Shannon Sahlqvist, Alison McMinn, Simon Griffin, and David Ogilvie. 2010. "Interventions to Promote Cycling: Systematic Review." *British Medical Journal* 341:5293.

Zavestoski, Stephen, and Julian Agyeman, eds. 2015. *Incomplete Streets: Processes, Practices, and Possibilities.* Abingdon: Routledge.

Zigon, Jarret. 2010. "Moral and Ethical Assemblages: A Response to Fassin and Stoczkowski." *Anthropological Theory* 10, nos. 1–2: 3–15.

Index

Page numbers in italic indicate illustrations

BUMP. *See* Bicycle Use Master Plan
(BUMP)
Burrard Bridge (Vancouver), 141
business, cycling and, 161

Cabana Road (Windsor), 90
Canada: automobile use within, 5–6;
colonization of, 53–54; cycling
scholarship within, 7–8; ecological concerns within, 235–36;
good roads movement and, 36,
52, 60–61, 92; immigration and,
142; Indigenous peoples and, 53;
market characteristics of, 232;
national city cycling plan, 234–
35; population factors within,
234–35, 236–37; power relations
within, 221; transport strategies
of, 156; urban fabric of, 7; women,
workforce and, 46–47, 61
Canadian Charter of Rights and
Freedoms, 117
Canadian Pacific Railway, 142
Canadian Taxpayers Federation, 170
capital, cycling, 153–58
capitalism: connexionist spirit of,
181; driving for, 18–24; industrial, 23, 227; industrial worth
of, 20–21; market worth of, 22;
neoliberal, 23–24, 28; "third way"
market, 176
cargo bike, 55–58, *57*, 60
carrier cycling, 54–55
cars, 5–6, 15, 43, 112, 118–19, 126
casualties, cycling, 118, 127–28
Catherine (research participant),
55–62, *57*

Celestina (research participant),
story of, 63–69
child care, challenges of, 47, 61–62
children, cycling with, 47, 54–63
China, bike share system in, 167
Chinatown (Vancouver), 140–47, *144*
Chinese Cultural Center, 142
Chinese Exclusion Act, 142
Chrysler Corp., 19
Citizens for Safe Cycling, 129
City Cyclery, 135–38
CityPlace (Vancouver), 174–75
civic inequities, 228
civic mobilities, 37, 147–49
civic worth, 26–27, 117, 118
civil rights, 117
co-cycling, 54–63, 225, 239–40n2
Cogswell Interchange (Halifax), 80–81
common good: abstract, 15; anthropocentric walls of, 54; civic worth
and, 118; communitarianism and,
121; ecological, 12–13, 29; market
and, 22, 154, 160; mobility and,
181–82; moralities of, 12
communitarianism, 121
commuting, 11, 97, 122
Complete Streets movement, 139
complex mobility systems, 106–7
Concord Pacific (developer), 174
connexionist cyclists, 157–58
consumption, 151
Copenhagen, 2, 12, 186
corking, 134
Corner, James, 173
Critical Mass ride, 134
CycleHop bike system, 166
cycle planning: Cycling Plan
(Ottawa), 127, 129; first-wave, 37, 84,